THE LEGAL RECOGNITION
OF SAME-SEX RELATIONSHIPS

This book analyses the key issues affecting same-sex families in Ireland and beyond today: marriage; formalised and non-formalised same-sex relationships outside of marriage; parental rights for same-sex couples with donor-conceived or surrogate-born children; and the protections afforded to same-sex families under European human rights law.

It critically examines the Irish and Australian citizen-led approaches to achieving marriage equality, which made Ireland and Australia the first and second countries in the world, respectively, to extend the institution of marriage to same-sex couples on foot of a popular vote.

It analyses the pragmatic and symbolic effects of civil partnership, which was the premier means of formalising same-sex unions in Ireland. Ireland's hurried 'divorce' from civil partnership in the aftermath of marriage equality is examined in light of evidence from the U.K. indicating that this mode of relationship recognition remains popular with both same-sex and opposite-sex couples in that jurisdiction.

The book goes on to consider the legal position of same-sex couples who are parenting children born via assisted reproductive techniques (ARTs) like donor-assisted human reproduction (DAHR) and surrogacy.

Finally, it looks at the impact (or lack thereof) of the European Convention on Human Rights (ECHR) as regards the protection of same-sex relationships, marriage and parental rights for same-sex couples. It does this to determine what is required of Ireland and other states party to the ECHR to comply with European human rights obligations when it comes to legally recognising couples, and parents, of the same sex.

The Legal Recognition of Same-Sex Relationships

Emerging Families in Ireland and Beyond

Brian Tobin

·HART·

OXFORD · LONDON · NEW YORK · NEW DELHI · SYDNEY

HART PUBLISHING

Bloomsbury Publishing Plc

Kemp House, Chawley Park, Cumnor Hill, Oxford, OX2 9PH, UK

1385 Broadway, New York, NY 10018, USA

29 Earlsfort Terrace, Dublin 2, Ireland

HART PUBLISHING, the Hart/Stag logo, BLOOMSBURY and the Diana logo are
trademarks of Bloomsbury Publishing Plc

First published in Great Britain 2023

First published in hardback, 2023

Paperback edition, 2024

Copyright © Brian Tobin, 2023

A catalogue record for this book is available from the British Library.

A catalogue record for this book is available from the Library of Congress.

Library of Congress Control Number: 2022948648

ISBN: PB: 978-1-50995-257-1
        ePDF: 978-1-50995-255-7
        ePub: 978-1-50995-254-0

Typeset by Compuscript Ltd, Shannon

To find out more about our authors and books visit www.hartpublishing.co.uk.
Here you will find extracts, author information, details of forthcoming events
and the option to sign up for our newsletters.

For my family, constitutional and beyond

FOREWORD

In June 2024 the Supreme Court will mark the hundred years of its first inception. As I survey the ranked masses of the Irish Reports in my office and reflect upon all of the many hard, difficult and tragic cases which are contained in those volumes, in some ways I cannot help think that the facts of *The State (Nicolaou) v. An Bord Uchtala* [1966] IR 567 are amongst the saddest of them all. Here a child was put up for adoption against the wishes of a father who clearly cared for that child. Yet the challenge to the constitutionality of the Adoption Act 1952 on which this entire process rested ultimately failed. (The entire story is told from a human perspective in MacCormaic's *The Supreme Court* (Dublin, 2016), Chp. 6). Had that legislation been found to be unconstitutional, the history of Ireland would have been fairer, better and happier. The same is quite obviously true of the Court's decision in *Norris v. Attorney General* [1984] IR 36.

While these decisions were of their time, they in their own way show not only a judicial failure but also a wider societal failure to recognise the importance of associational rights to the human condition. Human beings are by definition social creatures who need to associate with others. This finds expression most obviously in the protection at constitutional and legal level in the context of marriage, family and children, but it is also true of wider human friendships at all levels. Once one accepts that the diversity of life throws up a Gaussian distribution curve of human emotions, commitments, sexuality and needs, then the rational case against the legal recognition of same-sex marriage rather crumbles. I distinctly recall that during the hearing of *Zappone v. Revenue Commissioners* [2008] 2 IR 417 Michael Collins SC – our leading and very brilliant counsel – quoted Holmes' *Path of the Law* in a manner which seemed telling, forceful and appropriate:

> "It is revolting to have no better reason for a rule of law than that so it was laid down in the time of Henry IV. It is still more revolting if the grounds upon which it was laid down have vanished long since, and the rule simply persists from blind imitation of the past."

In the end that challenge did not prevail. But perhaps the *Zappone* litigation was not entirely in vain, because by opening the minds of the population to what the then Tanaiste Eamon Gilmore TD once described as the greatest human rights challenge of our time, perhaps in its own way it paved the way for the marriage equality referendum.

CONTENTS

1

Introduction

It is 30 years since consensual same-sex sexual activity was decriminalised in Ireland. However, little more than a decade ago, Ireland still had no legal framework for formally recognising committed same-sex relationships. Since 2011, the rate of progress to improve the legal position of same-sex couples has been remarkable; not only was legislation commenced to simultaneously provide for same-sex civil partnerships and legal protections for certain cohabiting same-sex (and opposite-sex) couples but, less than five years later, Ireland became the first country in the world to enshrine marriage equality in its national constitution on foot of a popular vote in a referendum.

This book analyses key themes pertaining to same-sex families in Ireland and beyond: marriage; formalised and non-formalised same-sex relationships outside of marriage; and parental rights for same-sex couples with children. Regarding the former themes, which largely concern the legal relationships between adults, the book aims to critically examine the various mechanisms used to achieve the legal recognition of same-sex relationships in Ireland. These include participatory democratic processes such as a Constitutional Convention and a referendum to secure marriage equality, and, prior to that, legislation which enabled same-sex couples to formalise their relationships through the marriage-like institution of civil partnership, while also establishing a scheme to recognise and protect certain same-sex and opposite-sex cohabitants who qualify for redress. Regarding the latter theme, which concerns legal adult-child relationships in same-sex families, the book predominantly focuses on the regulation of surrogacy and donor-conception, as these are the methods used by same-sex couples to procreate with assistance and are the most common routes to same-sex parenting. The book aims to critique Irish legislation introduced to recognise the relationship between same-sex parents and their donor-conceived children, as well as proposed legislative initiatives to recognise the relationship between same-sex parents and their surrogate-born children; considered, pragmatic and inclusive recommendations for law reform are proffered.

As will become clear from the chapter outlines, each thematically linked chapter adopts a comparative perspective, where relevant. The book considers those jurisdictions beyond Ireland in which legislation, case law or law reform processes are most relevant to an analysis of the Irish situation or, conversely, where such jurisdictions could benefit from a consideration of the Irish approach to legally recognising and protecting same-sex families. The book also analyses other recent, significant developments in international law and best practice, where relevant to the theme under discussion. In that regard, an international human rights instrument most relevant to the themes in the book is the European Convention on Human Rights (ECHR), to which Ireland is a party, and which was granted some domestic effect through legislation enacted in 2003.[1] Thus, the book further extends beyond Ireland by critically analysing the jurisprudence of the European Court of Human Rights (ECtHR) in the areas of same-sex relationships, marriage equality, and legal parental rights for same-sex couples.

The analysis in this book of the themes related to same-sex families is intended to contribute to furthering international debate on the legal recognition of same-sex relationships and same-sex couples as parents. The book presents its analysis and critique in an accessible manner that is designed to engage readers who are students, academics, activists, practitioners, policy-makers, NGOs and members of the public who are interested in the intersection between law and LGBT+ issues.

Chapter two critically examines the Irish and Australian citizen-led approaches to achieving marriage equality, which made Ireland and Australia the first and second countries in the world, respectively, to extend marriage to same-sex couples on foot of a popular vote. While the journey towards marriage equality in Ireland and Australia was remarkably similar, the politically convenient exercises in participatory democracy that were employed to extend marriage to same-sex couples in each jurisdiction were crude, unnecessary and uncertain, and other jurisdictions should be cognisant of this if considering similar mechanisms. However, these processes were also undeniably successful, and resulted in the ultimate societal affirmation of the legitimacy of same-sex relationships by a majority of the members of the electorate both in Ireland and in Australia.

Chapter three analyses the pragmatic and symbolic effects of civil partnership, the marriage-like regime that served as the premier form of 'opt-in' legal recognition for committed same-sex relationships in Ireland. In 2016, following the Marriage Referendum, the option of entering into a civil partnership was discontinued for constitutional reasons. However, civil partnership was retained in the UK in the aftermath of marriage equality, and recently extended to opposite-sex couples there. In light of available evidence from the UK, and recent recommendations in Ireland from both the Citizens' Assembly and the Joint Oireachtas Committee on Gender Equality for a referendum to extend the constitutional definition of the 'Family' beyond 'Marriage', this chapter aims to reignite the debate surrounding civil partnership or an equivalent mechanism as an alternative for same-sex and opposite-sex couples in Ireland who wish to formalise their relationships outside of marriage.

Further, this chapter considers the efficacy of the Irish redress scheme for same-sex cohabitants who meet the specified statutory criteria. This was introduced into Irish law at the same time as civil partnership in order to protect

---

[1] European Convention on Human Rights Act 2003.

persons in cohabiting relationships, whether they are of the same or opposite sex, and it is argued that the scheme's criteria ensure that it achieves a fair equilibrium between providing protection for a truly vulnerable cohabitant while avoiding any undue state interference in non-formalised relationships. In addition, the scheme's phased approach to the remedies available to qualifying cohabitants ensures that there is no undue encroachment on a respondent's pension or property rights. Overall, the Irish approach to redress for cohabitants is likely to be of interest to those currently considering cohabitation law reform in the UK and elsewhere.[2]

Chapter four moves from examining the mechanisms used to recognise adult same-sex relationships in Ireland to critiquing those employed to recognise the parent-child relationship between same-sex couples and their children, but before doing so the more common arguments against same-sex parenting are refuted in order to demonstrate that there is no 'harm' to a child raised in a same-sex relationship.

The chapter largely focuses on the legal position of same-sex couples who are parenting children born via assisted reproductive techniques (ARTs) like donor-assisted human reproduction (DAHR) and surrogacy. The chapter critiques the complex 'hybrid' pre-conception state approval and post-birth Parental Order model for regulating domestic surrogacy that is proposed in Part 7 of the Health (Assisted Human Reproduction) Bill 2022. This model is partly based on a flawed understanding of the Supreme Court's ruling on surrogacy in *MR v An t-Ard Chláraitheoir*, and replicates contentious aspects of the statutory model for regulating surrogacy arrangements in the UK. In proposing an alternative model for regulating domestic surrogacy arrangements, which arguably achieves a better balance between the rights of the surrogate, the intended parents and the surrogate-born child, the chapter engages with significant, recent international developments, such as the publication of the Verona Principles and the New Zealand Law Commission's 'Review of Surrogacy'.[3] Further, the Law Commission of England and Wales and Scottish Law Commission's Consultation Paper, 'Building Families through Surrogacy: A New Law', and the Irish Special Rapporteur for Child Protection's 'Review of Children's Rights and Best Interests in the Context of Donor-Assisted Human Reproduction and Surrogacy in Irish Law' are of considerable import not only to the discussion of this alternative model, but also to the analysis of international surrogacy arrangements and whether these can be regulated under domestic law in a manner that assuages any associated legal and ethical concerns.

The chapter subsequently analyses certain shortcomings as regards parental rights in the Children and Family Relationships Act 2015, the existing legislation that regulates DAHR. In particular, the chapter discusses the rationale for the apparent exclusion of 'reciprocal IVF' and the decisive exclusion of non-clinical

---

[2] The Women and Equalities Committee is currently considering cohabitation law reform in England and Wales, as is the Scottish Law Commission in Scotland.

[3] New Zealand Law Commission, 'Review of Surrogacy' Report, NZLC R146 (2022).

DAHR procedures from the ambit of the legislation. The chapter examines amendments to the Act that could decisively provide for reciprocal IVF, and proposes a potential, balanced statutory model for prospectively regulating non-clinical DAHR procedures where a known donor is used. The discussion of statutory models for regulating domestic surrogacy and domestic non-clinical DAHR procedures is cognisant of the child's right to knowledge of genetic identity throughout.

Chapter five focuses on the impact of the European Convention on Human Rights (ECHR) as regards same-sex relationships, marriage and parental rights for same-sex couples, in order to determine what is required of states party to the ECHR when it comes to legally recognising couples, and parents, of the same sex. Although Ireland has outpaced the requirements of the ECHR as regards making legal provision for adult same-sex relationships, recent case law of the ECtHR regarding the ECHR rights of surrogate-born children vis-à-vis their parents is of significant import in Ireland and beyond, albeit that states are granted a wide margin of appreciation in this complex area of the law. Further, the analysis in this part of the book of the ECHR's provisions on the right to marry, the right to respect for private and family life, and non-discrimination are relevant to those states *beyond Ireland* that are party to the ECHR and where the rights of LGBT+ families have not yet reached the high-water mark of protection that is available under Irish domestic law.

2

Marriage Equality by Popular Vote

The Irish and Australian Experiences

I. Introduction

Marriage equality between same-sex and opposite-sex couples is perhaps the ultimate affirmation of the socio-legal assimilation of same-sex relationships in any society and, in 2015 and 2017 respectively, marriage equality became a reality in Ireland and Australia. The success of the Marriage Referendum made Ireland the first country in the world to recognise marriage equality following a popular vote and, in 2017, Australia followed suit by becoming the second country in the world to do so, following a successful postal plebiscite. In Ireland, the successful referendum result meant that Article 41 of the Constitution, which only protects the 'Family' based on 'Marriage', was amended and updated by the insertion of Article 41.4, which provides that 'marriage may be contracted in accordance with law by two persons without distinction as to their sex',[1] and the enactment of the Marriage Act 2015 saw the legislative amendments necessary to facilitate marriage equality become part of Irish law. In Australia, the successful plebiscite result did not involve any change being made to 'marriage' in Section 51(xxi) of the Australian Constitution, but it did lead to the enactment of the Marriage Amendment (Definition and Religious Freedoms) Act 2017 and, consequently, the legal recognition of marriage equality in Australia.[2] This chapter analyses and illuminates the striking similarities between the politico-legal journeys towards marriage equality in Ireland and Australia, which culminated in the Marriage Referendum and postal plebiscite. Both were successful, participatory democratic processes that facilitated the emergence of same-sex married families in Ireland and Australia, respectively.

---

[1] See Thirty-fourth Amendment of the Constitution Act, 2015. Same-sex marriage has been legal in Northern Ireland, which is a part of the UK, since 2020. While an analysis of the journey towards same-sex marriage in Northern Ireland is beyond the scope of this book, see C McCormick and T Stewart, 'The Legalisation of Same-Sex Marriage in Northern Ireland' (2020) 71 *Northern Ireland Legal Quarterly* 557.

[2] In any event, in *Commonwealth v Australian Capital Territory* (2013) 250 CLR 441, 461 [33] the High Court of Australia had recognised that 'marriage' under the Australian Constitution encompasses same-sex marriage.

The chapter initially examines the original constitutional parameters of the marital family in Ireland and discusses why growing international judicial recognition of same-sex marriage post-millennium may have fuelled the codification of the common law position on marriage in domestic legislation in 2004.[3] The chapter then discusses the significance of the High Court's deference to that legislative prohibition in *Zappone v Revenue Commissioners*, and argues that the Marriage Referendum was unnecessary because of judicial deference to legislative enactments in complex, controversial areas of social policy like marriage equality.[4]

The chapter then examines Australia's legislative response to the increasing international judicial recognition of same-sex marriage, enacted in the same year as its Irish counterpart, and equally as prohibitive, and explains why the High Court of Australia's deference to that legislation in *Commonwealth v Australian Capital Territory* rendered the postal plebiscite in Australia just as unnecessary as Ireland's Marriage Referendum. The chapter continues by analysing the similarities between the Marriage Referendum and the postal plebiscite and argues that these crude, risk-laden processes were, ultimately, successful socio-legal experiments that resulted not from political dynamism, but instead from a lack of political determination to try to resolve the issue of marriage equality in the Irish and Australian Parliaments respectively, and governmental recourse to citizen-led, politically convenient exercises in participatory democracy. The chapter concludes by suggesting that since the Australian Government was so resolutely determined to put the issue of marriage equality to a nationwide public vote, then Australia should have followed the Irish example by holding a constitutional referendum on the matter, as a successful referendum result would have guaranteed the greatest possible level of domestic legal protection for this fundamental human right.

II. The Contours of the Constitutional Family Prior to Marriage Equality in Ireland

Articles 41 and 42 of the Constitution of Ireland represent the basic law of the state pertaining to marriage, the family, and the education of any children within the family unit, and 'it is generally considered that these provisions were heavily influenced by Roman Catholic teaching and Papal encyclicals'.[5] Indeed, in Article 41.3.1 of the Constitution, 'The State pledges itself to guard with special

---

[3] The common law definition of marriage is 'the voluntary union for life of one man and one woman, to the exclusion of all others', as stated 156 years ago by Lord Penzance in *Hyde v Hyde* (1866) LR 1 P and D 130, 133. While this definition has been cited in courts throughout the common law world, including Ireland, Probert cogently argues that '*Hyde* should be seen for what it is: a case of considerable historical interest, that tells us a great deal about the attitudes of mid-Victorian England – but nothing about how marriage should be defined today': see R Probert, '*Hyde v Hyde*: Defining or Defending Marriage?' (2007) 19 *Child and Family Law Quarterly* 322, 336.

[4] *Zappone v Revenue Commissioners* [2008] 2 IR 417.

[5] 'Report of the Constitution Review Group' (Stationery Office, 1996) 319.

care the institution of Marriage, on which the Family is founded, and to protect it against attack'. While 'Marriage' and 'Family' are terms undefined by the Constitution, Article 41.3.1 places a strict parameter on the constitutional concept of 'Family' by making it clear that it is solely 'Marriage, on which the Family is founded'. Hence, as Doyle affirms, marriage is clearly a 'necessary condition for a group of persons to constitute a family unit protected by Art 41'[6] and so the right to marry is also recognised as being implicit from the terms of that provision.[7] Given the Catholic ethos of the Constitution, the document's conflation of the concepts of 'Marriage' and 'Family' is understandable since, as Duncan observes, 'Roman Catholic social teaching emphasises the central importance to society of the family based on indissoluble marriage'.[8] Further, it is clear from case law that the marital 'Family' originally envisaged by the Constitution was an opposite-sex, nuclear family unit because 'Marriage' was consistently recognised by the courts as 'the basis of the family and as a ... union of man and woman',[9] and the 'Family' was deemed to be comprised of parents and children and did not include other relationships beyond the nuclear family. In *McCombe v Sheehan*, Murnaghan J had 'no doubt' about the meaning to be attributed to the word 'Family' in Article 41 and found that it referred to 'parents and children'.[10] In *Jordan v O'Brien*, Lavery J, having considered Murnaghan J's pronouncement on the constitutional 'Family' in *McCombe*, stated as follows:

> I will accept, without deciding, that the word as used in the Constitution does mean parents and children and does not include other relationships. Certainly the Constitution has primarily in mind the natural unit of society – parents and children – which it protects.[11]

Similarly, in *Jordan v O'Brien* Kingsmill Moore J felt that 'Mr. Justice Murnaghan may have been correct in saying, as he did in *McCombe's Case*, that "Family" in Article 41 of the Constitution means "parents and children"'.[12] The understanding which the courts have attributed to the 'Family' in the Constitution reflects social reality at a time when the norm was for opposite-sex couples to marry and found a family through procreation, leading in turn to the establishment of the typical parent-child relationship. As the Constitution Review Group observed in 1996, 'Articles 41 and 42 were drafted with only one family in mind, namely, the family

---

[6] O Doyle, *Constitutional Law: Text, Cases and Materials* (Dublin, Clarus Press, 2008) 225.

[7] However, in *Ryan v Attorney General* [1965] IR 294, at 313, Kenny J referred to the right to marry as one of the unenumerated personal rights protected under Art 40.3.1. In *O'Shea v Ireland* [2007] 2 IR 313, Laffoy J confirmed that the right to marry is also protected by Art 40.3.1.

[8] Marriage in Ireland is no longer indissoluble since the introduction of divorce in 1996, following a referendum to remove the ban on divorce contained in Art 41.3.2 of the Constitution. The provision was replaced by a new Art 41.3.2 which expressly permits divorce in certain circumstances.

[9] *Murphy v Attorney General* [1982] IR 241, 286 (Kenny J).

[10] *McCombe v Sheehan* [1954] IR 183, 190.

[11] *Jordan v O'Brien* [1960] IR 363, 370.

[12] ibid, 375.

based on marriage *with* children.[13] Although Costello J in *Murray v Ireland* held that a married couple without children can also be considered a constitutional 'Family' unit,[14] his understanding of the concept of marriage was clearly that of an opposite-sex, potentially procreative partnership because elsewhere in his judgment he makes it clear that the constitutional concept of marriage is clearly derived from the 'Christian notion', according to which 'the procreation and education of children by the spouses is especially ordained'.[15] This understanding of marriage was later approved – albeit obiter – by the Supreme Court.[16] Therefore, it would appear that the sex of the parties was essential to the constitutional notion of the marital family because only opposite-sex couples are theoretically capable of procreating and establishing the 'natural unit of society – parents and children'.[17]

III. The Legislative Prohibition on Same-Sex Marriage

While the original parameters of the constitutional marital family unit recognised in Article 41 would appear clear from the discussion above, there was no express statutory prohibition on same-sex marriage in Ireland until section 2(2)(e) of the Civil Registration Act 2004 entered into force on 5 December 2005. The Civil Registration Act 2004 was mainly introduced to modernise the procedures for registering births, deaths and marriages; nonetheless, section 2(2)(e) expressly prevented same-sex couples from marrying in the following terms: 'For the purposes of this Act there is an impediment to a marriage if ... both parties are of the same sex'. Subsection (2)(e) was an amendment inserted into the Civil Registration Bill 2003 in early 2004, and the timing of such an amendment is curious given international developments in the area of marriage equality post-millennium. In 2001, the Netherlands became the first country in the world to recognise same-sex marriage – it was followed by Belgium in June 2003. However, it was the *judicial recognition* of same-sex marriage in Canadian provinces and the US State of Massachusetts in 2003 that was undoubtedly of more interest, or concern, for conservative parliamentarians in Ireland, given that the Constitution of Ireland contains a Bill of Rights which falls to be interpreted by the judiciary. Article 41 on The Family and Article 40.1 on Equality are part of that Bill of Rights. In 2003, Canadian courts had struck down the limitation of marriage to opposite-sex couples as being in violation of the equality guarantee contained in section 15 of the Canadian Charter of Rights and Freedoms.[18] That same year, the Massachusetts Supreme Court found that the exclusion of same-sex couples

---

[13] See *Report of the Constitution Review Group* (n 5) 336.
[14] *Murray v Ireland* [1985] IR 532, 537.
[15] ibid, 536.
[16] *TF v Ireland* [1995] IR 321, 373.
[17] *Jordan v O'Brien* (n 11) 370.
[18] *Halpern v Canada (AG)* [2003] OJ No 2268.

from marriage was contrary to the rights to dignity and equality contained in the Constitution of Massachusetts.[19] Given the timing of the insertion of subsection (2)(e) into the Civil Registration Bill 2003, it is not unreasonable to surmise that the Oireachtas may have been aware of these progressive international developments and likely had concerns pertaining to the judicial recognition of same-sex marriage in the Irish courts.

IV. The Legislative History of the Civil Registration Act 2004, s 2(2)

Section 2(2)(a)-(e) of the 2004 Act was an amendment to the legislation, introduced at Committee Stage to clarify 'what is an impediment to a marriage', as explained by the then Minister for Social and Family Affairs, Mary Coughlan.[20] During the Committee Stage, revisions of this proposed amendment were suggested. Deputy Penrose suggested that section 2(2)(a) should be amended to take account of the availability of divorce in Ireland since 1996 so that there would no longer be an impediment to a marriage between a person and the divorced spouse of that person's sibling.[21] Deputy Neville, obviously aware of contemporary, informed understandings of persons with impaired mental abilities, felt that the wording of subsection 2(d) was not appropriate for a modern piece of legislation because it sought to render void the marriage of 'lunatics'.[22] However, at no point during the Committee's debate was the impediment to same-sex marriage contained in subsection 2(e) discussed. This is most disappointing because, akin to the above amendments that were tabled, socio-legal changes had taken place which arguably necessitated debate as to whether it was even justifiable to include subsection (2)(e) in the Bill. Such developments were indicative of an ever-increasing acceptance of the normality of the sexual identity of LGBT+ persons. In 1973 the American Psychiatric Association dropped homosexuality from the classification as a mental illness in its diagnostic and statistical manual. In 1993, in Ireland, private consensual same-sex sexual activity between males had been decriminalised by legislative enactment and legislative protections for LGBT+ persons were subsequently imposed in the fields of insurance, employment, and goods and services.[23]

In light of this, one might ask why the Oireachtas did not see fit to debate the proposed ban on same-sex marriage, possibly one of the greatest obstacles to the full assimilation of LGBT+ citizens into Irish society? It must be remembered

---

[19] *Goodridge v Dept of Public Health*, 798 NE 2d 941 (Mass 2003).
[20] Select Committee on Social and Family Affairs Debate, 3 February 2004, available at www.oireachtas.ie/en/debates/debate/select_committee_on_social_and_family_affairs/2004-02-03/3.
[21] ibid.
[22] ibid.
[23] Criminal Law (Sexual Offences) Act 1993; see also B Tobin, 'EB v France: Endorsing Un-"Convention"-al Families?' (2008) 11 *Irish Journal of Family Law* 78, 79.

that, when section 2(2) was being debated on 3 February 2004, the global recognition of same-sex marriage was little more than embryonic. As demonstrated, only two countries in the world had come to recognise same-sex marriage, in 2001 and 2003 respectively.[24] Hence, even if parliamentarians had sought to contest the contemporary meaning of marriage, it was clear that, on a global scale, the meaning of marriage remained predominantly unchanged. In addition, when the Civil Registration Bill 2003 was being debated, the deputies did not have the benefit of the judgment in *Zappone v Revenue Commissioners*,[25] which, as we shall see, accords the Oireachtas primacy in determining the future understanding of marriage. Indeed, parliamentarians may not have felt the need to address section 2(2)(e) at all because they were aware of the role of the Oireachtas in enacting legislation that was in compliance with the Constitution, and at the time, 'Marriage' under Article 41 was constitutionally understood as being a union between a man and a woman. On this analysis section 2(2)(e), as enacted, was clearly in compliance with the Constitution.

V. Same-Sex Marriage in the Irish Courts: *Zappone v Revenue Commissioners*

In 2006, section 2(2)(e) was a crucial deciding factor in a High Court action taken by a female same-sex couple to have their Canadian marriage recognised in Ireland. Dr Katherine Zappone and Dr Ann Louise Gilligan had married in British Columbia in 2003, following the opening up of the institution of marriage to same-sex couples in that jurisdiction. Upon their return to Ireland, they wrote to the Office of the Registrar General seeking confirmation that their marriage was legally binding, but they were informed by letter-response that a declaration on the validity of foreign marriages was a matter for the courts by virtue of family law legislation.[26] The plaintiffs also wrote to the Revenue Commissioners seeking the recognition of their marriage in order to obtain the various tax benefits available to married couples in Ireland. However, the Revenue Commissioners replied with an interpretation that confined the provisions of tax law relating to married couples to a 'husband' and a 'wife' only, citing the *Oxford English Dictionary*'s gender-specific definitions of such terms.

The plaintiffs sought a judicial review of the Revenue Commissioners' decision. When the matter came on for hearing before the High Court, the plaintiffs argued, inter alia, that the Revenue Commissioners' decision was in breach of their right to marry and their right to equality before the law under the Constitution.

---

[24] The Netherlands opened up marriage to same-sex couples in 2001 and was followed by Belgium in 2003.

[25] *Zappone v Revenue Commissioners* (n 4).

[26] Family Law Act 1995, s 29.

They sought to have the impugned provisions of Irish tax law declared unconstitutional for excluding same-sex marriages from their ambit.[27]

In the High Court, Dunne J considered the question at the heart of the action: does the right to marry inherent in the Constitution encompass a right to marry for same-sex couples? Dunne J observed that

> what was always understood by the framers of the Constitution was the traditional understanding of marriage as exemplified in cases such as Hyde v. Hyde ... namely 'the voluntary union of one man and one woman, to the exclusion of all others'.[28]

Indeed, Dunne J observed that 'as recently as 2003' in *DT v CT*, Murray J had described marriage as 'a solemn contract of partnership entered into between man and woman with a special status recognised by the Constitution'.[29] Consequently, Dunne J held that the notion of marriage as a union between parties of the opposite-sex was not 'some kind of fossilised understanding of marriage'[30] and the plaintiffs wanted the High Court to 'redefine marriage to mean something which it has never done to date'.[31]

However, the plaintiffs argued that the Constitution was a 'living instrument' and, accordingly, that the right to marry should be considered to have changed to embrace the concept of same-sex marriage due to the existence of a changing international consensus. Dunne J accepted that the Constitution is a 'living instrument' and proceeded to consider whether the meaning of marriage could therefore be regarded as having been updated. Dunne J had recourse to the *dicta* of Walsh J in *McGee v Attorney General*.[32] In *McGee*, Walsh J enunciated 'the principle that the meaning of the Constitution is open to evolution through interpretation'[33] by stating that 'no interpretation of the Constitution is intended to be final for all time. It is given in the light of prevailing ideas and concepts'.[34]

However, Dunne J could not find a basis for concluding that same-sex marriage was actually a prevailing idea or concept because, globally, there was in fact 'limited support for the concept of same-sex marriage' in late 2006.[35] At the time, merely six jurisdictions worldwide had come to recognise same-sex marriage.[36] On that basis she held that it was difficult to see this 'limited support for the concept of

---

[27] Art 34.3.2 of the Constitution of Ireland grants the Irish superior courts the power to review the constitutional validity of laws.

[28] *Zappone v Revenue Commissioners* (n 4) 501. The common law definition of marriage was enunciated by Lord Penzance in *Hyde v Hyde* (1866) LR 1 P and D 130, 133.

[29] *DT v CT* [2003] 1 ILRM 321, 374. However, it should be noted that this case was concerned with making proper financial provision for the divorcing spouses and did not involve any challenge to the legal definition of marriage.

[30] *Zappone v Revenue Commissioners* (n 4) 504.

[31] ibid, 505.

[32] *McGee v Attorney General* [1974] IR 284.

[33] C O'Mahony, 'Societal Change and Constitutional Interpretation' (2010) 1 *Irish Journal of Legal Studies* 71, 74.

[34] *McGee v Attorney General* [1974] IR 284, 319.

[35] *Zappone v Revenue Commissioners* (n 4) 506.

[36] The Netherlands, Belgium, Canada, Massachusetts (United States), Spain and South Africa.

same-sex marriage … as a consensus, changing or otherwise'.[37] Therefore Dunne J rejected the plaintiffs' argument that the meaning of marriage should be updated because of a 'changing consensus', pointing out that 'the consensus around the world does not support a widespread move towards same-sex marriage'.[38]

A. Equality before the Law

In those jurisdictions where same-sex marriage was recognised by virtue of a constitutional equality guarantee there was, *unlike Ireland*, no constitutional provision explicitly protecting the traditional family based on marriage.[39] In *Zappone*, Dunne J did not consider the potential for the constitutional equality guarantee contained in Article 40.1 to embrace same-sex marriage as this would have conflicted with the meaning of the 'Family' in Article 41. Dunne J swiftly disposed of the plaintiffs' equality argument by simply stating as follows

> if there is in fact any form of discriminatory distinction between same-sex couples and opposite-sex couples by reason of the exclusion of same-sex couples from the right to marry, then Article 41 in its clear terms as to guarding the family provides the necessary justification.[40]

Thus, by holding that Article 40.1 occupies a subordinate position to Article 41, Dunne J essentially treated the constitutional equality guarantee as surplusage and was easily able to dispose of any egalitarian arguments in support of same-sex marriage. This strategy has previously found favour in the Irish courts. Indeed, a prime example of this judicial approach is to be found in *O'Brien v Stoutt*.[41] Here Walsh J found that a discrimination under succession law against children born outside of marriage was justified by reference to the constitutional protection of the family based on marriage in Article 41 and, as Doyle observes, in doing so the learned justice 'did not consider the possibility that Art. 40.1 might limit the constitutional protection afforded to the marital family'.[42] Therefore, as Doyle observes, Irish case law clearly illustrates that 'equality-derogating classifications that are not justified by reference to a difference between the persons distinguished might nonetheless be legitimate where they support … another constitutional value'.[43]

This approach is rather unsurprising when examined against the backdrop of the harmonious approach to constitutional interpretation. For the Irish courts to recognise same-sex marriage via a general equality guarantee like Article 40.1

---

[37] *Zappone v Revenue Commissioners* (n 4) 506.
[38] ibid.
[39] The jurisdictions are Massachusetts (US), Canada and South Africa, respectively.
[40] *Zappone v Revenue Commissioners* (n 4) 507.
[41] *O'Brien v Stoutt* [1984] IR 316.
[42] O Doyle, *Constitutional Equality Law* (Dublin, Thomson Round Hall, 2004) 94. Indeed, the Irish courts have often failed to realise the potential of the equality guarantee contained in Art 40.1: see G Hogan, 'The Supreme Court and the Equality Clause' (1999) 4 *Bar Review* 116.
[43] ibid, 99.

when Article 41 expressly protects the marital family, interpreted as being an opposite-sex union by the courts, would be repugnant to what Henchy J described in *Tormey v Ireland* as the

> fundamental rule of constitutional interpretation that the Constitution must be read as a whole and that its several provisions must not be looked at in isolation, but be treated as interlocking parts of the general constitutional scheme.[44]

In essence, it would have been incongruous for the High Court to require same-sex marriage via the back door of the equality guarantee when it was unable to do so under Article 41. Adherence to the harmonious approach necessitates the subordination of Article 40.1 in cases involving atypical family units due to the fact that Article 41 only recognises marital families. For an Irish court to recognise same-sex marriage via the constitutional equality clause would be as incongruous as the European Court of Human Rights (ECtHR) recognising this under a general provision such as Article 8 of the European Convention on Human Rights (ECHR), which guarantees to everyone a right to respect for their private and family life. Indeed, as I shall explain in chapter five, the ECtHR has declined to adopt this very course of action because it has stressed that Article 12 of the ECHR explicitly protects the right to marry and to found a family.[45] Akin to the Irish domestic courts, the ECtHR in *Schalk and Kopf v Austria* adopted a harmonious approach to the interpretation of the ECHR and subordinated Article 8 to Article 12 in the same respective manner as the Irish courts tend to treat Articles 40.1 and 41 in cases involving marriage and the family.[46] While Dunne J's judgment in *Zappone* arguably disappoints by failing to recognise the equality guarantee as having any 'substantive, egalitarian content which could weigh against other ... provisions of the Constitution',[47] her approach was arguably necessary in order to achieve what Henchy J described in *Tormey v Ireland* as 'the smooth and harmonious operation of the Constitution'.[48]

B. Judicial Deference to Legislation

However, the main factor that led Dunne J to find against the plaintiffs was the legislative prohibition on same-sex marriage contained in section 2(2)(e) of the 2004 Act. Judicial deference to legislative enactments is not unusual because, as O' Mahony observes, 'when invited to re-interpret a provision of the Constitution from its original or established interpretation, deference theory states that the courts should look to the legislative position for guidance'. Although the

---

[44] *Tormey v Ireland* [1985] IR 289, 295.
[45] *Schalk and Kopf v Austria* App No 30141/04 (ECtHR, 24 June 2010). This judgment, the ECtHR's premier ruling on same-sex marriage, will be considered in ch 5.
[46] ibid, [101].
[47] O Doyle, *Constitutional Equality Law* (2004) 75.
[48] *Tormey v Ireland* [1985] IR 289, 295.

constitutionality of section 2(2)(e) had not been challenged in the proceedings, Dunne J found that 'the Act of 2004 is in force, is entitled to a presumption of constitutionality and is to my mind an expression of the prevailing view as to the basis for capacity to marry'.[49]

Indeed, Dunne J's deference towards the 2004 Act's traditional notion of marriage was never more apparent than when she posed, *and quite emphatically answered*, the following question: 'Is [section 2(2)(e)] not *of itself* an indication of the prevailing idea and concept in relation to what marriage is and how it should be defined? *I think it is*'.[50] Therefore, Dunne J actually viewed section 2(2)(e) as *the* legal expression of the prevailing view as to the basis for capacity to marry. However, Dunne J's strict adherence to the approach to marriage enshrined in section 2(2)(e) of the 2004 Act is frustrating when one considers the manner in which this provision came about. As discussed, section 2 (2)(e) was never debated by the Oireachtas prior to its enactment, hence Dunne J's assertion that the provision represented the prevailing legislative view on the capacity to marry is not necessarily accurate. As O'Mahony argues, section 2(2)(e) 'did not represent a considered legislative judgment on the issue to which the court could defer'.[51] Foley has also quite cogently emphasised that

> the essence of deference, however, is deference to a *decision actually made*. If the legislature *does not actually* decide on matters of rights, then it starts to make less sense to 'defer' to its decisions because they *do not exist*.[52]

While all of this is true, it must be remembered that in treating section 2(2)(e) as evidence of a legislative consensus, Dunne J could not have made herself aware of the unsatisfactory manner in which this statutory provision came about. This is because, in Ireland, a judge is precluded from having regard to the parliamentary debates concerning a statutory provision.[53]

C. A Synergy between the Constitutional and Statutory Understandings of Marriage?

Dunne J's deference to the legislature's understanding of marriage was most significant, and because of the synergy between any future legislation altering the capacity to marry and the constitutional understanding of marriage that she envisaged, the Marriage Referendum of 2015 may not have been at all necessary. Since Dunne J appeared to view section 2(2)(e) of the Civil Registration Act 2004 as

---

[49] *Zappone v Revenue Commissioners* (n 4) 506.

[50] ibid; emphasis added.

[51] C O'Mahony, 'Principled Expediency: How the Irish Courts can Compromise on Same-Sex Marriage' (2012) *Dublin University Law Journal* 198, 213.

[52] B Foley, *Deference and the Presumption of Constitutionality* (Dublin, Institute of Public Administration, 2008) 230.

[53] See *Crilly v Farrington Ltd* [2001] 3 IR 25.

cementing '*of itself*'[54] the concept of marriage as a union between two parties of the opposite sex, she appears to be granting the Oireachtas primacy in this contentious matter. Carolan makes the following pertinent observation:

> [T]he fact that Dunne J. relied so heavily on the Civil Registration Act 2004 as indicative of the nature of the existing social consensus suggests a pre-eminent role for the Oireachtas in determining the social (and thus constitutional) appropriateness of any future amendments to the meaning of marriage.[55]

Further, and perhaps unsurprisingly given her adherence to the legislative concept of marriage contained in section 2(2)(e) of the 2004 Act, Dunne J concluded that 'ultimately, it is for the legislature to determine the extent'[56] of the legal recognition to be accorded to same-sex unions. Thus, it is submitted that Dunne J appeared to be indicating that, if the Oireachtas chose to alter the capacity to marry by legislating for same-sex marriage, then the courts would abide by this and recognise any legislation as being in harmony with the Constitution. As Carolan points out, Dunne J 'appears to posit the existence of a more complex and dynamic relationship [between the Oireachtas and the courts] in which statute in some way informs the meaning of the constitutional text'.[57] On this reading it would appear that same-sex marriage legislation could have been introduced by the Oireachtas absent a constitutional referendum and it would not have been rendered unconstitutional by the courts for updating the legal understanding of marriage. Dunne J was giving 'due respect to the superior institutional capacity of the Oireachtas to reflect public opinion, and its democratic primacy on matters of political controversy'.[58] In 2006, Dunne J had good reason to pass an issue as controversial as same-sex marriage to the Oireachtas because, as Kavanagh observes,

> if there is intense social controversy about an issue, suggesting that people may not be ready to accept a particular change in the law (or at least may not be prepared to accept it from an unelected court) considerations about democratic legitimacy and social acceptance may lead the courts to exercise caution before making the decision themselves.[59]

Thus, the Oireachtas could have introduced same-sex marriage through legislation, just as the Westminster Parliament did in July 2013 when it passed the Marriage (Same-Sex Couples) Act 2013 and provided for same-sex marriage in England and Wales. Since Dunne J left remarkable leeway to the Oireachtas to determine the appropriate legal status for same-sex relationships, I shall now try to deduce why the then Irish Government did not take advantage of this judicial

---

[54] *Zappone v Revenue Commissioners* (n 4) 506.

[55] E Carolan, 'Committed Non-Marital Couples and the Irish Constitution' in O Doyle and W Binchy (eds), *Committed Relationships and the Law* (Dublin, Four Courts Press, 2007) 256, 265–66.

[56] ibid, 513.

[57] Carolan, 'Committed Non-Marital Couples' (2007) 266.

[58] O'Mahony, 'Principled Expediency' (2012) 226.

[59] A Kavanagh, 'Strasbourg, the House of Lords or elected Politicians: Who decides about rights after *Re P*?' (2009) 72 *Modern Law Review* 828, 843.

deference towards legislative enactments and proceed to legislate for same-sex marriage following the *Zappone* judgment.

VI. Legal Recognition of Same-Sex Relationships Post-*Zappone*

A. Marriage Equality – A Political 'Hot Potato'

In 2007, with the *Zappone* judgment under appeal to the Supreme Court,[60] a new Fianna Fáil/Green Party coalition Government was formed in Ireland. The coalition's Programme for Government contained a commitment to introduce civil partnership legislation for same-sex couples: 'Taking into account the Options Paper prepared by the Colley Group, and the pending Supreme Court case, we will legislate for civil partnerships at the earliest possible date in the lifetime of this Government'.[61] This statement on civil partnership legislation is interesting because the coalition claimed to be committing to its introduction in light of the Working Group on Domestic Partnership's Options Paper and the *Zappone* appeal. Granted, the Options Paper concluded that full civil partnership was the best mode of relationship recognition for same-sex couples because the introduction of same-sex marriage was likely to be vulnerable to constitutional challenge. However, this recommendation was published on 28 November 2006, a few weeks before the release of the High Court's decision in *Zappone*, which seems to grant the legislature primacy in determining the meaning of marriage.[62] Dunne J's deferential judgment surely abrogates what might otherwise have been a sound recommendation. Thus, it is unclear why the Government committed to civil partnership over marriage when one considers the High Court's judgment. Nonetheless, the 'pending Supreme Court case' was another reason why the Government claimed to be committing to civil partnerships. Although Dunne J's judgment left the issue of same-sex marriage to the legislature, such a pronunciation indicates that the Government was, in turn, waiting for this divisive issue to be decided at Supreme Court level. Indeed, the upshot of all this circuitousness is that neither branch of

---

[60] The *Zappone* appeal was never heard by the Supreme Court. It was dropped in June 2012 as the parties wished to initiate a new High Court action challenging the Civil Registration Act 2004, s 2(2)(e) instead. However, this action was never progressed and is now unnecessary in light of the result of the Marriage Referendum: C Taylor, 'Couple to Issue renewed Legal Challenge to Civil Registration Act in Bid for Marriage' *Irish Times* (7 June 2012) 8.

[61] See 'Programme for Government 2007–2012' (Stationery Office, 2007) 87. The Options Paper was a 2006 report prepared for the previous government by a working group chaired by a former TD, Anne Colley. The working group was tasked with recommending options for the legal recognition of same-sex relationships.

[62] The High Court handed down judgment in *Zappone v Revenue Commissioners* [2008] 2 IR 417 on 14 December 2006.

government was willing to be responsible for making what would undoubtedly have been a significant social change.

B. Attorney General's Advice – A Political Smokescreen

In 2008, when civil partnership legislation was proposed, the then Minister for Justice, Dermot Ahern, claimed that the Government was acting on the advice of the then Attorney General, who was of the view that 'anything that would provide, or try to replicate "marriage" in this legislation would not stand constitutional scrutiny'.[63] It is respectfully submitted that the Attorney General, and consequently the Government, failed to accord adequate weight to the statute-sensitive approach to marriage evident in *Zappone*. Hence, the non-introduction of same-sex marriage can either be attributed to a (perhaps inadvertent) lack of appreciation as to the ramifications of the High Court judgment,[64] or a lack of political will on the part of the Fianna Fáil/Green Party coalition Government. The latter is probably closer to the truth. The Attorney General's advice 'is almost never published' and, as Kenny and Casey point out, 'this means that parliamentarians and the public cannot consider the correctness of the AG's advice for themselves'.[65] Thus, it is submitted that it might have been convenient for a government opposed to marriage equality to hide behind the Attorney General's overly cautious advice, using it as 'a pretext for inaction, letting the blame fall on the law rather than on the government if nothing is done'.[66] This view is not without merit – the author of the Green Party's policy on marriage and partnership rights claimed that its coalition partners, Fianna Fáil, stood opposed to the introduction of same-sex marriage when the Programme for Government was being negotiated, and the Green Party was the minority party in the coalition Government from 2007 to 2011.[67] Fianna Fáil is known for often taking a conservative stance on significant social issues. More than half the members of the Fianna Fáil parliamentary party backed a

---

[63] M Hennessy and C O'Brien, 'Bill to Grant Legal Protection to Same-Sex Couples', *Irish Times* (25 June 2008) 3. In Ireland, under Art 30 of the Constitution, the Attorney General is the Government's legal advisor and advises it as to legal and constitutional issues that might arise with proposed legislation.

[64] The Attorney General is not infallible – the current AG disagreed with legal advice given by his immediate predecessor that allowing adopted people to access their birth records would require a change to the Constitution. As Kenny and Casey point out, 'advice changes depending on who gives it'; see D Kenny and C Casey, 'The role of Attorney General should be more transparent – let's start by publishing the advice', *TheJournal.ie*, available at www.thejournal.ie/readme/attorney-general-ireland-5336108-Jan2021.

[65] ibid.

[66] ibid. Kenny and Casey argue that the AG's ability to act as an obstacle to proposed laws by being too cautious with their legal advice to the government makes the AG 'something of a one-person supreme court'. The authors cogently argue that the AG's legal advice should be published to facilitate greater transparency, and to enable such advice to be scrutinised and challenged, when appropriate.

[67] See 'Green Party Decision' *Gay Community News* (February 2008) 2.

'no' vote in a more recent referendum to remove the ban on abortion from the Constitution of Ireland.[68]

VII. Would the Supreme Court have Declared Same-Sex Marriage Legislation Unconstitutional?

The Government may have been apprehensive about introducing same-sex marriage legislation because any Bill purporting to do so could have been referred to the Supreme Court by the President of Ireland via the Article 26 reference procedure. Article 26 of the Constitution provides that, before signing it into law, the President may refer a Bill to the Supreme Court for a decision as to whether the Bill or any specified provision thereof is repugnant to the Constitution. However, the Article 26 reference procedure is rarely invoked; there have been 15 such references in the Constitution's 85–year history. Only one of the 15 Bills referred to the Supreme Court has ever been deemed entirely unconstitutional – the Matrimonial Homes Bill 1993 (Ireland).[69] The Bill sought to give non-owning wives equal legal rights to family homes owned by their husbands, and it was declared unconstitutional because it effectively forced all married couples into joint ownership of the family home, thus interfering in the autonomous decision-making of the family unit.[70] The Bill was found to be repugnant to Article 41 of the Constitution, wherein the state pledges to protect the family against 'attack'. Therefore, if an Article 26 reference was made in respect of a same-sex marriage Bill, it is possible that the Bill might have been deemed unconstitutional by the Supreme Court because marriage in Ireland has traditionally been understood as being opposite-sex in nature.[71] The highest court in the land could have slammed the door firmly shut on same-sex marriage, declaring it an 'attack' on the age-old institution of marriage which the State 'pledges itself to guard with special care' in Article 41.3.1.

---

[68] P Ryan, 'More than half of Fianna Fáil parliamentary party backing "no" vote in referendum', *Irish Independent* (online) (3 May 2018), available at www.independent.ie/irish-news/abortion-referendum/more-than-half-of-fianna-fil-parliamentary-party-backing-no-vote-in-referendum-36870462.html. However, the referendum to remove the constitutional protection for the unborn was successful. Fianna Fáil's lack of appetite for legislating for marriage equality at the time might be somewhat understandable in light of the findings contained in the All-Party Oireachtas Committee's report on 'The Family' in 2006. The All-Party Oireachtas Committee reported that in the submissions made to it as to whether the constitutional definition of the family should be extended in order to be capable of embracing same-sex marriage, there was 'a sharp division' and that many wished Art 41 on Marriage and The Family to remain unchanged as 'They fear that any change would threaten the position of the family based on marriage. It would undermine the stability of the traditional family and all the enhancement of the common good that flows from it': All-Party Oireachtas Committee on the Constitution, 'Tenth Progress Report: The Family' (Stationery Office, 2006) 121.

[69] See *Re Article 26 of the Constitution and the Matrimonial Home Bill, 1993* [1994] 1 IR 305.

[70] C Coulter, 'Possible blessing in disguise for Cabinet', *The Irish Times* (online) (23 December 2004), available at www.irishtimes.com/news/possible-blessing-in-disguise-for-cabinet-1.1171049.

[71] See *DT v CT* [2003] ILRM 321, 374 (Murray J).

Doyle believes that any attempt to introduce same-sex marriage legislation would have been struck down by the courts as unconstitutional.[72] He states that the statutory definition of marriage as evinced in section 2(2)(e) of the 2004 Act was but one of the reasons why the High Court rejected the plaintiff's claim in *Zappone*. While this is accurate, I have demonstrated that a close reading of the *Zappone* judgment makes it clear that the statutory definition was *the main reason* why the High Court ruled against the plaintiffs, with Dunne J emphasising that section 2(2)(e) was '*of itself*' an indication as to how marriage should be defined, and that '*ultimately*, it is for the legislature to determine the extent'[73] of the legal recognition to be accorded to same-sex relationships in Ireland. Overall, Dunne J's judgment is evidence of *substantial* judicial deference to legislative enactments.

Further, Doyle argues that any legislation introducing same-sex marriage would have been at odds with statements by the Supreme Court defining marriage as a union between parties of the opposite sex, and the traditional, gendered 'natural law ethos' of Article 41.[74] However, all of the Supreme Court's statements on marriage as a union between opposite-sex partners were obiter dicta, and Carolan emphasises that the judicial approach to marriage in *Zappone* 'certainly implies that a court should exercise considerable constraint in preferring its own perception of society's norms to that evinced in a statutory instrument'.[75] Doyle is correct in stating that Article 41 has a 'natural law ethos', because its terminology clearly conceives of marriage in traditional terms as an institution that is preoccupied with gender-determined roles and child-rearing.[76] This is particularly clear from Article 41.2.1, which refers to a 'woman' and 'her life within the home' as contributing to the 'common good', and Article 41.2.2, which obliges the state to 'endeavour to ensure that mothers shall not be obliged by economic necessity to engage in labour to the neglect of their duties in the home'. However, Article 41.2 has been described as being 'outdated, stereotypical, biologically deterministic' and 'insulting to women'.[77] Indeed, the Citizens' Assembly, the Constitutional Convention and, most recently, the Joint Oireachtas Committee on Gender Equality have all recommended that the provision should be amended to appear in a gender-neutral form that would include other carers both in and outside of the home.[78] Therefore, it is submitted that Article 41.2, a provision which specified

---

[72] O Doyle, 'Minority Rights and Democratic Consensus: The Irish Same-Sex Marriage Referendum' (2020) 15 *National Taiwan University Law Review* 21, 28.

[73] *Zappone v Revenue Commissioners* (n 4) 505.

[74] O Doyle, 'Minority Rights and Democratic Consensus' (2020).

[75] Carolan (n 55) 266.

[76] Indeed, in *McD v L* [2010] 1 ILRM 461, Denham J (at 488) in the Supreme Court made an obiter remark that '*arising from the terms of the Constitution*, "family" means a family based on marriage, the marriage of a man and a woman'.

[77] All-Party Oireachtas Committee on the Constitution (n 68) 106.

[78] See 'Second Report of the Convention on the Constitution' (Convention on the Constitution, May 2013), available at www.constitutionalconvention.ie/AttachmentDownload.ashx?mid=268d930 8-c9b7-e211-a5a0-005056a32ee4. See also Recommendations of the Citizens' Assembly on Gender Equality (Citizens Assembly, 2021), available at www.citizensassembly.ie/en/news-publications/press-releases/recommendations-of-the-citizens-assembly-on-gender-equality.html. The Constitutional

a particular enumerated safeguard for marriage that had in mind the majority of family types at the time, and which is clearly derided in modern Ireland, would not have been interpreted by the Supreme Court as circumscribing any contemporary legislative conception of marriage within the 1937 ideal.[79] For all of the abovementioned reasons, I respectfully disagree with the arguments proffered by Doyle and believe that instead, the Supreme Court would have replicated the High Court's approach to marriage in *Zappone* and 'used statute rather than its own experience as evidence of the prevailing social view'.[80] Indeed, in its policy on marriage and partnership rights in 2006, the Green Party claimed to anticipate the adoption of this manner of judicial approach to a same-sex marriage Bill:

> [W]e believe that the Supreme Court would be unlikely to strike down such an expression of the democratic will of the Oireachtas on the grounds that marriage under Article 41 can only be defined in relation to Christian beliefs.[81]

Doyle's belief that any attempt to introduce same-sex marriage via legislation would have been struck down by the courts also fails to take into account that the courts are most deferential to the Oireachtas when it comes to deciding the *capacity* to benefit from rights guaranteed by the Constitution, and on matters of social policy.[82] Dunne J's approach in *Zappone* is similar to Murray J's in *Sinnott v Minster for Education*,[83] in that both judges respect the statutory bar placed on one's capacity to enjoy a constitutional right.

In *Sinnott*, the petitioner was a 22-year-old male with severe autism. The state was appealing the High Court judgment in which it was held to have an open-ended duty to provide the petitioner with free primary education beyond the age of 18. Reversing the High Court decision, Murray J, and indeed a majority of the Supreme Court, held that in the context of the constitutional right to free primary education which is guaranteed under Article 42.4, the state's duty expires when a person reaches the age of 18, *which is the age of majority set by legislation*. Thus, the Supreme Court respected the decision of the Oireachtas regarding a person's

---

Convention (2012–16) and the Citizens' Assemblies (2016–18; 2019–21) were exercises in participative democracy designed to consider changes to the Constitution and the law in specified areas. The former body was comprised of a Chairperson, 33 members of the Oireachtas and 66 citizens, and the Citizens' Assemblies were comprised of a Chairperson and 99 citizens. See also Joint Committee on Gender Equality, 'Interim Report on Constitutional Change' (Joint Committee on Gender Equality, 2022) 22.

[79] I would like to thank my colleague, Dr Eoin Daly, for his valuable insight on this matter.

[80] Carolan (n 55) 266. The Irish courts have been *largely* willing to defer to the legislature on matters of social policy and the appropriate balancing of constitutional rights for many decades. In *Tuohy v Courtney* [1994] 3 IR 1 at 47, the Supreme Court held that in an action challenging the constitutionality of any statute, 'the role of the courts is not to impose their view of the correct or desirable balance in substitution for the view of the legislature as displayed in their legislation but rather to determine from an objective stance whether the balance contained in the impugned legislation is *so contrary to reason and fairness* as to constitute an unjust attack on some individual's constitutional rights'. Thus, the courts will generally defer *unless* the approach of the legislature is 'so contrary to reason and fairness'.

[81] Green Party, 'Valuing Families: A Policy on Marriage and Partnership Rights' (Green Party, 2006) 8.

[82] *Sinnott v Minister for Education* [2001] 2 IR 545; *D v Ireland* [2012] IESC 10.

[83] *Sinnott v Minister for Education* [2001] 2 IR 545.

capacity to benefit from the constitutional right to free primary education under Article 42.4. Similarly, in *Zappone*, the High Court respected the decision of the Oireachtas, as contained in the Civil Registration Act 2004, prescribing a couple's capacity to enter into a constitutionally protected marriage under Article 41, and strongly indicated that it was solely for the Oireachtas to decide the capacity to marry.

Further, the courts' deference to the Oireachtas on complex, controversial social issues is apparent from the more recent case of *MR & Ors v An tArd Chláraitheoir & Ors*.[84] There is currently no legislation regulating surrogacy in Ireland, and in this case the Supreme Court reversed the High Court's decision that the genetic mother of twins born to a gestational surrogate be registered as the mother on the twins' birth certificates. Existing legislation only permits the birth mother, ie the gestational surrogate in this instance, to be registered on the twins' birth certificates. Nonetheless, in the Supreme Court, Denham CJ held that:

> Such lacuna should be addressed in legislation and not by this Court … Under the current legislative framework it is not possible to address issues arising on surrogacy, including the issue of who is the mother for the purpose of the registration of the birth. *The issues raised in this case are important, complex and social, which are matters of public policy for the Oireachtas.*[85]

Not only is it highly unlikely that the Supreme Court would have struck down same-sex marriage legislation as being unconstitutional but, internationally, constitutional challenges to same-sex marriage laws have foundered. The superior courts of countries like Spain, Portugal and France all upheld the validity of same-sex marriage legislation when constitutional challenges were mounted against it. In Spain, the Constitutional Court confirmed that the Constitution did not require same-sex marriage, but same-sex marriage 'was a legislative option that did not infringe the Constitution either.'[86] Similarly, in Portugal, the Constitutional Court held that although the Constitution 'did not require the opening up of marriage, it also did not impede such reform, which could be decided by Parliament as part of the ordinary exercise of its legislative powers.'[87] In France, the Constitutional Court was of the view that the Constitution did not prohibit same-sex marriage and confirmed that the legislature had the power to open up the institution of marriage.[88] In *Zappone*, the High Court was clearly of the view that the Constitution did not require same-sex marriage, yet it strongly intimated that same-sex marriage was a matter for the Oireachtas. The judicial approach to

---

[84] *MR v An t-Ard Chláraitheoir* [2014] IESC 60.

[85] ibid, [116]–[118]; emphasis added.

[86] CG Beilfuss, 'Southern Jurisdictions: Consolidation in the West, Progress in the East' in K Boele-Welki and M Fuchs (eds), *Same-Sex Relationships and Beyond: Gender Matters in the EU*, 3rd edn (Cambridge, Intersentia, 2017) 42. See Case no 198/2012, 6 November 2012, SCT.

[87] ibid, 43.

[88] Case no 2013-669 DC, 17 May 2013. See generally A Sperti, *Constitutional Courts, Gay Rights and Sexual Orientation Equality* (Oxford, Hart, 2017) 92–97.

marriage equality in Spain, Portugal, France and Ireland was similar – the superior courts were in favour of the matter being resolved by the national Parliaments. In France, as Sperti points out, 'it is worth noting that the Conseil constitutionnel took a firm stance in recognising the power of Parliament to regulate sensitive social issues (questions de société)',[89] and similarly in Ireland, complex social issues are seen by the courts as 'matters of public policy for the Oireachtas'.[90] Thus, one is inclined to agree with Encarnacion that 'in sum, it is not unthinkable that a same-sex marriage law in Ireland could have survived constitutional scrutiny, just as similar laws have in other countries'.[91]

VIII.   Constitutional Convention

The Civil Partnership and Certain Rights and Obligations of Cohabitants Act 2010 entered into force on 1 January 2011, enabling same-sex couples to enter into civil partnerships and gain formal legal recognition of their relationship. Despite this positive development (pragmatically, if not symbolically) the struggle for same-sex marriage continued unabated with advocacy groups like Marriage Equality continuing to mobilise.[92] Hence when a Fine Gael/Labour coalition Government came to power in February 2011 it established a Constitutional Convention to consider comprehensive constitutional reform. It was agreed between the parties in the Programme for Government that the issue of same-sex marriage would go to the Constitutional Convention.[93] The Convention was a venture in participatory democracy tasked with considering certain aspects of the Constitution to ensure that the basic law of the state was fully equipped for the twenty-first century. Once it debated an aspect of the Constitution, the Convention prepared a report containing recommendations for consideration by the Oireachtas. The Convention was required to report back to the Oireachtas on each aspect of the Constitution under its consideration within a 12-month period. The Convention was comprised of a chairman, 33 Members of Parliament and 66 citizens who were randomly selected by a polling company using the electoral register. The citizen members were broadly representative of Irish society and generally balanced in terms of gender, age, region, social class and occupational status.

The Convention was slow to begin its work, which led to the body being dubbed as the '"garden shed", a dumping ground for any issue likely to cause Coalition

---

[89] ibid, 96.

[90] *MR v An t-Ard Chláraitheoir* [2014] IESC 60, [118]. See also *Roche v Roche* [2009] IESC 82.

[91] OG Encarnacion, 'There's Something about Marriage', *Foreign Affairs*, available at www.foreign affairs.com/articles/ireland/2015-05-31/theres-something-about-marriage.

[92] See G Healy, B Sheehan and N Whelan, *Ireland Says Yes: The Inside Story of how the Vote for Marriage Equality was Won* (Dublin, Merrion Press, 2015).

[93] See 'Programme for Government 2011–2016', available at www.merrionstreet.ie/en/wp-content/uploads/2010/05/programme_for_government_2011.pdf.

grief until it's safe to resurrect it – ideally, sometime in the next term.[94] Despite these initial misgivings, in 2013, having considered the issue, the Constitutional Convention voted by an overwhelming majority for express constitutional provision to be made for same-sex marriage. Indeed, in the Third Report of the Convention on the Constitution it was reported that 'a strong majority favoured amendment of the Constitution to provide for same-sex marriage. A similarly strong majority favoured *directive or mandatory wording* in the event of such amendment going ahead'.[95]

Thus, rather than vote in favour of a permissive amendment providing that the state *may* enact laws providing for same-sex marriage, the vast majority of the Convention's members (78 out of 100) voted in favour of a directive amendment providing that the state *shall* enact laws providing for same-sex marriage.[96] The Third Report of the Convention on the Constitution, which contains this recommendation, was deposited in the library of the Houses of the Oireachtas in June 2013. Shortly thereafter the Fine Gael/Labour Coalition Government committed itself to holding a referendum on same-sex marriage in 2015,[97] because in order for *express provision* for same-sex marriage to be made in the Constitution a majority of the Irish people would have to approve this change to Article 41 via a referendum.[98]

IX. Marriage Referendum

The Marriage Referendum was held on 22 May 2015 and there was cause for concern regarding voter turnout because the previous referendum, the Children's Referendum in November 2012,[99] saw a mere 33.49 per cent of the Irish electorate turn out to cast their votes.[100] Any concern as to voter turnout proved unfounded, as more than 60 per cent of the Irish people cast a vote in the Marriage Referendum.[101] Voter turnout was among the highest since the Constitution was enacted in 1937, with young and working class voters coming out in force to

---

[94] K Sheridan, 'How Gay Marriage went Mainstream', *Irish Times* (14 July 2012) 2.

[95] 'Third Report of the Convention on the Constitution: Amending the Constitution to Provide for Same-Sex Marriage' (Convention on the Constitution, 2013), available at www.constitutionalconvention. ie/AttachmentDownload.ashx?mid=c90ab08b-ece2-e211-a5a0-005056a32ee4.

[96] ibid.

[97] K Rose, 'Historic Step in Remarkable Journey to Equal Marriage: Ireland has made huge progress in evolving toward full equality for LGBT people', *Irish Times* (8 November 2013) 18.

[98] See Art 46, Constitution of Ireland.

[99] This was a referendum which proposed the insertion of a new article into the Constitution, Art 42A, to provide express constitutional protection for the rights of the child. The referendum was successful and Art 42A now forms part of the Constitution of Ireland.

[100] M O'Halloran, 'Young Voter Surge Pushes Turnout into Top Five Highest', *Irish Times* (25 May 2015) 2.

[101] ibid.

show solidarity with the LGBT+ community.[102] By noon on 23 May it was abundantly clear that the Irish people had voted in favour of allowing constitutional recognition of, and protection for, same-sex marriage. The national electorate comprises some 3,222,681 people, and 1,949,725 of them turned out to vote. There were 13,818 spoiled votes.[103] The final result saw 1,201,607 votes to allow same-sex marriage, with 734,300 votes against, giving the 'yes' campaign a victory with a very comfortable margin of 62.07 per cent to 37.93per cent.[104] Ireland made history by becoming the first country in the world to introduce same-sex marriage by means of a popular vote. The Thirty-fourth Amendment of the Constitution (Marriage Equality) Act 2015 (Ireland) was signed into law by the President of Ireland on 29 August 2015, and the 'Marriage Equality Amendment', Article 41.4, officially became part of the Constitution of Ireland. Article 41.4 provides that 'marriage may be contracted in accordance with law by two persons without distinction as to their sex'. In November 2015, the Marriage Act 2015 amended existing marriage laws to give effect to the constitutional amendment. The first same-sex marriages took place on 17 November 2015.

X. Marriage Equality in Australia

This chapter has critiqued the manner in which marriage equality became a reality in Ireland. In less than a decade, Ireland moved from commencing a legislative prohibition on same-sex marriage to enacting the Marriage Act and extending the right to marry to same-sex couples.[105] In the interim, there was much meandering between the various branches of government and, ultimately, marriage equality really came about as a result of a citizen-led exercise in participative democracy and a popular vote. However, Ireland's situation is not really unique; there are striking parallels between the journey towards marriage equality in Ireland and that in another common law jurisdiction – Australia.

As discussed, the increasing judicial recognition post-millennium of a right to same-sex marriage in other jurisdictions likely influenced the enactment of Ireland's premier statutory prohibition on same-sex marriage in 2004. At this time, akin to Ireland, Australia did not have any statutory prohibition on same-sex marriage. Witzleb observes that in Australia, 'the then Liberal/National Government became

---

[102] Over 100,000 new voters were registered in the months prior to the referendum, most of whom were young, first-time voters and students. Further, the percentage of 'Yes' votes in some of the most socially deprived areas of the capital, Dublin, was quite remarkable. 87% of voters in Dublin's Jobstown voted 'Yes', with 88% of voters in Coolock and The Liberties voting the same way, while 85% of voters in Ballyfermot also voted 'Yes'.

[103] F Kelly, 'Kenny hails vote as pioneering: 62% of voters support constitutional amendment with 38% against', *Irish Times* (25 May 2015) 2.

[104] ibid.

[105] Section 2(2)(e) of the Civil Registration Act 2004 was commenced on 5 December 2005. The Marriage Act 2015 was commenced on 16 November 2015.

concerned that Australian courts might follow Canadian decisions' and hence the Marriage Amendment Act 2004 was enacted by the federal Parliament to amend the Marriage Act 1961 so that section 5(1) defined marriage as 'the union of a man and a woman to the exclusion of all others, voluntarily entered into for life'.[106] As Witzleb points out in the Australian context, 'the amendment gave the common law definition statutory force and thus put it beyond the reach of reform-minded courts'.[107] Indeed, the intention of Australia's federal Parliament was clear from the Explanatory Memorandum to the Marriage Amendment Bill 2004, because this states that the purpose of the amending legislation was to 'protect the institution of marriage by ensuring that marriage means a union of a man and a woman and that same sex relationships cannot be equated with marriage'.[108] The fact that two court applications seeking the recognition of foreign same-sex marriages had already been filed when the Marriage Amendment Bill 2004 was being debated in the Australian Parliament strongly indicates that the then Australian Government had significant concerns regarding the potential for judicial recognition of same-sex marriage in the courts.[109]

Nonetheless, Australia's first statutory prohibition on same-sex marriage, enacted in the same year as its equivalent statutory prohibition in Ireland, resulted in a similar outcome in same-sex marriage litigation in that jurisdiction. In 2013, the Australian High Court's deference to this legislative amendment was abundantly evident in Australia's same-sex marriage case, *Commonwealth v Australian Capital Territory*.[110]

A. Same-Sex Marriage in the Australian Courts: *Commonwealth v Australian Capital Territory*

The Australian Capital Territory (ACT) legislated for same-sex marriage in October 2013, when its Legislative Assembly passed the Marriage Equality (Same Sex) Act 2013 (ACT). The ACT legislation authorised marriage within the Australian Capital Territory for same-sex couples who were unable to marry under the Marriage Act 1961, as amended. Shortly thereafter, the federal Parliament challenged the ACT legislation in the High Court on the ground that it was inconsistent

---

[106] N Witzleb, 'Marriage as the "Last Frontier"? Same-Sex Relationship Recognition in Australia' (2011) 25 *International Journal of Law, Policy and the Family* 135, 153–54. Following the success of the postal plebiscite on same-sex marriage, the Marriage Amendment (Definition and Religious Freedoms) Act 2017 (Cth) amended this definition of marriage in s 5(1) of the 1961 Act by replacing the words 'a man and a woman' with '2 people'.

[107] ibid, 154.

[108] See Explanatory Memorandum, Marriage Amendment Bill 2004, available at www.legislation.gov.au/Details/C2004B01703/Explanatory%20Memorandum/Text.

[109] See Commonwealth, 'Parliamentary Debates', House of Representatives (24 June 2004) 31461 (Nicola Roxon), available at parlinfo.aph.gov.au/parlInfo/download/chamber/hansardr/2004-06-24/toc_pdf/3496-4.pdf;fileType=application%2Fpdf.

[110] (2013) 250 CLR 441.

with the Marriage Act 1961. The ACT legislation was struck down by a unanimous High Court on 12 December 2013.

Similar to the Constitution of Ireland, the Australian Constitution does not define marriage. Nonetheless, and in contrast to Ireland, the High Court of Australia expressly held that the constitutional concept of marriage in s. 51(xxi) could include same-sex marriage, as

> 'marriage' is to be understood in s 51(xxi) of the *Constitution* as referring to a consensual union formed between natural persons in accordance with legally prescribed requirements which is not only a union the law recognises as intended to endure and be terminable only in accordance with law but also a union to which the law accords a status affecting and defining mutual rights and obligations ... When used in s 51(xxi), 'marriage' is a term which includes a marriage between persons of the same sex.[111]

Section 51(xxi) of the Australian Constitution gives the federal Parliament the power to legislate in respect of marriage. Indeed, the High Court's conclusion made it clear that *only* the federal Parliament could legislate for same-sex marriage. This finding was anathema to the legal validity of the ACT legislation:

> It is necessary to bear steadily in mind that the federal Parliament has power under s 51(xxi) to make a national law with respect to same sex marriage ... The federal Parliament has not made a law permitting same sex marriage. But the absence of a provision permitting same sex marriage does not mean that the Territory legislature may make such a provision. It does not mean that a Territory law permitting same sex marriage can operate concurrently with the federal law.[112]

The High Court noted that the Marriage Act had been amended in 2004 to expressly stipulate that for its purposes marriage is an opposite-sex union, and to expressly prohibit foreign same-sex marriages from being recognised in Australia. According to the High Court, the upshot of the 2004 amendments to the Marriage Act was that

> the kind of marriage provided for by the Act is the *only* kind of marriage that may be formed or recognised in Australia. It follows that the provisions of the ACT Act which provide for marriage under that Act cannot operate concurrently with the Marriage Act and accordingly are inoperative.[113]

Hence the Marriage Act 1961 constitutes *the* national law as regards the capacity to marry. The High Court deemed this piece of legislation 'a comprehensive and exhaustive statement of the law with respect to the creation and recognition of the legal status of marriage'.[114] In the aftermath of this case, Parkinson and Aroney correctly observed that 'the future of marriage is now firmly with the Federal Parliament'.[115]

---

[111] ibid 461 [33], 463 [38].
[112] ibid 467 [56].
[113] ibid 468 [59].
[114] ibid 467 [57].
[115] P Parkinson and N Aroney, 'The Territory of Marriage: Constitutional Law, Marriage Law and Family Policy in the ACT Same-Sex Marriage Case' (2014) 28 *Australian Journal of Family Law* 160.

The High Court's approach in this case is very similar to the Irish High Court's earlier decision in *Zappone v Revenue Commissioners*.[116] Both Courts treated the statutory amendments to the definition of marriage in their respective jurisdictions in 2004 as clearly delineating the *only* type of marriage that can be entered into – hence both Courts were highly deferential to the legislative view of marriage as espoused by their respective national Parliaments. Further, the Irish High Court strongly indicated that the Irish Parliament could legislate for same-sex marriage and the understanding of marriage in Article 41 of the Constitution of Ireland would be deemed 'updated' by such legislation, while the Australian High Court expressly stated that the federal Parliament has the power to legislate for same-sex marriage and the constitutional understanding of marriage in s 51(xxi) *already* embraces this concept. However, the reason why the Australian High Court was willing to accept that same-sex marriage was encompassed by s 51(xxi) of the *Australian Constitution* was because

> other legal systems now provide for marriage between persons of the same sex. This may properly be described as being a recent development of the law of marriage in those jurisdictions. It is not useful or relevant for this Court to examine how or why this has happened. What matters is that the juristic concept of marriage (the concept to which s 51(xxi) refers) embraces such unions.[117]

The High Court referred to marriage equality laws in place in Canada, New Zealand and England and Wales, adding that examples of such laws could be 'multiplied'. Unlike Dunne J's finding in the Irish High Court in December 2006, by 2013 there was significant global support for the concept of same-sex marriage, and the High Court acknowledged this and its effect on the interpretation of marriage under section 51(xxi). Despite these significant, similar rulings in each jurisdiction, the Irish and Australian Parliaments did not proceed to legislate for marriage equality. Instead, they once again adopted a similar, citizen-led approach to the dilemma posed by same-sex marriage. For Ireland, it was the Constitutional Convention, and for Australia, it was the postal plebiscite.

B. Australia's Postal Plebiscite on Marriage Equality

The postal plebiscite on same-sex marriage was Australia's version of the 'Constitutional Convention', so to speak. It was merely a different, far more costly means of gauging public opinion on a divisive human rights issue before the Government would commit itself to a specific course of action. The postal plebiscite

---

In *Commonwealth v Australian Capital Territory* (2013) 250 CLR 441, 452 [1], the High Court itself had made it very clear that marriage equality was a matter for the Federal Parliament: 'Under the Constitution and federal law as it now stands, whether same sex marriage should be provided for by law … is a matter for the federal Parliament'.

[116] [2008] 2 IR 417.

[117] *Commonwealth v Australian Capital Territory* (2013) 250 CLR 441, 462 [37].

was preceded by plans to hold a traditional, in-person plebiscite. Prior to the Australian Federal Election in July 2016 the Liberal/National coalition Government, led by Malcolm Turnbull, proposed a national plebiscite on same-sex marriage, one for which voter turnout would be compulsory. However, after the Liberal/National coalition won the Federal Election it was unable to pass the legislation necessary to give effect to its proposal. The Plebiscite (Same-Sex Marriage) Bill 2016 (Cth) was passed by the House of Representatives but defeated in the Senate by Labour, the Greens and Senate crossbenchers, all of whom favoured a parliamentary vote on marriage equality instead of a plebiscite process. Despite this, the coalition Government remained committed to the notion of a national vote, and consequently the postal plebiscite was announced by the Government on 7 August 2017. This was a voluntary national postal survey on whether same-sex marriage should be legalised. The coalition Government instructed the Australian Bureau of Statistics (ABS) to carry out what became known as the Australian Marriage Law Postal Survey.[118] The ABS distributed survey forms with 'reply-paid' envelopes to over 16 million Australian citizens from 13 September 2017. Survey forms had to be returned by 7 November. The ABS revealed the result of the postal survey on 15 November 2017, which was strikingly similar to that achieved in Ireland in 2015. Australia had voted in favour of marriage equality, with 61.6 per cent of those who participated in the postal survey voting 'yes', and 38.4 per cent voting 'no'. Over 12.7 million Australians, or 79.5 per cent of voters, had participated in the postal survey.[119] The Marriage Amendment (Definition and Religious Freedoms) Bill 2017 (Cth) was passed on 7 December 2017; it received royal assent on 8 December, and the Act came into force on 9 December. The first same-sex marriage ceremony took place in Australia on 15 December 2017.[120]

XI. Plebiscites, Referenda, Political Opportunism and Human Rights Issues

The Irish coalition Government should not be lauded for its willingness to hold a referendum on marriage equality when one acknowledges that it only agreed to do so because the Constitutional Convention, a body comprised largely of ordinary

---

[118] There were a number of unsuccessful legal challenges to the postal survey in Australia – *Wilkie v Commonwealth* (2017) 349 ALR 1 – these cases were heard simultaneously by the High Court of Australia. A discussion of these cases is beyond the scope of this chapter.

[119] H Davidson, 'Australia's same-sex marriage postal survey: 61.6% yes, 38.4% no – as it happened', *The Guardian* (online) (15 November 2017), available at www.theguardian.com/australia-news/live/2017/nov/15/australias-same-sex-marriage-postal-survey-results-live. There was far higher voter participation in the Australian postal plebiscite than there was in the Irish Marriage Referendum, where voter turnout was at 60%.

[120] P Williams, 'The first same-sex couple to wed in Australia were only married for 48 days before death parted them', ABC News (online) (7 March 2018), available at www.abc.net.au/news/2018-03-07/heartbreaking-story-behind-australias-first-same-sex-marriage/9523098.

Irish citizens, voted in favour of making legal provision for same-sex marriage. Indeed, sending this contentious matter to the Constitutional Convention for deliberation was something of a political masterstroke. If the Fine Gael/Labour coalition had simply announced that it was holding a referendum on the issue without any intervention from the Convention, it might have lost much public support from those opposed to such a move. Instead, the Government made it look as though it was giving the people the chance to 'have their say' through a constitutional referendum, because this is what the people, as represented by the members of the Constitutional Convention, had indicated that they were in favour of. Given that the coalition Government failed to act on recommendations in relation to *seven of the nine areas* that the Convention reported back on, and the fact that marriage equality was the only recommendation from the Constitutional Convention that ultimately became law,[121] one might further surmise that this exercise in participatory democracy was predominantly set up to deal with the issue of same-sex marriage in a politically sensitive and convenient manner.

The same logic can be applied to the Australian coalition Government's willingness to move to legislate for same-sex marriage – it only arose from the result of the postal plebiscite, a nationwide public opinion poll on marriage equality. The Australian coalition Government was unwilling to move to introduce marriage equality legislation without first utilising such a public process because it wanted to save political face. Thus, the Constitutional Convention and the postal plebiscite can really be viewed as politically convenient methods of participatory democracy, opportunistically employed to deal with a divisive human rights issue before the state would commit itself to any specific course of action.

Although the recommendations from Ireland's Constitutional Convention and the result of Australia's postal plebiscite were in favour of marriage equality, these positive outcomes did not mean that a change in the law was *guaranteed*. The recommendations of the Constitutional Convention were not binding on the Irish Government, but it rather swiftly committed to holding a referendum on marriage equality. Similarly, the result of a plebiscite is non-binding and needs to be passed through Parliament, although the then Australian Prime Minister Malcolm Turnbull was consistent in his declarations that if a plebiscite was ultimately successful then Australian MPs would be allowed a free vote in Parliament on whether the Marriage Act should be amended to embrace marriage equality.

The Marriage Referendum and the postal plebiscite can best be described as crude but effective methods of introducing marriage equality. The processes were crude because placing the rights of a minority group in the hands of the majority seems almost ludicrous, as a sizeable number of the electorate could have simply voted against the issue without being properly informed in the way that elected

---

[121] B Tobin, 'Fine Gael and Labour's approach to marriage equality was crude, uncertain and politically opportune', Irish Times (online) (17 November 2015), available at www.irishtimes.com/opinion/fine-gael-and-labour-s-approach-to-marriage-equality-was-crude-uncertain-and-politically-opportune-1.2433221.

politicians are expected to be when legislating.[122] Indeed, the 'No' campaign in Ireland was actively attempting to misinform citizens.[123] These public processes force a historically oppressed minority group to rally together to plead with the majority for access to the institution of marriage. The Irish 'Yes' campaign literally had its members knocking on doors nationwide – LGBT+ people were reduced to 'begging' for Irish society's approval of their intimate relationships. A survey of the negative social and psychological impacts of Ireland's 'No' campaign, which was conducted by Australian academics at the University of Queensland and Victoria University in conjunction with Irish marriage equality activists and LGBT+ organisations, found that of the 1,657 participants, 71 per cent reported that they often or always felt negative in the months leading up to the Marriage Referendum due to the 'No' campaign. Two-thirds of the participants reported feeling anxiety and distress due to the 'No' campaign posters.[124] Similarly, in Australia, research has demonstrated that frequent exposure to negative anti-LGBT+ media messages during the postal plebiscite was associated with greater psychological stress in LGBT+ persons.[125]

Based on these findings it seems clear that if a majority of the electorate had voted against marriage equality in either jurisdiction, then LGBT+ citizens throughout Ireland and Australia would undoubtedly have felt a profound sense of public rejection in the aftermath of the results. Indeed, in August 2017, the Senate Finance and Public Administration References Committee launched an inquiry into the process that the Australian Government chose to adopt in order to bring about marriage equality legislation, that is, the holding of a non-binding postal plebiscite. The Committee issued its report in February 2018, wherein it concluded that a non-compulsory, non-binding postal survey had never previously been used to inform parliamentary processes on a matter of human rights for a minority group; the Committee was firmly of the view that a plebiscite process should not be used this way in the future.[126]

---

[122] B Tobin, 'Australia doesn't need a plebiscite on same-sex marriage – Ireland's experience shows why', *The Conversation* (26 June 2016), available at theconversation.com/australia-doesnt-need-a-plebiscite-on-same-sex-marriage-irelands-experience-shows-why-61499.

[123] S Bardon, 'Surrogacy and adoption rights will not be affected: Minister accuses No side of trying to confuse voters with irrelevant issues', *The Irish Times* (13 May 2015) 4.

[124] S Dane, L Short and G Healy, 'Swimming with Sharks: The negative social and psychological impacts of Ireland's marriage equality referendum "NO" campaign' Survey Report (University of Queensland, 7 October 2016), available at espace.library.uq.edu.au/view/UQ:408120/Ireland_Survey_Final_F_compressed.pdf.

[125] S Verrelli et al, 'Minority Stress, Social Support, and the Mental Health of Lesbian, Gay and Bisexual Australians during the Australian Marriage Law Postal Survey' (2019) 54 *Australian Psychologist* 336, 341.

[126] Senate Finance and Public Administration References Committee, Parliament of Australia, 'Arrangements for the postal survey' (Commonwealth of Australia, 2018) 33, available at www.aph.gov.au/Parliamentary_Business/Committees/Senate/Finance_and_Public_Administration/postalsurvey/~/media/Committees/fapa_ctte/postalsurvey/report.pdf.

XII. The Potential Pitfalls Associated with Australia's Postal Plebiscite and Ireland's Marriage Referendum

Although allowing the people to ultimately decide via a national vote as to whether same-sex marriage should be granted legal protection was transparent, politically convenient and ultimately successful, it was a somewhat risky venture. In Ireland, prior to the Marriage Referendum, the Gay and Lesbian Equality Network had noted that no referendum anywhere in the world had passed same-sex marriage.[127] Further, in 2006 the All-Party Oireachtas Committee on the Constitution had observed in its 'Tenth Progress Report: The Family', that the 'Irish experience of constitutional amendments shows that they may be extremely divisive and that however well-intentioned they may be, they can have unexpected outcomes'.[128] This is true because, as Ryan points out regarding Ireland's constitutional prohibition on divorce, 'the removal of the ban on divorce, most notably, took two attempts, in 1986 and 1995, the ban eventually being discarded in 1995 by the tiniest of margins'.[129] Further, voter turnout for the Children's Referendum in 2012 was as low as 33 per cent, and the 'Children's Amendment', Article 42A, was not passed by an overwhelming number of voters – 58 per cent of those who turned out voted in favour of the amendment, and 42 per cent voted against. In 2006, the All-Party Oireachtas Committee reported that in the submissions made to it as to whether the constitutional definition of the family should be expanded there was 'a sharp division' and that many wished Articles 41 and 42 to remain unchanged as 'they fear that any change would threaten the position of the family based on marriage. It would undermine the stability of the traditional family and all the enhancement of the common good that flows from it'.[130] This led the All-Party Oireachtas Committee to conclude that a proposed constitutional amendment to extend the definition of the 'Family' would cause deep and long-lasting division in Irish society and would not necessarily be passed by a majority of voters in a referendum. However, Keane was critical of the Committee for ultimately recommending civil partnership legislation over a constitutional referendum on Article 41 because 'virtually every proposal to amend the Constitution provokes opposition from some quarters ... That is an inevitable consequence of the democratic process: it is not a justification for leaving untouched the framework of [Article 41]'.[131]

Nonetheless, a referendum may have proved rather divisive because the Committee's conclusions suggested that traditional views on the marital family

---

[127] K Sheridan, 'How gay marriage went mainstream', *The Irish Times* (14 July 2012) 2.

[128] All-Party Oireachtas Committee on the Constitution (n 68) 122.

[129] F Ryan, '21st Century Families, 19th Century Values: Modern Family Law in the Shadow of the Constitution' in O Doyle and E Carolan (eds), *The Irish Constitution: Governance and Values* (Dublin, Thomson Round Hall, 2008) 374–75.

[130] All-Party Oireachtas Committee on the Constitution (n 68) 122.

[131] R Keane, 'The Constitution and the Family: The Case for a New Approach' in O Doyle and E Carolan (eds), *The Irish Constitution: Governance and Values* (Dublin, Thomson Round Hall, 2008) 355.

remained dominant in a society where, merely four years pre-referendum, Census results indicated that 84 per cent of the population still identified as Roman Catholic.[132] Indeed, Croatia, a country where 86 per cent of the population identified as Roman Catholic in 2011,[133] held the first referendum on the constitutional definition of marriage on 1 December 2013, a mere 18 months before Ireland's Marriage Referendum, and the majority of voters there voted for the constitutional definition of marriage in Article 62 of the Croatian Constitution as a union between a man and a woman.[134]

Conversely, in the five-year period prior to the Marriage Referendum, Irish opinion polls leaned heavily in favour of marriage equality. In 2010, an opinion poll in *The Irish Times* indicated that just over two-thirds (67 per cent) of the Irish people believed that same-sex couples should be allowed to marry.[135] In 2011, Red C, a research and marketing group based in Dublin, conducted another opinion poll on same-sex marriage, which found that 73 per cent of the population was in favour.[136] In 2014, an opinion poll in *The Irish Times* indicated that 76 per cent of the electorate supported the introduction of same-sex marriage.[137] In 2015, the last opinion poll published by Red C just prior to the Marriage Referendum indicated that support for a 'Yes' vote had dropped slightly to 69 per cent.[138] In Australia, a poll by Ipsos in 2013 indicated that 54 per cent of Australians were in favour of marriage equality.[139] In 2015, a poll by Essential Media Communications showed support for same-sex marriage in Australia at 59 per cent.[140] In September 2017, a poll conducted by *The Guardian* shortly after the commencement of the postal vote showed that 55 per cent of Australian people were in favour of marriage equality.[141] It is unsurprising that support for a 'Yes' vote dropped

---

[132] Census 2011, 'This is Ireland: Part 1' (CSO, 2012).

[133] For the 2011 Census results in Croatia see www.dzs.hr/eng/censuses/census2011/results/htm/e01_01_10/e01_01_10_RH.html.

[134] Voter turnout was low (37.9%) but 65.87% of voters were in favour of amending Art 62 of the Croatian Constitution to provide for a constitutional definition of marriage as a union between a man and a woman. See further S Kralijić, 'Same-Sex Partnerships in Eastern Europe: Marriage, Registration or no Regulation' in K Boele-Welki and M Fuchs (eds), *Same-Sex Relationships and Beyond: Gender Matters in the EU*, 3rd edn (Cambridge, Intersentia, 2017) 62.

[135] C O'Brien, 'Two-thirds support gay marriage, poll finds', *The Irish Times* (Dublin, 15 September 2010) 1.

[136] M Marsh, J Suiter and T Reidy, 'Report on Reasons Behind Voter Behaviour in the Oireachtas Inquiry Referendum 2011' (Red C, January 2012), available at per.gov.ie/wp-content/uploads/OIReferendum-Report-Final-2003-corrected.

[137] S Collins, 'Support for same-sex marriage increasing, poll finds', *The Irish Times* (7 April 2014) 1.

[138] A Nardelli, 'Could polls be wrong about outcome of Ireland's gay marriage referendum?', *The Guardian* (online) (18 May 2015), available at www.theguardian.com/society/2015/may/18/could-polls-be-wrong-irelands-gay-marriage-referendum-vote-same-sex.

[139] See Ipsos, 'Same-Sex Marriage: Citizens in 16 Countries Assess Their Views on Same-Sex Marriage for a Total Global Perspective' Survey Report (June 2013), available at web.archive.org/web/20160314051755/http://www.ipsos-na.com/download/pr.aspx?id=12795.

[140] See Essential Research, 'The Essential Report' (Essential Media Communications, 27 October 2015), available at essentialvision.com.au/documents/essential_report_151027.pdf.

[141] K Murphy, 'Marriage equality support falls but yes vote still leads – Guardian Essentials poll', *The Guardian* (online) (18 September 2017), available at www.theguardian.com/australia-news/2017/sep/19/marriage-equality-support-falls-but-yes-vote-still-leads-guardian-essential-poll.

slightly in Ireland and Australia in the lead up to each jurisdiction's national vote on marriage equality since the Irish and Australian 'No' campaigns would have been most active at that point. Nonetheless, all of these opinion polls showed strong support for marriage equality, thus indicating that the Irish and Australian people had adopted a more tolerant, liberal attitude towards LGBT+ relationships. However, favourable opinion polls were no guarantee of a positive outcome for same-sex couples seeking equal access to marriage since, arguably 'the idea that opinion polls amount to indicators of the "will of the people" is itself repugnant to democracy – they are cybernetic indicators based on scientific sampling techniques and devoid of democratic content or status'.[142]

XIII. An Australian Referendum on Marriage Equality?

Since the Australian Government was so resolutely committed to letting the nation decide the issue of marriage equality by means of a postal plebiscite, I believe that it might have been better to go one significant step further and hold a referendum on marriage equality, whereby the nation's decision would be legally binding and lead to marriage equality being expressly enshrined in the Australian Constitution, just as it was enshrined in the Constitution of Ireland following the result of the Marriage Referendum in 2015.[143]

Although Australian LGBT+ people would have been subjected to heated and often hateful anti-LGBT+ debate during a referendum campaign, just as their Irish counterparts were, they were subjected to this in any event while the postal plebiscite was being conducted, and at least a successful referendum result would provide far greater domestic protection for marriage equality than ordinary legislation. If a government is doggedly determined to let a human rights issue be decided by the nation, and if the nation decides in favour of recognising and protecting that right, then it is arguable that such a fundamental right should be accorded the greatest domestic legal protection possible by being expressly enshrined in the national constitution. Indeed, the Marriage Amendment (Definition and Religious Freedoms) Act 2017 could hypothetically be repealed by a future anti-LGBT+ administration in Australia. Making marriage equality part of the Australian Constitution would ensure that only the Australian people themselves, through

---

[142] J Waters, 'Let Norris enter race – and be treated like anyone else', *The Irish Times* (16 September 2011) 16.

[143] Although the High Court of Australia held that s 51 of the Constitution *implicitly* recognises same-sex marriage in *Commonwealth v Australian Capital Territory* (2013) 250 CLR 441, this does not mean that a future anti-LGBT+ administration cannot repeal the Marriage Amendment (Definition and Religious Freedoms) Act 2017 because s 51 expressly provides that it is the Australian Parliament that shall make laws with respect to marriage. This can be contrasted with the situation in Ireland, where any attempt to repeal the Marriage Act 2015 would undoubtedly be unconstitutional in light of the express protection for same-sex marriage contained in Art 41.4, an amendment inserted into the Constitution to reflect the will of the people as a result of a referendum process.

a future successful referendum, could ever remove the constitutional protection for marriage equality. Nonetheless, there are significant differences between holding a referendum on this issue in Ireland and Australia given the latter country's 'constitutional culture', specifically, as Stephenson points out '[Australia's] deep ambivalence about using the Constitution as a source and embodiment of society's values and principles'.[144]

Unlike the Irish Constitution, which contains a Bill of Rights, the Australian Constitution does not – it is a document primarily concerned with delineating Federal power and state power. Further, Stephenson points out that, via referenda, 'the Australian people have rejected attempts to bolster the Constitution's protection for rights (in 1944 and 1988) and to introduce a preamble outlining society's values and principles (in 1999)'.[145] Indeed, constitutional referenda in Australia have often failed (a mere eight referenda out of the 44 that have been held have been successful). In contrast, Stephenson observes that the Irish people are accustomed to updating their Constitution, 'approving amendments on a regular basis' to the Bill of Rights contained in Articles 40–44.[146] He argues that 'the referendum on same-sex marriage is the latest episode in the Irish people's continuing engagement with, and commitment to, the Irish Constitution as a source and embodiment of society's values and principles'.[147] Further, in Australia a 'double majority' is required for a referendum to be successful. This means that an overall majority of voters *and* a majority of voters in a majority of Australia's six states would have to approve of a 'marriage equality' amendment to the Australian Constitution. Although the threshold for success in an Australian Referendum is undoubtedly high, this does not mean that a referendum could not have been held to expressly define 'marriage' in section 51(xxi) akin to the definition in Article 41.4 of the Irish Constitution and, given the very positive result of the postal plebiscite, and the fact that voting in Australian referenda is compulsory for all those enrolled to vote, it is not unreasonable to conclude that a referendum on marriage equality would most likely have succeeded.

XIV. Conclusion

Ireland and Australia followed remarkably similar routes to achieving marriage equality. Both jurisdictions' initial knee-jerk reaction to international developments in the area was to legislate to expressly prohibit marriage equality from being recognised by the courts, although even in the absence of such legislation it

---

[144] S Stephenson, 'The Constitutional Referendum in Comparative Perspective: Same-Sex Marriage in Ireland and Australia', *International Journal of Constitutional Law* Blog (4 June 2015), available at www.iconnectblog.com/2015/06/the-constitutional-referendum-in-comparative-perspective-same-sex-marriage-in-ireland-and-australia.

[145] ibid.

[146] ibid.

[147] ibid.

was highly unlikely that the High Court in *Zappone* would have declared a constitutional right to same-sex marriage given the limited international consensus on the matter in 2006, and a subordinated constitutional equality guarantee. Although the political will to champion marriage equality eventually surfaced in Ireland and Australia, the Irish and Australian Governments should not be lauded for this. This political determination really only resulted from the recommendations of the Constitutional Convention in Ireland and the result of the postal plebiscite in Australia – both of which were citizen-led processes and, indubitably, a politically convenient means to an end. The postal plebiscite, and the Marriage Referendum that resulted from the recommendations of the Constitutional Convention, were crude, uncertain and largely inappropriate methods of deciding a fundamental human rights issue. For Ireland and Australia's LGBT+ communities, a far less distressing route to marriage equality would have been for the Irish and Australian Parliaments to simply legislate in that regard. However, at least the successful Irish referendum process resulted in the greatest possible form of domestic legal protection for this fundamental right; in that respect, the daring experiment that was the Marriage Referendum of 2015 was a resounding success, rightly praised by Encarnacion as 'a milestone in Irish history, a monumental achievement in the country's social and political development, and a repudiation of the Catholic Church's outmoded views on homosexuality'.[148]

---

[148] OG Encarnacion (n 91).

3

Same-Sex Relationships
Beyond Marriage

Civil Partnership and Cohabitation in Ireland

I. Introduction

In 2011, the Civil Partnership and Certain Rights and Obligations of Cohabitants Act 2010 (the '2010 Act') finally enabled same-sex couples to formalise their relationships by entering into a registered civil partnership. The legislation also introduced a redress scheme for opposite-sex and same-sex cohabitants in order to enable a financially dependent party who satisfies the requisite statutory criteria to seek certain relief from the other party following the termination of their cohabitation. In 2008, in the High Court proceedings in *McD v L*, Hedigan J remarked obiter that 'the State has a strong interest in the recognition, maintenance and protection of all *de facto* families that exist since they are inherently supportive units albeit unrecognised by the Constitution', and by enacting the 2010 Act a few years later the Oireachtas confirmed this to be the case.[1]

This chapter will briefly discuss the unsatisfactory state of the law for same-sex couples prior to this statute's enactment. It will then explain the impetus for the legislation and the constitutional imperative for restricting civil partnership to same-sex couples only. The chapter will continue by critically analysing the key legal and practical differences between civil partnership and marriage. Further, the controversial question as to whether civil partnership is a more appropriate form of relationship recognition for same-sex couples than civil marriage will be scrutinised. The chapter will then discuss why civil partnership was quickly phased out in post-marriage equality Ireland, and assess whether this outcome is regrettable in light of evidence from Ireland and the UK suggesting that there is demand for this egalitarian form of relationship recognition among same-sex *and* opposite-sex couples.

The chapter will subsequently critique the redress scheme for cohabitants to ascertain whether it achieves an equitable balance between respecting the autonomy ordinarily associated with non-formalised relationships and providing

---

[1] *McD v L* [2008] IEHC 96 (Hedigan J).

protection for vulnerable cohabitants, while assuaging constitutional concerns. Finally, the likely impact of this scheme on Irish cohabitants and, in particular, same-sex cohabitants, will be gauged in light of the available empirical evidence relating to the growing phenomenon of cohabitation in Ireland.

II. The Constitution and Non-Marital Unions

In Ireland prior to marriage equality, same-sex relationships, like their non-marital opposite-sex counterparts, were completely devoid of constitutional protection because, as discussed in the previous chapter, the protection afforded to the 'Family' in Article 41 applies only to that which is based on marriage.[2] In the seminal case of *State (Nicolaou) v An Bord Uchtála*, Walsh J outlined the parameters of Article 41:

> While it is quite true that unmarried persons cohabiting together and the children of their union may often be referred to as a family and have many, if not all, of the outward appearances of a family, and may indeed for the purposes of a particular law be regarded as such, nevertheless so far as Article 41 is concerned the guarantees therein contained are confined to families based upon marriage.[3]

This exclusive constitutional position was particularly harsh on same-sex couples because they were unable to form a family unit based on marriage; the understanding that the constitutional right to marry was restricted to opposite-sex couples was confirmed by Dunne J in *Zappone v Revenue Commissioners*, placing substantial reliance on the statutory definition of marriage contained in section 2(2)(e) of the Civil Registration Act 2004.[4] However, in the last chapter it was demonstrated that the Oireachtas appears to have been granted leeway by the High Court to alter this understanding, *if it chose to do so*. While opposite-sex couples could acquire constitutional protection and legal obligations in respect of each other by simply marrying, prior to the success of the Marriage Referendum in 2015 this option was out of reach for same-sex couples, hence why the introduction of civil partnership legislation was so significant. It enabled same-sex couples to gain formal legal recognition of their relationship and acquire legal rights and duties towards each other. However, although civil partnership is, like marriage, a means of registering and formalising a committed relationship, Ryan points out a 'key distinction' between the two institutions, because, despite their similarities, 'unlike marriage, the household based on civil partnership (like any household not based

---

[2] *State (Nicolaou) v An Bord Uchtála* [1966] IR 567.

[3] ibid, 643.

[4] As Ryan points out, 'the common law ban [on marriage between persons of the same sex] was copper-fastened by s. 2(2)(e) of the Civil Registration Act 2004, which confirmed that being of the same sex as one's partner was (prior to 2015) an impediment to a valid marriage': see F Ryan, 'The Rise and Fall of Civil Partnership' (2016) 19 *Irish Journal of Family Law* 50.

on marriage) does not enjoy constitutional protection as a 'family' under Art. 41 of the Constitution'.[5]

III. The Disparate Legislative Treatment of Non-Marital Couples in Ireland pre-2010

As will be demonstrated later in this chapter, a phenomenal number of opposite-sex couples now choose to cohabit outside of marriage.[6] As cohabitation rates increased, the legislature had, 'increasingly, as a matter of policy'[7] extended protections ordinarily associated with marriage to such couples since the mid-1990s, *but not* to same-sex cohabiting couples (prior to the introduction of the 2010 Act). Some prime examples of this exclusionary approach included the Domestic Violence Act 1996, which provided that a barring order may be granted to an applicant who 'has lived with the respondent as husband or wife';[8] the Civil Liability (Amendment) Act 1996, which enabled the opposite-sex surviving partner of a person killed due to the negligence of others to sue for their wrongful death;[9] the Residential Tenancies Act 2004, which allowed an unmarried partner who had been living with the deceased tenant 'as husband and wife in the dwelling' for six months preceding the death to succeed to the tenancy;[10] and section 11 of the Social Welfare Act 1993, which recognised as a couple for the purposes of social welfare law 'a man and woman who are not married to each other but are cohabiting as husband and wife'. The practical effect of each of these provisions was to consistently exclude all same-sex cohabiting couples from their ambit. In fact, as concerns the Residential Tenancies Act 2004, the then Minister for the Environment, Heritage and Local Government, Noel Ahern, stated in the Dáil that the provisions in the statute 'provide for security in the case of established, family-type relationships, rather than homosexual or other relationships'.[11] It appears that an appreciation of any potential functional similarities between committed

---

[5] F Ryan, 'Repackaged Goods? – Interrogating the Heteronormative Underpinnings of Marriage' in F Hamilton and G Nota La Diega (eds), *Same-Sex Relationships, Law and Social Change* (London, Routledge, 2020) 231, 233.

[6] The results of the 2016 Census indicate that there are 152,302 opposite-sex cohabiting couples, almost five times the figure of 31,300 recorded just two decades earlier in the 1996 Census: see Census 2016, 'Summary Results – Part 1' (CSO, 2016) 41, available at www.cso.ie/en/media/csoie/newsevents/documents/census2016summaryresultspart1/Census2016SummaryPart1.pdf.

[7] J Nestor, *An Introduction to Irish Family Law*, 1st edn (Dublin, Gill and Macmillan, 2000) 9.

[8] Domestic Violence Act 1996, s 3.

[9] It should be noted that at the time these legislative developments benefitting opposite-sex couples took place in 1996 merely 150 unmarried couples identified as being of the same sex, compared to the figure of 31,300 unmarried opposite-sex couples recorded in the 1996 Census. See B Tobin, 'Relationship Recognition for Same-Sex Couples in Ireland: The Proposed Models Critiqued' (2008) 11 *Irish Journal of Family Law* 10.

[10] Residential Tenancies Act 2004, s 39.

[11] Dáil Debate, vol 588, col 1043, 1 July 2004.

same-sex and opposite-sex relationships seems to have completely escaped the former Minister in this instance.[12]

IV. Progressing Towards Civil Partnership

Although Denmark made socio-legal history by becoming the first country in the world (and in the EU) to introduce civil partnership for same-sex couples in 1989, the introduction of this mode of relationship recognition really only gained impetus in other EU Member States post-millennium, with Estonia becoming the most recent jurisdiction to embrace it.[13] However, the need for Ireland to embrace civil partnership did not stem from an EU obligation or, *at the time*, a requirement under the European Convention on Human Rights (ECHR).[14] Rather, it was necessitated by the coming into force of the Civil Partnership Act 2004 in our neighbouring jurisdiction, the UK. As I have pointed out elsewhere,[15] it was ironic that, on 5 December 2005, the very date that this legislation entered into force and enabled same-sex couples in Northern Ireland to obtain a status akin to marriage, the Civil Registration Act 2004 also acquired the force of law in the Republic of Ireland and precluded same-sex marriage under section 2(2)(e).[16] It is submitted that the contrast between the legal position of same-sex couples on the island of Ireland was at its most stark at this point in time. This arguably placed the Irish Government in breach of the Good Friday Agreement, by virtue of which the Government undertook to provide in the Republic of Ireland at least an equivalent level of human rights protection as that pertaining in Northern Ireland and, as Ryan points out, 'same-sex couples in the Republic legitimately asked why they could, in 2005, formalise their relationships in Derry but not in neighbouring Donegal'.[17] Indeed, O'Cinnéide argued that the introduction of the

---

[12] However, Ryan observes that subsequently, the Parental Leave (Amendment) Act 2006, by recognising same-sex relationships and de facto parents for the purpose of *force majeure* leave and parental leave respectively, 'suggested a growing sensitivity to the issue of recognition of same-sex unions': see Ryan, 'The Rise and Fall of Civil Partnership' (2016) 51. In addition, the 2006 Census recorded 2,090 cohabiting same-sex couples compared to just 150 such couples in the 1996 Census: see Tobin, 'Relationship Recognition for Same-Sex Couples' (2008) 10.

[13] The Registered Partnership Act entered into force in Estonia on 1 January 2016. Of the EU Member States other than Denmark that introduced civil partnership, all have only done so 'post-millennium', since 2001, with Estonia being the most recent Member State to do so.

[14] See ch 5.

[15] B Tobin, 'Same-Sex Couples and the Law: Recent Developments in the British Isles' (2009) 23 *International Journal of Law, Policy and the Family* 309, 318.

[16] The island of Ireland is comprised of 32 counties. The Republic of Ireland is comprised of 26 counties and is independent of the UK, whereas Northern Ireland is comprised of six counties and along with Scotland, England and Wales, forms part of the UK. For a discussion of the application of the Civil Partnership Act 2004 to Northern Ireland, see B Sloan, 'Registered Partnerships in Northern Ireland' in JM Scherpe and A Hayward (eds), *The Future of Registered Partnerships* (Cambridge, Intersentia, 2017) 253.

[17] Ryan (n 4) 51. Derry is a county in Northern Ireland and Donegal is a neighbouring county in the Republic of Ireland.

Civil Partnership Act 2004 in Northern Ireland and the failure to enact corresponding legislation in the Republic of Ireland constituted a 'lack of equivalence' in breach of the Good Friday Agreement.[18] On this analysis, the introduction of civil partnership legislation in the Republic of Ireland was necessary to ensure the Irish Government's continued compliance with the terms of the Good Friday Agreement.

In 2006, the All-Party Oireachtas Committee on the Constitution and the Working Group on Domestic Partnership both recommended the introduction of civil partnership legislation for same-sex couples in Ireland.[19] Although the last chapter highlighted that the High Court appeared willing to countenance the introduction of same-sex marriage via an Act of the Oireachtas, due to either a lack of political will or an inadvertent failure to appreciate this important aspect of the *Zappone* judgment, in 2007 the Fianna Fáil/Green Party coalition Government proceeded to include plans to introduce civil partnership legislation for same-sex couples in the Programme for Government. Less than two months after the coalition was formed the then Taoiseach, Bertie Ahern, committed to implementing such legislation as early as possible in the lifetime of the Government.[20] In 2008, the General Scheme of the Civil Partnership Bill was unveiled, and the Civil Partnership Bill was then published in June 2009.[21] Of the 2009 Bill, Ryan stated at the time that 'it is clear from the heavy borrowing from current marriage legislation, that civil partnership is based largely on the same blueprint.[22]

A. Ineligibility of Opposite-Sex Couples

In Ireland, the ability to enter into a civil partnership was confined to same-sex couples. In 2006, the All-Party Oireachtas Committee had recommended civil

---

[18] C O'Cinnéide, 'Equivalence in Promoting Equality: The Implications of the Multi-Party Agreement for the Further Development of Equality Measures for Northern Ireland and Ireland' (Equality Authority and Equality Commission for Northern Ireland, 2005).

[19] The All-Party Oireachtas Committee on the Constitution was established in 1996 to undertake a full review of the Constitution in order to establish areas where constitutional change may be desirable or necessary. The Committee recommended civil partnership in the All-Party Oireachtas Committee on the Constitution, 'Tenth Progress Report: The Family' (Stationery Office, 2006). The Working Group on Domestic Partnership was established in March 2006 and charged with preparing an Options Paper for the Tánaiste and Minister for Justice, Equality and Law Reform by October 2006. The Working Group was tasked with considering and recommending various options for the legal regulation of non-marital opposite-sex and same-sex relationships. See Working Group on Domestic Partnership, 'Options Paper' (Stationery Office, 2006), available at www.justice.ie/en/JELR/OptionsPaper.pdf/Files/OptionsPaper.pdf.

[20] A Healy, 'Ahern Backs Legal Recognition of Gay Partners' *Irish Times* (17 July 2007) 3. On 16 July 2007, while speaking at the official opening of a refurbished Outhouse, the LGBT+ community resource centre in Dublin's Capel Street, Mr Ahern stated that 'we will legislate for civil partnerships at the earliest possible date in the lifetime of this government'.

[21] In Ireland a 'General Scheme' refers to a draft Bill.

[22] F Ryan, 'The General Scheme of the Civil Partnership 2008: Brave New Dawn or Missed Opportunity?' (2008) 11 *Irish Journal of Family Law* 51, 52.

partnership legislation for opposite-sex couples, though this would most likely have been constitutionally unsound. Civil partnership is very similar to marriage and, as demonstrated, the marital 'family' occupies a special position under Article 41 of the Constitution. If introduced for opposite-sex couples it would have provided them with an alternative to marriage, thus constituting what Mee describes as 'a competing State-sponsored institution'[23] that may induce those couples who have ideological (and other) objections to marriage to shun it and opt to become civil partners instead. Case law suggests that an inducement not to marry can render a law incompatible with Article 41.[24] Hence, as Walsh and Ryan have observed, 'too ready an equation between marriage and alternative family forms',[25] ie civil partnership, may constitute an 'attack' by the state on the institution of marriage, which it 'pledges itself to guard with special care' in Article 41.3.1. It is perhaps with these concerns in mind that the Oireachtas proceeded to confine civil partnership in Ireland to same-sex couples only. Since same-sex couples were excluded from the institution of marriage (prior to 2015), the same constitutional concerns did not arise in that context.

Ireland was not alone in confining civil partnership to same-sex couples for constitutional reasons because in 2007, the Hungarian Parliament adopted a Bill that would enable same-sex *and* opposite-sex couples to enter into civil partnerships, but the Hungarian Constitutional Court struck down the Bill on the grounds that it would diminish the value of the institutions of marriage and the family, as protected under Article 15 of the then Constitution of Hungary.[26] The Hungarian Parliament subsequently passed an amended Bill that confined civil partnership registration solely to same-sex couples.[27] The constitutionality of a civil partnership regime solely for same-sex couples in another jurisdiction that provides constitutional protection for marriage and the family was tested before the German Constitutional Court in 2001. Article 6(1) of the German Constitution provides that 'marriage and the family shall enjoy the special protection of the State'. German legislation that allowed same-sex couples to register a 'life partnership' was challenged in the courts as being contrary to Article 6(1). However, the Constitutional Court held that because the concept of a 'life partnership' was only available to same-sex couples, it was not in competition with

---

[23] J Mee, 'Cohabitation, Civil Partnership and the Constitution' in O Doyle and W Binchy (eds), *Committed Relationships and the Law* (Dublin, Four Courts Press, 2007) 204.

[24] *Murphy v Attorney General* [1982] IR 241; *Muckley v Ireland* [1985] IR 471; *Mhic Mhathúna v Ireland* [1989] IR 504. If a law is declared 'unconstitutional' by the courts for being incompatible with a provision of the Constitution it is rendered invalid and of no legal effect.

[25] J Walsh and F Ryan, *The Rights of De Facto Couples* (Dublin, IHRC, 2006) 81–82.

[26] Article 15 of the Constitution of Hungary 1949 provided that 'the Republic of Hungary shall protect the institutions of marriage and the family'. A new Constitution of Hungary entered into force on 1 January 2012.

[27] See S Kralijić, 'Same-Sex Partnerships in Eastern Europe: Marriage, Registration or No Regulation?' in K Boele-Welki and A Fuchs (eds), *Same-Sex Relationships and Beyond: Gender Matters in the EU*, 3rd edn (Cambridge, Intersentia, 2017) 55, 72.

the institution of marriage which, by definition, was available to opposite-sex couples only.[28]

B. Arguments for a Conscientious Objection Clause

Ryan observes that in the Oireachtas, the Civil Partnership Bill 'had a relatively smooth and speedy passage through the Dáil' (Lower House), but that its passage through the Seanad (Upper House) 'proved to be somewhat bumpier', largely because opponents of the Bill sought to include a conscientious objection clause that would prevent persons who for reasons of religious conscience refused to facilitate a same-sex civil partnership from being sued or prosecuted in respect of their refusal.[29] If the state was introducing same-sex marriage at the time, such a clause would arguably have been necessary to enable *religious solemnisers* to abstain from presiding over a same-sex marriage. Indeed, this is the situation in Canada, South Africa, and Norway, all of which have come to recognise same-sex marriage.[30] However, *civil registrars* are public servants and, as such, they are under a duty to perform marriage ceremonies in accordance with law, irrespective of their personal religious views. In the Seanad, Senator Alex White illuminated the fallacy of legislation that would allow a public servant to refuse to perform their civic duties because of a conscientious objection to doing so:

> [It] is simply inconceivable, however, that if someone is appointed to be a judge, for example, of the Circuit Court which administers the divorce legislation, he or she would refuse to make an order for divorce in circumstances in which he or she has a difficulty or objection to it on a personal basis or as a matter of conscience.[31]

The Senator described the campaign for a conscientious objection clause as 'a contrivance masquerading as a basis for opposing legislation'[32] and the 2010 Act contains no provisions enabling a person to declare a conscientious objection in order to discriminate against civil partners.

---

[28] Bundesverfassungsgericht (BVerfG – Federal Constitutional Court) Case No 1 BvF 1/01, 17 July 2002, 105 BVERFGE 313, 345–46 (Ger). See also the discussion in G Hogan and G Whyte, *JM Kelly – The Irish Constitution*, 4th edn (Dublin, Butterworths, 2003) 1837. This case implies that had the 'life partnership' been available to opposite-sex couples then this would have been contrary to Art 6(1) of the German Constitution.

[29] F Ryan, *Annotated Legislation: Civil Partnership and Certain Rights and Obligations of Cohabitants Act 2010* (Dublin, Thomson Round Hall, 2011) 12–13.

[30] M Sáez, 'Same-Sex Marriage, Same-Sex Cohabitation and Same-Sex Families Around the World: Why "Same" is so Different' (2011) 19 *American University Journal of Gender Social Policy and Law* 7, 7–8. Similarly, the Marriage Act 2015, s 7 provides that, in Ireland, a religious solemniser shall not be obliged to solemnise a marriage in accordance with a form of marriage ceremony which is not recognised by the religious body of which the religious solemniser is a member.

[31] Seanad Debate, vol 204, col 176, 7 July 2010.

[32] ibid.

C. Civil Partnership for Siblings or Friends?

During the passage of the Bill through the Oireachtas, some politicians also considered non-sexual relationships to be as worthy of legislative protection as intimate unions. However, Bala observes that globally, adults residing together in non-conjugal relationships are not actively seeking legislative protection. He acknowledges that amongst such persons 'in particular, there seems to be no interest or expectation that there should be any obligations, such as support claims, extending beyond the termination of cohabitation.'[33] Indeed, Graycar and Millbank observe that there is 'no empirical evidence to demonstrate an unmet legal need for broadly based recognition of non-couple relationships, nor any form of political or social mobilising by non-couples.'[34] Hence one is inclined to agree with the view expressed by Doyle that 'people in such relationships do not aspire to the same exclusivity that is generally accepted as the ideal in sexual relationships.'[35] The Civil Partnership and Certain Rights and Obligations of Cohabitants Act 2010 was ultimately signed into law by the President on 19 July 2010, and its provisions, except for section 5, came into force on 1 January 2011.[36]

V. An Overview of the Rights and Duties of Civil Partners

The parties to a civil partnership have rights and duties that reflect those of married couples. Civil partners are entitled to statutory protection for their 'shared home' and are under a legal obligation to maintain each other financially.[37] In addition, the 2010 Act also extends the provisions of the Domestic Violence Act 1996 to civil partners to enable them to avail of the various remedies for domestic violence.[38] One can also sue for the wrongful death of their civil partner under the Civil Liability Act 1961.[39] The 2010 Act also amends the Residential Tenancies

---

[33] N Bala, 'Controversy over Couples in Canada: The Evolution of Marriage and Other Adult Interdependent Relationships' (2003) 29 *Queen's Law Journal* 41, 98.

[34] R Graycar and J Millbank, 'From Functional Family to Spinster Sisters: Australia's Distinctive Path to Relationship Recognition' (2007) 24 *Journal of Law and Policy* 121, 153. See also the discussion in O Doyle, 'Sisterly Love: The Importance of Explicitly Assumed Commitment in the Legal Recognition of Personal Relationships' in S Fitzgibbon, LD Wardle and AS Loveless (eds), *The Jurisprudence of Marriage and Other Intimate Relationships* (New York, WS Hein & Co, 2010).

[35] O Doyle, 'Moral Argument and the Recognition of Same-Sex Partnerships' in O Doyle and W Binchy (eds), *Committed Relationships and the Law* (Dublin, Four Courts Press 2007) 155.

[36] Section 5 came into force on 13 January 2011 pursuant to the Civil Partnership (Recognition of Registered Foreign Relationships) Order 2010 (SI 2010 No 469). This statutory instrument recognised certain foreign legal relationships (including same-sex marriages) as civil partnerships for the purposes of the 2010 Act.

[37] See Pts 4-7 of the Civil Partnership and Certain Rights and Obligations of Cohabitants Act 2010.

[38] See Pt 9 of the Civil Partnership and Certain Rights and Obligations of Cohabitants Act 2010.

[39] See the Civil Liability Act 1961, s 47, as amended by the Civil Partnership and Certain Rights and Obligations of Cohabitants Act 2010, s 105.

Act 2004 to enable a civil partner, following their partner's death, to succeed to a tenancy in which the couple lived.[40] Part 10 of the 2010 Act provides that civil partners will be treated the same as husband and wife for the purposes of determining pension entitlements and treatment under equality legislation.[41] Civil partners and cohabiting same-sex couples are now recognised for the purposes of social welfare law by virtue of the Social Welfare and Pensions Act 2010, while the Finance (No 3) Act 2011 deals with civil partners in the same way as spouses for most taxation purposes.[42]

VI. Differences between Civil Partnership and Marriage

Aside from being an institution that was only available to same-sex couples from 2011 to 2016, there are a number of other notable differences between the laws on marriage and civil partnership which are worthy of some consideration and critique.

A. Nullity of Civil Partnership

Section 107 of the 2010 Act sets out the grounds for granting a decree of nullity of a civil partnership, and these are largely similar to marriage. The effect of a decree of nullity means that not only is the civil partnership declared not to have existed, but the parties are not entitled to avail of the various ancillary orders applicable upon dissolution of a civil partnership. It should be noted that a civil partnership cannot be avoided for non-consummation, most likely because consummation involves a single act of sexual intercourse between parties of the opposite sex.[43] Further, a civil partnership cannot be avoided where one of the parties is unable to form and sustain a normal and caring marital relationship, a ground upon which reliance has been placed by opposite-sex partners seeking nullity of marriage in Ireland for decades.[44] Ryan appears to welcome the exclusion of this ground for

---

[40] See the Residential Tenancies Act 2004, s 39, as amended by the Civil Partnership and Certain Rights and Obligations of Cohabitants Act 2010, s 40.

[41] See the Civil Partnership and Certain Rights and Obligations of Cohabitants Act 2010, ss 99, 100, 102 and 103.

[42] Ryan, *Annotated Legislation* (2011) 18–20. In his later work, Ryan also notes that 'official policy requires that civil partners be treated the same as spouses in relation to immigration, putting same-sex couples on a more secure footing in this context': see Ryan (n 4) 52. See further, 'Notice: Immigration Arrangements for Civil Partners', available at www.inis.gov.ie/en/inis/pages/civil%20partnership.

[43] See *MM v PM* (1986) ILRM 515. It is also the case that in the UK a civil partnership cannot be annulled for non-consummation, though with the recent extension of civil partnership to opposite-sex couples in that jurisdiction this position might need to be revisited: see the Civil Partnership Act 2004, ss 50 and 174.

[44] See further F Ryan, '"When Divorce is Away, Nullity's at Play": A New Ground for Annulment, its Dubious Past and its Uncertain Future' (1998) 1 *Trinity College Law Review* 15.

nullity in the case of civil partnership. He argues that the parameters of this ground are too vague and that the circumstances in which some annulments have been granted pursuant to it would suggest that the threshold for obtaining a decree is not particularly exacting. Ryan believes that the appropriate remedy in such cases is arguably a divorce or dissolution.[45]

B. Succession Rights

The Succession Act 1965 was amended by Part 8 of the 2010 Act to grant succession entitlements to a person on the death of their civil partner, which largely (but not entirely) mirror the existing succession rights of a surviving spouse. Part 8 of the 2010 Act provides a surviving civil partner with the virtual equivalent of a spouse's security against disinheritance because, *irrespective of the terms of the deceased's will*, the surviving partner is entitled to one-half of the deceased's estate, or one-third where the deceased has issue.[46] However, *unlike a spouse*, a surviving civil partner's share can be affected where a child of the deceased brings a section 117 application, thus creating a statutory inequality between surviving spouses and civil partners. Section 117 enables the court to make provision for a child where a parent has failed in their 'moral duty to make proper provision for the child in accordance with his means'. As enacted, section 117(3) of the 1965 Act provides that a court order under section 117 is not to affect the legal right of a surviving spouse. However, section 117(3A) of the 1965 Act, as inserted by section 86 of the 2010 Act, provides that

> an order under this section shall not affect the legal right of a surviving civil partner unless the court, after consideration of all the circumstances, including the testator's financial circumstances and his or her obligations to the surviving civil partner, is of the opinion that it would be unjust not to make the order.

As Byrne and Binchy observe, 'the effect of this provision is that the legal right of a civil partner (in contrast to that of a surviving spouse) may be affected by an order under section 117'.[47] However, section 69 of the Children and Family Relationships Act 2015 amended subsection 3A of the 1965 Act, such that where the surviving civil partner is a parent of the child bringing the section 117 application, then their legal right share cannot be affected. Nonetheless, the position remains unchanged where the civil partner is not a parent of the child.

In cases of intestacy, the surviving civil partner can inherit the deceased partner's entire estate where they die intestate and have no issue. Where a civil partner dies intestate and has issue, the surviving partner is entitled to two-thirds

---

[45] See Ryan (n 29) 178–79.

[46] Succession Act 1965, s 111A, as inserted by the Civil Partnership and Certain Rights and Obligations of Cohabitants Act 2010, s 81.

[47] R Byrne and W Binchy, 'Family Law' in R Byrne and W Binchy (eds), *Annual Review of Irish Law 2010* (Dublin, Thomson Round Hall, 2011) 391.

of the estate, and the remaining one-third will be distributed equally amongst the deceased's issue. This is identical to the entitlements of a surviving spouse in cases of intestacy. However, section 67A(2) of the 1965 Act, as inserted by section 73 of the 2010 Act, enables the court to order that provision for a child be made out of the intestate's estate – this would obviously have the effect of reducing the entitlement of the intestate's surviving civil partner. The court will only make such an order if it would be unjust not to do so after considering all the circumstances of the case. Nonetheless, section 67 of the Children and Family Relationships Act 2015 amended section 67A of the 1965 Act, such that an application for provision out of an intestate's estate may not be made by a child where that child is also the child of the surviving civil partner. The position remains unchanged where the surviving civil partner is not a parent of the child.

Arguably, there are constitutional justifications for permitting a child of the deceased civil partner to be able to encroach upon the succession rights of a surviving civil partner. In cases where a child of the deceased civil partner was born as a result of the deceased civil partner's previous *marriage* to another party, then such child would be part of a constitutionally protected family unit, and their Article 41 rights in respect of their deceased parent could trump the legal position of a surviving civil partner whose relationship with the deceased is devoid of constitutional protection. This might explain why the amendments to the 2010 Act that were introduced by the Children and Family Relationships Act 2015 left unchanged the succession rights of a deceased civil partner's child where that person is not the child of the surviving civil partner, but provided that a child who was born into a civil partnership cannot affect their surviving civil partner parent's succession rights – the child in this latter scenario would have no Article 41 rights in respect of its deceased parent that could be invoked to trump its surviving civil partner parent's succession rights.

C. Dissolution of Civil Partnership

Akin to married couples, civil partners can enter into separation agreements to agree to live apart and settle their financial and property affairs, but their civil partnership, like a marriage, can only be dissolved through the courts. A civil partnership can be brought to an end by the granting of a dissolution, and the same court-ordered remedies that are available on divorce, which include property and financial relief, can be obtained by the parties following dissolution or indeed at any time thereafter, and this is identical to the 'no clean break' policy that applies to married couples following their divorce. Hence a former civil partner who has not married or entered into a new civil partnership may apply for certain court-ordered remedies long after the civil partnership has been dissolved by the courts.

Part 12 of the 2010 Act enables the court to grant a dissolution where the parties have been 'living apart' for two out of the previous three years, and where 'proper provision' has been or will be made for each of the civil partners and any dependent children of the civil partners.[48] When it was introduced, the 'living apart' requirement for seeking a dissolution of a civil partnership was more favourable than that which applied to married couples seeking a divorce. Married couples had to be 'living apart' for four of the previous five years before they could institute divorce proceedings under Irish Law until the Family Law Act 2019 reduced this waiting period to two out of the previous three years and equated the temporal requirements for divorce with those for dissolution of a civil partnership.[49]

However, when seeking a divorce, Article 41.3.2 of the Constitution and section 5 of the Family Law (Divorce) Act 1996 require the divorcing parties to show that there is 'no reasonable prospect of reconciliation', whereas this is not required of separating civil partners under the provisions of the 2010 Act. The omission of this requirement holds symbolic significance because it indicates that Irish law does not place the same value on civil partnerships as constitutionally protected marriages. Whereas divorce proceedings can only be commenced once the parties' solicitors certify that they have advised their clients regarding all the alternatives to a divorce, this is not required when dissolving a civil partnership. Although Irish law does not deem civil partnerships worthy of any salvage attempts before dissolution proceedings are commenced, section 111 of the 2010 Act enables the court to adjourn dissolution proceedings to enable the civil partners to attempt, if they both so wish, to reconcile, and so the potential for the partners' reconciliation even when dissolution proceedings are in progress is at least *acknowledged*.

VII. The Recognition of Foreign Civil Partnerships and Same-Sex Marriages

Section 5 of the 2010 Act permits certain classes of foreign legal relationship to be recognised by ministerial order as civil partnerships in Ireland. The criteria for recognition are that the relationship must be exclusive and permanent in nature

---

[48] Civil Partnership and Certain Rights and Obligations of Cohabitants Act 2010, s 110. As enacted, this provision did not require a court to take into account any children being raised by the civil partners when deciding whether 'proper provision' had been made. However, the Children and Family Relationships Act 2015, s 150 amended s 110 of the 2010 Act such that the court must now be satisfied before granting a dissolution that 'proper provision' exists or will be made for the civil partners *and* any dependent child of the civil partners.

[49] As the original 'living apart' requirement contained in s 5 of the Family Law (Divorce) Act 1996 derived from Art 41.3.2 of the Constitution, a referendum was held in May 2019 to remove this requirement from the Constitution, thus enabling legislative reform. The Thirty-Eighth Amendment of the Constitution (Dissolution of Marriage) Bill 2019 was approved by over 82% of the electorate at this referendum, and it was signed into law by the President of Ireland in June 2019. The Family Law Act 2019 was enacted later that year and s 3 amended s 5 of the Family Law (Divorce) Act 1996 to reduce the 'living apart' requirement from four out of the previous five years to two out of the previous three years.

and can only be dissolved in a court. The foreign legal relationship does not need to be identical to an Irish civil partnership provided that the rights and obligations are largely similar. Relationships that can be dissolved either by contractual agreement or administrative order will not be recognised as civil partnerships in Ireland (a French *Pacte de Civil Solidarité*, for example). Further, although civil partnership may be open to opposite-sex couples in some jurisdictions, section 5 only permits the recognition of foreign civil partnerships entered into between parties of the same sex who do not fall within the prohibited degrees of relationship set out in section 26 of the 2010 Act. There are no restrictions on recognition based on the age of the parties so, although the minimum age for civil partnership in Ireland is 18, civil partnerships entered into in other jurisdictions by persons below that age can be recognised.

As explained below, the introduction of marriage equality resulted in civil partnership being rather quickly phased out in Ireland. Section 13 of the Marriage Act 2015 (the '2015 Act') provides that section 5 of the 2010 Act, and any order made thereunder, shall not apply to a legal relationship that is entered into by the parties on or after the date that is six months after the commencement of section 8 of the 2015 Act. Section 8 of the Marriage Act 2015 repeals those provisions of the Civil Registration Act 2004 (as inserted by the 2010 Act) that enabled same-sex couples to enter into domestic civil partnerships. The Marriage Act 2015 entered into force on 16 November 2015 and, by virtue of the changes section 13 of that Act made to section 5 of the 2010 Act, all civil partnerships that were contracted abroad after 16 May 2016 will not be recognised under Irish law.[50]

This is most likely for constitutional reasons, because to recognise foreign civil partnerships in a country where marriage is now available to opposite-sex and same-sex couples, and foreign same-sex marriages are now recognised, might incentivise those Irish persons who disapprove of marriage to contract civil partnerships abroad and subsequently seek to have them recognised in Ireland. This might prove to be contrary to public policy, constituting an 'attack' on the institution of marriage that the state pledges itself to guard with special care under Article 41.3.1 of the Irish Constitution.

Same-sex marriages celebrated in jurisdictions that allow same-sex marriage were previously downgraded to civil partnership status by virtue of section 5 of the 2010 Act and the ministerial orders made thereunder. However, since the introduction of marriage equality, Irish law provides that a marriage in another jurisdiction between two persons of the same sex may now be recognised as a marriage in Ireland.[51] Further, a foreign same-sex marriage shall not be precluded from being recognised where it falls within a class of legal relationship in respect of which a ministerial order was previously made under section 5 of the 2010 Act.

[50] See the Marriage Act 2015, s 13.
[51] See the Marriage Act 2015, s 12.

VIII. The Dissolution of Foreign Civil Partnerships and Same-Sex Marriages

Where a foreign legal relationship was recognised in Ireland as equivalent to a civil partnership, and such relationship is later dissolved in the jurisdiction where it was originally formalised, the dissolution will be recognised as if it were a dissolution under Irish law.[52] The same applies where a foreign legal relationship that is recognised under section 5 is later dissolved in any jurisdiction that enables same-sex couples to enter into the type of legal relationship that is recognised under section 5 (ie civil partnerships or same-sex marriages). Hence it would appear that same-sex couples who have their civil partnerships dissolved abroad will be able to seek, in an Irish court, the various ancillary orders that are available to those civil partners who have had their civil partnership dissolved in Ireland (ie periodical payment orders, lump sum orders, property adjustment orders, pension adjustment orders, etc). However, the civil partners will only be able to seek such remedies where at least one of them is either domiciled in or ordinarily resident in Ireland for one year preceding the application.[53]

IX. Civil Partnership: Separate, but Equal?

Whether one is a proponent of civil partnership or not, it was availed of by many same-sex couples in Ireland during its relatively short life span, most likely because it was a mode of relationship recognition that improved the *practical* legal situation of same-sex couples who hitherto were largely shunned by domestic law. Indeed, Eskridge points out that in the US, '*functionally*, [civil partnership] ameliorates rather than ratifies a sexuality caste system'.[54] These analyses are equally applicable in Ireland. On a symbolic level, Chan observes that the equivalent civil partnership legislation in the UK, the Civil Partnership Act 2004 provides,

> an official statement of acceptance: by approving the recognition of marriage-like relationships, the [2004 Act] endorses a form of life, a loving and committed relationship. It endorses that relationship with the authoritative voice of the State, throwing public weight behind the partners' membership of, and integration with, the community.[55]

Indeed, the exact same could be said of the impact that the 2010 Act had in Ireland. However, offering same-sex couples most of 'the rights, privileges and benefits of the institution of marriage'[56] under the nomenclature of civil partnership is

---

[52] See the Civil Partnership and Certain Rights and Obligations of Cohabitants Act 2010 s 5(4).

[53] See the Civil Partnership and Certain Rights and Obligations of Cohabitants Act 2010, s 140(3).

[54] WN Eskridge, Jr, 'Equality Practice: Liberal Reflections on the Jurisprudence of Civil Unions' (2001) 64 *Albany Law Review* 853, 863.

[55] W Chan, 'Cohabitation, Civil Partnership, Marriage and the Equal Sharing Principle' (2013) 33 *Legal Studies* 46, 50.

[56] *Halpern and Ors v AG of Canada* (2002) CanLII 42749 (ON SCDC) [187].

'a version of the separate but equal doctrine'[57] and this arguably falls short of true equality. Indeed, the Massachusetts Supreme Court has stated that 'the dissimilitude between the terms 'civil marriage' and 'civil union' is not innocuous; it is a considered choice of language that reflects a demonstrable assigning of same-sex, largely homosexual, couples to second-class status'.[58] Indeed, it has been argued that granting partnership as opposed to marriage rights leaves a 'lingering odour of homophobia'.[59] However, one might contend, in response to this, that civil partnership is quite acceptable when viewed as a necessary *interim* measure on the road to same-sex marriage, one that contributes to the greater social acceptance of same-sex relationships and ultimately paves the way for the introduction of same-sex marriage. In the early days of European civil partnership regimes it was argued by Wintemute that, in many jurisdictions civil partnership laws for same-sex couples might largely 'have been passed for a very negative reason: avoiding the opening up of legal marriage to same-sex couples'.[60] As Ryan observed, 'civil partnership represents a consolation prize of sorts, detracting attention from the exclusion of same-sex couples from marriage'.[61] Speaking in the context of the UK, Cretney believed that by arguably meeting the needs of the LGBT+ community with civil partnership laws, the British Government 'no doubt thought it would avoid the demands' for same-sex marriage.[62] All these concerns were valid at the time when very few European countries had even introduced civil partnership, let alone made the transition from partnership laws to same-sex marriage.

Today, it can be said with much certainty that civil partnership laws ordinarily result in the eventual introduction of same-sex marriage, because each of the EU Member States that has come to recognise same-sex marriage initially had a form of civil partnership.[63] Although many of the EU Member States that moved from civil partnership to marriage did so in a rather short space of time, Denmark was an outlier, because despite making history by becoming the first country in the world to introduce civil partnership for same-sex couples in 1989, it only introduced same-sex marriage a staggering 23 years later, in 2012.

---

[57] ibid [192] (LaForme J, quoting Linden JA in *Egan v Canada* [1993] 3 FC 401).

[58] *Opinions of the Justices to the Senate*, 802 NE2d 565, 570 (Mass 2004). The Justices were disapproving a civil union bill drafted by the Massachusetts legislature in response to the Massachusetts Supreme Court's finding that the ban on same-sex marriage violated the State's Constitution.

[59] L Crompton, 'Civil Partnership Bill 2004: The Illusion of Equality' (2004) 34 *Family Law* 888, 889.

[60] R Wintemute, 'Marriage or "Civil Partnership" for Same-Sex Couples: Will Ireland Lead or Follow the United Kingdom?' in O Doyle and W Binchy (eds), *Committed Relationships and the Law* (Dublin, Four Courts Press, 2007) 97.

[61] Ryan, 'The General Scheme of the Civil Partnership 2008' (2008) 51.

[62] S Cretney, 'Comment: Sex is Important' (2004) 34 *Family Law* 777. Indeed, the British Government was unable to avoid such demand and same-sex marriage became legal in England and Wales on 29 March 2014. Scotland followed suit in the autumn of 2014 and same-sex marriage became legal in Northern Ireland in 2020.

[63] These states are Austria, Finland, France, Germany, Ireland, Luxembourg, Malta, Belgium, Denmark, Spain, Portugal, Sweden and the Netherlands. Although it recently left the EU, the UK also introduced civil partnership legislation in England and Wales, Scotland and Northern Ireland in 2004 before the introduction of same-sex marriage in these jurisdictions in more recent years.

As discussed, there are judges and academics who believed that the enactment of civil partnership legislation conferred an unequal, second-class status on same-sex couples.[64] An analysis of the sociological concept of the 'functional family' demonstrates that there is merit in their view, as same-sex couples are in an analogous situation to opposite-sex couples. As Millbank points out, the kernel of 'functional family' claims in law is that rights should flow from the way a relationship functions rather than being limited by its legal form.[65] Ryan observes that this approach involves 'referring not to the respective characteristics of the parties to the relationship but rather to the characteristics of the relationship itself'.[66] Glennon believes that the functional family model has 'the capacity to transcend discriminatory assumptions based on sexual orientation'.[67] The functional family approach to same-sex relationships was prominent in cases in the UK involving challenges to provisions of the Rent Acts by a same-sex partner seeking the right to succeed to his deceased partner's tenancy as either his 'spouse' or a member of his 'family'. In *Fitzpatrick v Sterling Housing Association*, the House of Lords held that the plaintiff was entitled to succeed to the tenancy as a member of his deceased same-sex partner's 'family'.[68] Their Lordships came to this conclusion by having recourse to the 'functional family' model. Lord Nicholls held that irrespective of a couple's sexual orientation 'there is the scope for the intimate love and affection and long-term commitment which typically characterise the relationship of husband and wife',[69] while Lord Slynn recognised that same-sex unions can have the hallmarks of a familial relationship, such as 'a degree of mutual interdependence, of the sharing of lives, of caring and love, of commitment and support'.[70] In the later rent-control case of *Ghaidan v Godin-Mendoza*,[71] which involved an identical claim but where the plaintiff was found eligible to succeed to his partner's tenancy as a 'spouse', Baroness Hale further endorsed the functional equality between intimate, stable opposite-sex and same-sex relationships by stressing that 'homosexual couples can have exactly the same sort of inter-dependent couple relationship as heterosexuals can' filled with the love, warmth and 'sense of belonging to one another which is the essence of being a couple'.[72]

In Ireland's same-sex marriage case, *Zappone v Revenue Commissioners*, Dunne J found that the same-sex couple seeking recognition of their Canadian

---

[64] See *Opinions of the Justices to the Senate*, 802 NE2d 565, 570 (Mass 2004); Crompton, 'Civil Partnership Bill 2004' (2004).

[65] J Millbank, 'The Role of 'Functional Family' in Same-Sex Family Recognition Trends' (2008) 20(2) *Child and Family Law Quarterly* 155.

[66] F Ryan, 'Sexuality, Ideology and the Legal Construction of Family: *Fitzpatrick v. Sterling Housing Association*' (2000) 3 *Irish Journal of Family Law* 2, 6.

[67] L Glennon, '*Fitzpatrick v Sterling Housing Association Ltd* – An Endorsement of the Functional Family?' (2000) 14 *International Journal of Law, Policy and the Family* 226, 245.

[68] [1999] 4 All ER 705.

[69] ibid 720.

[70] ibid 714.

[71] [2004] 2 AC 557.

[72] ibid, 608.

marriage under Irish law clearly had 'a long-lasting loving relationship of mutual commitment'.[73] More recently, in *Schalk and Kopf v Austria*, the first same-sex marriage case to come before it, the European Court of Human Rights acknowledged 'that same-sex couples are just as capable as different-sex couples of entering into stable committed relationships' and as a result they have a 'need for legal recognition and protection of their relationship'.[74] All of these judicial analyses and implicit approvals of the 'functional family' model could lead one to conclude, as Ward LJ did in the Court of Appeal in *Fitzpatrick v Sterling Housing Association*, that 'no distinction can sensibly be drawn between [same-sex and opposite-sex] couples in terms of love, nurturing, fidelity, durability, emotional and economic interdependence'.[75] Therefore, *on this analysis* the introduction of civil partnership instead of same-sex marriage by the Fianna Fáil/Green Party coalition Government appears arbitrary.

However, there are judges and academics who do not subscribe to the concept of the 'functional family' and hence for them civil partnership is an adequate mode of same-sex relationship recognition because the issue is very much what a couple *is*, and not what it *does*. This is true of Lord Millett, who dissented in *Ghaidan v Godin-Mendoza*. His Lordship felt that the then pending Civil Partnership Act 2004 in the UK was quite a logical 'separate but equal' form of relationship recognition for same-sex couples when he expressed the view that

> persons cannot be or be treated as married to each other or live together as husband and wife unless they are of the opposite sex. It is noticeable that, now that Parliament is introducing remedial legislation, it has not sought to do anything as silly as to treat same-sex relationships as marriages, whether legal or *de facto*. It pays them the respect to which they are entitled by treating them as conceptually different but entitled to equality of treatment.[76]

Lord Millett did not elaborate as to why, in his view, it is essential to marriage that the parties are of the opposite sex and consequently his strict adherence to a form-over-substance approach to marriage is unsatisfying from a theoretical perspective. Similarly, Wardle, a US academic, is of the opinion that 'the heterosexual dimensions of the relationship are at the very core of what makes "marriage" what it is',[77] and explains that, for him, opposite-sex marriage is unique, because:

> It is the *integration* of the universe of gender differences (profound and subtle, biological and cultural, psychological and genetic) associated with sexual identity that constitutes the core and essence of marriage ... Thus, cross-gender uniting in marriage is not merely a matter of arbitrary definition or semantic word-play; it goes to the heart of the very *concept* or *nature* of the marriage relationship itself.[78]

---

[73] *Zappone v Revenue Commissioners and Others* [2008] 2 IR 417, 501.
[74] *Schalk and Kopf v Austria* App No 30141/04 (ECHR, 24 June 2010) [99].
[75] [1998] 1 FLR 6, 39.
[76] [2004] 2 AC 557, 589 (Lord Millett, dissenting).
[77] LD Wardle, 'Form and Substance in Committed Relationships in American Law' in O Doyle and W Binchy (eds), *Committed Relationships and the Law* (Dublin, Four Courts Press, 2007) 61, 76.
[78] ibid.

Hence for Wardle, 'form reflects substance'.[79] However, it is respectfully submitted that Wardle's reasoning here is thin, and that a (slightly) more plausible ground for differentiating between same-sex relationships and opposite-sex marriage based on this notion of the 'complementarity of the sexes' is that of the 'unique procreative potential' which is always associated with male-female relationships, an argument to which this chapter shall now turn.

A. Public Interest and Moral Arguments for Privileging Opposite-Sex Marriage

Stith makes an interesting *public interest* argument for the continued legal restriction of marriage to opposite-sex couples only, as

> sexual relations between women and men may generate children, beings at once highly vulnerable and essential for the future of every human community. The good of those children as well as the common good thus require that the State do all it can to channel such relations into stable and secure relationships.[80]

Stith argues that marriage enables children 'to know who their true father is and thus to know on whom they have a legal and moral claim for support' and 'to have their true father at home, where he can do them the most good'.[81] Further, he states that because of the time and effort involved in responsible childrearing and the eventual benefits of this for the whole community through the production of 'educated and disciplined citizens' it makes sense for the state to reward married couples through the provision of tax and social security benefits. He concludes that 'the child-centred reasons for channelling heterosexual intercourse into exclusive and stable unions do not apply to sexual acts between persons of the same sex, since such acts can never generate children'.[82] If we accept that the public interest in the state's approval of and support for sexual relationships through its marriage laws is child-centred then, arguably, civil partnership is an adequate form of relationship recognition for same-sex couples because, according to Stith, there 'is no possible child-related reason why the public community should care when [same-sex unions] are formed or dissolved'.[83]

---

[79] ibid, 86.

[80] R Stith, 'On the Legal Validation of Sexual Relationships' in S Fitzgibbon, LD Wardle and AS Loveless (eds), *The Jurisprudence of Marriage and Other Intimate Relationships* (Buffalo, WS Hein & Co, 2010) 143, 147.

[81] Marriage encourages men to remain with women for the good of the children of the union and therefore the institution is arguably a state-imposed means of disciplining sexuality. See further M Murray, 'Marriage as Punishment' (2012) 112 *Columbia Law Review* 1.

[82] See also the discussion in RJ Araujo, 'Same-Sex Marriage-From Privacy to Equality: The Failure of the "Equality" Justifications for Same-Sex Marriage' in S Fitzgibbon, LD Wardle and A Scott Loveless (eds), *The Jurisprudence of Marriage and Other Intimate Relationships* (Buffalo, WS Hein & Co, 2010) 195, 202–03.

[83] R Stith, 'Legal Validation' (2010) 154.

However, numerous same-sex couples are raising the biological child of one of the partners from a previous opposite-sex relationship, and same-sex couples can also choose to have children via recourse to adoption or donor-assisted human reproduction and surrogacy. There is nothing to suggest that same-sex couples cannot raise their children to be responsible citizens who benefit the community at large. Although none of these children are generated by the sexual acts between the same-sex partners, the fact is that children can be brought into a same-sex household and thus there is a contemporary, child-related, public interest argument for recognising and supporting same-sex relationships through marriage. For the good of the normative development of these children, and indeed the common good, it is 'good social policy to give gay relationships the ultimate seal of approval'[84] by allowing them to be recognised by the state as marriages. In addition, as the Massachusetts Supreme Court acknowledged in *Goodridge v Dept of Public Health*, same-sex couples seeking access to marriage are 'not seeking to destroy the institution of marriage, but to share in its benefits and protections'[85] and embrace everything that it stands for, and this 'is a testament to the enduring place of marriage in our laws and in the human spirit'.[86] Indeed, Ryan observes that 'marriage represents an identification with, and a symbolic reaffirmation of, prevailing social understandings and moral norms'.[87] Marriage equality helps to further assimilate same-sex couples into the societies that embrace it – this is of benefit to the common good and represents an additional contemporary (albeit not necessarily a child-related) public interest argument for granting same-sex couples access to marriage.

In any event, Stith argues that civil partnership is a more appropriate form of relationship recognition for same-sex couples, *even those same-sex couples raising children*. It is here that his true position is revealed because he *overtly* employs a moral argument to discourage recognition of same-sex marriages. For Stith, the term 'marriage' carries with it a moral meaning that is inappropriate and misleading in the context of same-sex couples.[88] He argues that the term 'marriage' connotes a sense of new-found moral approval for sexual acts that take place within such unions (most likely because such acts can lead to the birth of children in a stable familial environment) and the same cannot be said for same-sex sexual acts that take place within marriage.[89] According to Stith, 'traditional natural law morality argues that our sexual fulfilment lies in engaging in only the

---

[84] N Cox, 'A Question of Definition: Same-Sex Marriage and the Law' in O Doyle and W Binchy (eds), *Committed Relationships and the Law* (Dublin, Four Courts Press, 2007) 104, 121.

[85] ME Wojcik, 'Wedding Bells Heard Around the World: Years from Now, Will we Wonder why we Worried about Same-Sex Marriage?' (2003–04) 24 *Northern Illinois University Law Review* 589, 680.

[86] *Goodridge v Department of Public Health* (2003) 798 NE2d 941, 965.

[87] F Ryan, 'From Stonewall(s) to Picket Fences: The Mainstreaming of Same-Sex Couples in Contemporary Legal Discourses' in O Doyle and W Binchy (eds), *Committed Relationships and the Law* (Dublin, Four Courts Press, 2007) 1, 58.

[88] Stith (n 81) 154–55.

[89] ibid 154.

sort of sex acts for which we are designed in mind and body, namely intercourse within committed different-sex marriage.'[90]

Thus, Stith's objection to same-sex marriage appears to be based more on a moral repugnance of same-sex sexual activity than any genuine child-centric public interest in promoting opposite-sex marriages as an ideal. Stith's position is similar to that of Wardle, who proffers a further allegedly child-related argument for not recognising same-sex marriage which is actually moral repugnance in disguise, and to which this chapter shall now turn.

B. Child-Centric Arguments for Restricting Marriage to Opposite-Sex Couples

Wardle's argument against permitting same-sex marriage, one that is (allegedly) based on same-sex parenting and child development, is that

> until the research clearly and honestly shows no significant increase in potential for harm of the children, it would be irresponsible to give legal status and benefits to other 'committed relationships' comparable to that accorded to married conjugal parents.[91]

However, this author cannot help but feel that, in light of a growing body of affirmative evidence pertaining to same-sex parents and child development,[92] the child welfare argument put forward by Wardle to discourage the global introduction of same-sex marriage is really nothing more than a stalling mechanism designed to mask an underlying moral disapproval. Indeed, Wardle's disdain for same-sex relationships is evident in much of his writing.[93] He castigates all same-sex relationships, stating that

> promiscuity, infidelity, multiple sexual partners, and dangerous sexual practices are the behavioural norms among gay couples (and also, to a lesser extent, lesbian couples) rather than monogamy and self-control which are the norms fostered by and nurtured in heterosexual marriages.[94]

---

[90] ibid 159.

[91] L.D. Wardle, 'Form and Substance' (2007) 79.

[92] See E Short et al, 'Lesbian, Gay, Bisexual and Transgender (LGBT) Parented Families: A Literature Review prepared for The Australian Psychological Society' (The Australian Psychological Society, 2007), available at psychology.org.au/getmedia/47196902-158d-4cbb-86e6-2f3f1c71ffd1/lgbt-families-literature-review.pdf; TJ Biblarz and J Stacey, 'How does the Gender of Parents Matter?' (2010) 72 *Journal of Marriage and Family* 3; J Tobin and R McNair, 'Public International Law and the Regulation of Private Spaces: Does the Convention on the Rights of the Child Impose an Obligation on States to Allow Gay and Lesbian Couples to Adopt?' (2009) 23 *International Journal of Law, Policy and the Family* 110.

[93] LD Wardle, 'The Boundaries of Belonging: Allegiance, Purpose and the Definition of Marriage' (2011) 25 *Brigham Young University Journal of Public Law* 287, 315; LD Wardle, 'Gender Neutrality and the Jurisprudence of Marriage' in S Fitzgibbon, LD Wardle and AS Loveless (eds), *The Jurisprudence of Marriage and Other Intimate Relationships* (Buffalo, WS Hein & Co, 2010); LD Wardle, 'The Attack on Marriage as the Union of a Man and a Woman' (2007) 83 *North Dakota Law Review* 1365, 1374.

[94] Wardle, 'The Attack on Marriage' (2007) 1374.

He cautions that 'redefining marriage to include gay and lesbian couples will have a profound impact upon sexual morality and public health in society'.[95] Indeed, his moral disapproval of same-sex marriage is so intense that Wardle strongly tries to discourage legislators from providing for marriage equality by solemnly warning that 'as goes marriage so goes the family, and as goes the family so goes the nation, and the world'.[96] Consequently, child-related interests do not really appear to be at the top of Wardle's agenda, and one might be far more inclined to agree with Pennings' assertion that 'the basic position against homosexual parenting is not determined by the expected outcome on the welfare of the children but by moral repugnance and a belief in the inherent wrongness of homosexuality'.[97]

On balance, it would have been more appropriate for Irish law to embrace same-sex marriage rather than civil partnership, though as seen, there may be several reasons as to why this did not occur following the *Zappone* case. The functional similarities between same-sex and opposite-sex couples are well documented above, and I have also proffered some contemporary public interest arguments for allowing same-sex couples access to marriage.

Civil partnership proved a necessary measure on the path to marriage equality in Ireland. Despite its timely practical benefits for the many same-sex couples who availed of it, civil partnership was a separate legal institution that symbolically confined same-sex couples who wished to marry to second-class legal status. However, this is not to say that the phasing-out of civil partnership post-marriage equality was necessarily a desirable move because, as I shall now demonstrate, it continues to hold significant value for many same-sex couples and, as Ryan observes, the demise of civil partnership 'leaves family law with less diversity and, crucially, compounds the dominant position of marriage in the Irish legal order'.[98]

X. Civil Partnership in Post-Marriage Equality Ireland

In light of the success of the Marriage Referendum, the Oireachtas had no option but to disallow the registration of any further civil partnerships in a jurisdiction where the state constitutionally 'pledges itself to guard with special care the institution of Marriage, on which the Family is founded, and to protect it against attack'.[99] Since marriage is now available to same-sex couples, it would most likely have been unconstitutional to retain civil partnership as an alternative option for formalising a relationship because, as Dunne observes, it might 'induce' same-sex couples 'not to enter the married state'.[100] Consequently, civil partnership cannot

---

[95] ibid 1377.

[96] Wardle, 'The Boundaries of Belonging' (2011) 287, 315.

[97] G Pennings, 'Evaluating the Welfare of the Child in Same-Sex Families' (2011) 26 *Human Reproduction* 1609, 1610.

[98] Ryan (n 4) 50.

[99] See Art 41.3.1, Constitution of Ireland.

[100] P Dunne, 'Civil Partnership in an Ireland of Equal Marriage Rights' (2015) 53 *Irish Jurist* 77, 81.

operate as an alternative to marriage; indeed, there can be no new civil partnerships; a same-sex couple can no longer enter into a civil partnership because the Marriage Act 2015 Act repeals the relevant statutory provisions which enabled them to do so in 2011–16.[101]

In addition, if Ireland was to retain same-sex civil partnership post-marriage equality, this would not only be susceptible to constitutional challenge but may also fall foul of Articles 8 (right to respect for private and family life) and 14 (freedom from discrimination) of the ECHR. This is because same-sex couples would have two options to formalise their relationship – marriage or civil partnership – whereas opposite-sex couples would only be permitted to marry. This is the situation that arose in England, Wales and Scotland. In *R (on the application of Steinfeld and Keidan) v Secretary of State for International Development* ('*Steinfeld*') the UK Supreme Court found that by continuing to restrict civil partnerships to same-sex couples post-marriage equality, the Civil Partnership Act 2004 breached Articles 8 and 14 of the ECHR.[102] Since marriage was equally available to opposite-sex and same-sex couples since 2014, the Supreme Court found that the Westminster Parliament had created 'a situation of inequality ... where none had previously existed',[103] by allowing same-sex couples to continue to enter into civil partnerships as a means of formalising their relationships post-marriage equality, while failing to extend the same legal privilege to their opposite-sex counterparts. Lord Kerr made it 'unequivocally clear' that from the moment marriage equality was introduced the Government was under an obligation to 'eliminate the inequality of treatment *immediately*'.[104] This could have been achieved by phasing out civil partnerships or by opening up the institution to opposite-sex couples, but the Westminster Parliament chose to pursue neither option. This significant persuasive decision from the UK Supreme Court demonstrates that, in Ireland, phasing out civil partnership simultaneous to the introduction of marriage equality ensured that the state remained compliant with its obligations under Articles 8 and 14 of the ECHR.[105]

---

[101] See the Marriage Act 2015, s 8.

[102] *R (on the application of Steinfeld and Keidan) v Secretary of State for International Development* [2018] UKSC 32.

[103] ibid [36].

[104] ibid [50], emphasis in original.

[105] However, in *Ratzenböck and Seydl v Austria* App No 28475/12, 26 October 2017 the ECtHR found that the inability of an opposite-sex couple in Austria to enter into a civil partnership, an option available to same-sex couples, did not violate Arts 8 and 14 because the couple could marry, whereas same-sex couples had no right to marry and needed civil partnership as an alternative means of legal recognition for their relationship. Thus, the applicants were not in a comparable situation to a same-sex couple. However, in a jurisdiction where marriage and civil partnership are both available to same-sex couples it is submitted that denying the latter to opposite-sex couples and only allowing them to marry would most likely be in breach of Arts 8 and 14. Therefore, Fenwick and Hayward conclude that the *Ratzenböck* decision 'can readily be found to be inapplicable to the situation in *Steinfeld*' and this author would agree, adding that retaining civil partnership in Ireland post-marriage equality and allowing same-sex couples to marry *or* enter into a civil partnership, while only allowing opposite-sex couples to marry would similarly violate Arts 8 and 14. For a discussion of *Ratzenböck* see H Fenwick

A. Conversion of Civil Partnership to Marriage?

Although new civil partnerships have not been recognised since 16 May 2016, subsisting civil partnerships are of course preserved under Irish law. However, the parties to such civil partnerships may marry each other, whereupon the subsisting civil partnership shall stand dissolved on and from the date of their marriage.[106] Unlike the situation in England and Wales, where a conversion from civil partnership to marriage is permitted and even has the effect of backdating the marriage to the date on which the parties entered into their civil partnership, in Ireland it is not possible to simply convert a subsisting civil partnership into a marriage: the parties must undergo a civil marriage ceremony.[107]

Perhaps due to the constitutional preference for marriage, the Marriage Act 2015 grants a dispensation to subsisting civil partners who wish to enter into a same-sex marriage by exempting them from the three-month notice requirement ordinarily applicable to marriage.[108] The Act stipulates that where the parties to the intended marriage are parties to a subsisting civil partnership they may notify *an tArd-Chláraitheoir* (the Registrar General) of their intention to marry *at any time* prior to the date on which the marriage is to be solemnised. As a result of this legislative dispensation, when the Marriage Act 2015 entered into force on 16 November 2015 the first same-sex marriages between subsisting civil partners were able to take place the following day: 17 November 2015.

Further, those couples who had given the requisite notice to *an tArd-Chláraitheoir* of their intention to become civil partners prior to the enactment of the Marriage Act 2015 also benefitted because the legislation provides that notification of an intention to enter into a civil partnership may, if requested by the parties concerned, be treated by a registrar as if it were a notification of the parties' intention to marry.[109] Between 17 November 2015 and the end of that year, there were 91 same-sex marriages in Ireland, all of which were between subsisting civil partners or parties who had notified an intention to enter into a civil partnership but requested that this be treated as an intention to marry.

B. An Ongoing Demand for Civil Partnership?

In the absence of a successful constitutional referendum to expand the definition of the family in Article 41 beyond the marital family unit, the fate of civil partnership was sealed upon the introduction of marriage equality in 2015.

---

and A Hayward, 'From Same-Sex Marriage to Equal Civil Partnerships: On a Path towards 'Perfecting' Equality?' (2018) 30 *Child and Family Law Quarterly* 97.

[106] See the Marriage Act 2015, s 11, inserting the Civil Partnership and Certain Rights and Obligations of Cohabitants Act 2010, s 109A.

[107] In England and Wales, conversion is possible under the Marriage (Same-Sex Couples) Act 2013, s 9.

[108] In Ireland, the Marriage Act 2015, s 9 amends the Civil Registration Act 2004, s 46(1) by substituting a new paragraph (a) for the existing one.

[109] See the Marriage Act 2015, s 10 which inserted Pt 7C into the Civil Registration Act 2004.

However, constitutional issues aside, Ireland acted entirely in line with the practice in many other jurisdictions that introduced marriage equality. Denmark, Norway, Sweden, Iceland, Finland and Germany and, very recently, Switzerland, all phased out civil partnership following the introduction of marriage equality.[110]

Nonetheless, it is worth briefly engaging with the arguments favouring not only the retention of civil partnership, but indeed its extension to opposite-sex couples if Article 41 was not a constitutional barrier to both options.[111] Evidence from the UK suggests that there is some demand among same-sex and opposite-sex couples for the retention of civil partnership. A UK Government consultation in 2012 revealed 61 per cent of respondents were in favour of extending civil partner-ship to opposite-sex couples, but Hayward argues that this percentage 'may need to be approached cautiously, as some respondents valued civil partnerships owing to their objection to same-sex marriage'.[112] In contrast, in 2014, a Department for Culture, Media and Sport consultation saw 76 per cent of respondents *opposed* to the extension of civil partnerships.[113] However, it is notable that 20 per cent of unmarried opposite-sex couples who responded to this latter consultation exercise favoured civil partnership over marriage.[114] Civil partnership was ulti-mately extended to opposite-sex couples in England and Wales following the UK Supreme Court's ruling in *Steinfeld*.[115] Indeed, on 31 December 2019, there were 167 opposite-sex civil partnerships formed in England and Wales, and this was only *the first day* on which it was possible for opposite-sex couples to become civil partners.[116] Recent evidence indicates that opposite-sex civil partnerships are now far more popular in England and Wales than their same-sex counterpart because in 2020, a total of 7,566 opposite-sex couples entered into civil partnerships in England and Wales, compared to a mere 785 same-sex civil partnerships.[117] The Office for National Statistics observed that 2020 saw the lowest number of

---

[110] Since the introduction of same-sex marriage in Switzerland on 1 July 2022, entering into a civil partnership is no longer possible in that jurisdiction.

[111] Jurisdictions such as New Zealand, Malta, Austria and the UK retained civil partnership post-marriage equality.

[112] A Hayward, 'The Steinfeld Effect: Equal Civil Partnerships and the Construction of the Cohabitant' (2019) *Child and Family Law Quarterly* 283, 297.

[113] Department for Culture, Media and Sport, 'Civil Partnership Review (England and Wales): Report on Conclusions' (DCMS, 2014) 11, [2.12].

[114] ibid 13. See also Ryan (n 4) 55.

[115] *R (on the application of Steinfeld and Keidan) v Secretary of State for International Development* [2018] UKSC 32. The Civil Partnership (Opposite Sex Couples) Regulations 2019 amended the Civil Partnership Act 2004 and enabled opposite-sex civil partnerships to occur in England and Wales. Opposite-sex civil partnerships are now an option throughout the UK. Opposite sex civil partner-ships became available in Northern Ireland on 13 January 2020 as a result of changes made to the Civil Partnership Act 2004 by the Marriage (Same-sex Couples) and Civil Partnership (Opposite-sex Couples) (Northern Ireland) Regulations 2019, and in Scotland on 1 June 2021 as a result of changes made to the Civil Partnership Act 2004 by the Civil Partnership (Scotland) Act 2020.

[116] See 'Civil Partnerships in England and Wales: 2019' (Office for National Statistics, 2020), available at www.ons.gov.uk/peoplepopulationandcommunity/birthsdeathsandmarriages/marriage cohabitationandcivilpartnerships/bulletins/civilpartnershipsinenglandandwales/2019.

[117] See 'Civil Partnerships in England and Wales: 2020' (Office for National Statistics, 2021), at www.ons.gov.uk/peoplepopulationandcommunity/birthsdeathsandmarriages/marriagecohabitation andcivilpartnerships/bulletins/civilpartnershipsinenglandandwales/2020.

same-sex civil partnerships recorded for England – 745 – since the introduction of the institution in 2005.[118] Nonetheless, Hayward notes that in the UK, only one in eight same-sex civil partnerships have been converted into marriages to date and, while he acknowledges that the reasons why couples are forgoing conversion are 'multi-faceted',[119] he believes that 'the fact that some same-sex civil partners have decided not to convert their civil partnerships into marriages indicates that they have *chosen* a particular family form'.[120] It is clear from these statistics and findings that in our neighbouring jurisdiction, the number of same-sex *and*, perhaps more so, opposite-sex couples that favour civil partnership over marriage is not insignificant.[121]

In Ireland, the demand among same-sex couples for the retention of civil partnership in the post-marriage equality era appears less significant. The uptake on civil partnership in Ireland over a relatively short period is notable – 2,077 same-sex civil partnerships were formed between the institution's inception in 2011 and its demise in 2016 at a time when marriage was off the table for same-sex couples. However, merely seven of these same-sex civil partnerships were formed in 2016, following the extension of marriage to same-sex couples.[122] This is compared to 376 such civil partnerships the previous year, most of which would have been formed prior to the introduction of marriage equality, given that the Marriage Act 2015 only entered into force towards the end of that year, on 16 November 2015.[123] Nonetheless, the Census in 2016 recorded same-sex couples in civil partnerships for the first time and 'the results show there were 4,226 persons in this category in 2016'.[124] This figure is a combination of civil partnerships that were entered into in

---

[118] ibid. This is interesting given that, following an initial decline after the introduction of marriage equality, the number of same-sex civil partnerships in England and Wales had been gradually increasing between 2016 and 2019. See 'Civil Partnerships in England and Wales' (Office for National Statistics, 2016–19), available at www.ons.gov.uk/peoplepopulationandcommunity/birthsdeathsandmarriages/marriagecohabitationandcivilpartnerships/bulletins/civilpartnershipsinenglandandwales/previousReleases.

[119] A Hayward, 'Relationships with Status: Civil Partnership in an Era of Same-Sex Marriage' in F Hamilton and G Nota La Diega (eds), *Same-Sex Relationships, Law and Social Change* (London, Routledge, 2020) 189, 200.

[120] A Hayward, 'The Steinfeld Effect' (2019) 283, 295; emphasis added.

[121] Only time will tell as to whether England and Wales will maintain this momentum by a notable number of same-sex and opposite-sex couples choosing civil partnership as a means of formalising their relationships. Indeed, Norrie points out that 'In the Netherlands civil partnership, though less popular than marriage, is chosen by a respectable number of couples *(of either gender mix)*' (emphasis added): see K Norrie, 'Registered Partnerships in Scotland' in JM Scherpe and A Hayward (eds), *The Future of Registered Partnerships* (Cambridge, Intersentia, 2017) 225, 251.

[122] The highest number of civil partnerships – 536 – was recorded in 2011; see Central Statistics Office, 'Statistics: Marriages and Civil Partnerships 2011', available at: www.cso.ie/en/releasesandpublications/er/mcp/marriagesandcivilpartnerships2011. There were seven civil partnership ceremonies in 2016; see Central Statistics Office, 'Statistics: Marriages and Civil Partnerships 2016' (2017), available at www.cso.ie/en/releasesandpublications/er/mcp/marriagesandcivilpartnerships2016.

[123] See Central Statistics Office, 'Statistics: Marriages and Civil Partnerships 2015' (CSO, 2016), available at www.cso.ie/en/releasesandpublications/er/mcp/marriagesandcivilpartnerships2015.

[124] See Census 2016, 'Summary Results – Part 1' (CSO, 2016) 28, available at www.cso.ie/en/releasesandpublications/er/mcp/marriagesandcivilpartnerships2016.

Ireland and abroad, but it is a significant figure that is indicative of support, and a preference for civil partnerships among some same-sex couples. That said, it must be approached with a degree of circumspection because the 2016 Census result is from the very early days of marriage equality in Ireland and a proportion of these civil partners might since have married.

While the number of civil partnerships formed in 2016 was minute, this does not necessarily indicate a preference for marriage among same-sex couples because it must be remembered that the option of notifying an intention to enter into a domestic civil partnership was foreclosed to same-sex couples in late 2015. Further, the notable result of the 2016 Census certainly indicates some preference for civil partnerships among same-sex couples, and the results of Census 2022, due for release in 2023, will be of significant interest. Thus, it is opined that the demand for civil partnership in Ireland should not be underestimated; after all, the reasons same-sex and opposite-sex couples may wish to choose civil partnership over marriage are varied and complex.[125]

Indeed, regarding the litigants in the *Steinfeld* case who sought access to civil partnership for *opposite-sex couples* in the UK, Hayward observes that 'justifying their decision to seek a civil partnership, the litigants emphasise the more egalitarian, secular and neutral nature of civil partnerships in comparison with what they view as the patriarchal, heteronormative and values-laden concept of marriage'.[126] Hayward believes that the secular nature of civil partnership is equally appealing to those *same-sex couples* ideologically opposed to marriage, 'particularly in light of the latter's relationship with the Church and its teaching on same-sex relationships'.[127] Further, Hayward observes that civil partnership might also appeal to religious same-sex couples who believe that marriage should remain an exclusively opposite-sex union.[128] Hayward's observations on the value that same-sex couples might place on civil partnership because of their religious views may hold particular relevance in a country like Ireland, where 78.3 per cent of the population identified as being of the Roman Catholic faith as recently as 2016.[129] As Hayward points out,

> it is true that civil partnerships are a statutory construct created by the State to protect a vulnerable group of citizens at a time when marriage was not available' but, as a means

---

[125] Indeed, Dunne argues that there is surely a 'policy imperative' for Irish policy-makers to encourage those couples who would never marry 'to enter into marriage-like structures so as to maximise their opportunity for relationship security. There is no threat to the institution of marriage, as these couples would otherwise not have married, but there is a significant societal benefit in seeing individuals adopt stable life-structures': see Dunne, 'Civil Partnership' (2015) 89.

[126] A Hayward, 'Relationships with Status' (2020) 199. However, see the arguments made by Norrie refuting the 'choice' and 'discrimination' arguments in favour of extending civil partnership to opposite-sex couples. Norrie favours phasing out civil partnership where marriage equality has been achieved: Norrie, 'Registered Partnerships in Scotland' (2017) 245–51.

[127] A Hayward, 'The Future of Civil Partnership in England and Wales' in JM Scherpe and A Hayward (eds), *The Future of Registered Partnerships* (Cambridge, Intersentia, 2017) 543.

[128] ibid.

[129] 'Census 2016 Summary Results – Part 1' (CSO, 2016) 72, available at www.cso.ie/en/media/csoie/newsevents/documents/census2016summaryresultspart1/Census2016SummaryPart1.pdf.

of formalising a relationship, civil partnership can, 'serve an important expressive function for couples.'[130]

The above statistics on the formation of opposite-sex civil partnerships and the annual increase in same-sex civil partnerships in the UK from 2016 to 2019 (excluding 2020) clearly lend support to this point of view.

C. The Recommendations of the Citizen's Assembly and the Joint Oireachtas Committee on Gender Equality

The outcome of the *Steinfeld* litigation in the UK, as well as the notable, ongoing demand for civil partnerships in that jurisdiction, might very well lead one to agree with Ryan's observation that 'the aspiration to form a union that is unequivocally egalitarian, as well as secular and anti-patriarchal in its origins, *is surely deserving of respect*.'[131] Indeed, it is worth noting that the members of the Citizens' Assembly recently demonstrated an understanding of, and respect for, alternative family structures by voting overwhelmingly in favour of broadening the constitutional definition of 'The Family' in Article 41 so that the provision 'would protect private and family life, with the protection afforded to the family not limited to the marital family'.[132] This recommendation is contained in the 'Report of the Citizen's Assembly on Gender Equality', which was laid before the Houses of the Oireachtas in 2021. The Joint Committee on Gender Equality was tasked with considering the recommendations contained in this report and, in July 2022, that body published an 'Interim Report on Constitutional Change' in which it recommended that a referendum should be held in 2023 in order to give effect to the Citizens' Assembly recommendations on constitutional change.[133] At the time of writing, one can only speculate as to whether such recommendation might be considered by or ultimately put to a referendum by the Irish Government, or whether it would be successful if it were, but it is encouraging to see such strong support for the constitutional recognition of family types that extend beyond the marital family,

---

[130] Hayward (n 119) 201. It is interesting to note that in 2020, more opposite-sex couples in Ireland availed of civil marriage ceremonies (41%) *over* Roman Catholic marriage ceremonies (35.8%). Given the demand for civil marriage ceremonies, it is not unreasonable to assume that some of these opposite-sex couples might have opted for civil partnership had the option been available to them in 2020: see 'Statistics: Marriages 2020' (CSO, 2021) available at www.cso.ie/en/releasesandpublications/ep/p-mar/marriages2020.

[131] Ryan (n 4) 57; emphasis added.

[132] See Citizen's Assembly, 'Report of the Citizen's Assembly on Gender Equality' (Citizen's Assembly, 2021) 50–53, available at citizensassembly.ie/en/about-the-citizens-assembly/report-of-the-citizens-assembly-on-gender-equality.pdf. 98.9% of the members of the Citizen's Assembly voted in favour of this potential amendment to the definition of 'The Family' in Art 41 of the Constitution. The Citizens' Assemblies (2016–2018; 2019–21) were exercises in participative democracy designed to consider changes to the Constitution and the law in specified areas. The Citizens' Assemblies were comprised of a Chairperson and 99 citizens.

[133] See Joint Committee on Gender Equality, 'Interim Report on Constitutional Change' (Dublin, Joint Committee on Gender Equality, 2022) 3, available at data.oireachtas.ie/ie/oireachtas/committee/dail/33/joint_committee_on_gender_equality/reports/2022/2022-07-13_interim-report-on-constitutional-change_en.pdf.

especially when the body making the initial recommendation was citizen-led. In light of these developments and the findings in the 2016 Census and from the UK, perhaps the swift phasing-out of civil partnership in Ireland should be somewhat lamented, even if it was constitutionally required.

XI. The Regulation of Cohabitation in Ireland

The difficulty with 'opt-in' registration models of relationship recognition like marriage and civil partnership has been identified by Walsh and Ryan: 'An inherent problem with using registration as the sole means of ameliorating the position of *de facto* couples is that it neglects the position of people that are not party to a formalised relationship'.[134] Accordingly, in 2006 the Irish Law Reform Commission recommended in its 'Report on the Rights and Duties of Cohabitants' that it would be wise to have a 'registration model and redress model' operating in conjunction with one another because 'rather than being mutually exclusive' they could logically coexist together with the latter system acting 'as a safety-net or default system for those couples who have not opted in' to the former regime.[135] In light of this pertinent recommendation and given the sheer numbers involved, it is perhaps unsurprising that the Irish legislature sought to make some legal provision for cohabitants in Part 15 of the 2010 Act. The 2006 Census highlighted that there were 121,800 cohabiting opposite-sex couples in Ireland, an almost quadruple increase on the figure of 31,300 recorded in the 1996 Census.[136] Indeed, the 2016 Census demonstrated that, although the rate of growth had slowed somewhat, the number of such couples stood at 152,302.[137] In addition, the number of cohabiting same-sex couples has almost trebled over the course of 10 years. The 2006 Census indicated that there were 2,090 such couples in Ireland; the 2016 Census states that there are 6,034 same-sex couples, and some 591 of these couples are raising children.[138]

Some academic commentators have nonetheless voiced concern over the introduction of a statutory regime for Irish cohabitants. Ryan observes that while spouses and civil partners enter into formal unions by consent, 'by contrast, cohabitants do not formally commit to legal rights and obligations, and as such, some caution must be exercised in imposing obligations on cohabitants in the absence of agreement'.[139] Mee advocates further research, urging legislative caution in the sphere of cohabitants' rights:

> In relation to cohabitation outside marriage/civil partnership, it is important to guard against the naïve assumption that immediate legislation is the appropriate response to any complex social phenomenon … prior to attempting to develop a new scheme for

---

[134] Walsh and Ryan, *De Facto Couples* (2006) 137.
[135] Law Reform Commission, 'Report on the Rights and Duties of Cohabitants' LRC 82-2006 (2006) 19.
[136] See Census 2006, 'Principal Demographic Results: Commentary' (CSO, 2007) 21.
[137] See Census 2016, 'Summary Results – Part 1' (Dublin, CSO, 2017) 41.
[138] ibid.
[139] Ryan (n 29) 16. See also the observations made by Dr Brian Tobin and Dr Andy Hayward in Scottish Law Commission, Report on Cohabitation (Scot Law Com No. 261, 2022) 18.

cohabitants, it would be highly desirable to commission empirical research on the social phenomenon of cohabitation, rather than attempting to shape a legislative scheme on the basis of guess-work as to the reality of cohabitants' lives.[140]

Similar concerns were voiced by Hörster when a legal framework for cohabitation was being debated by the Portuguese legislature. Hörster recognised that while cohabitation legislation might constitute a 'well-intentioned' attempt to protect cohabitants, 'legislators should avoid taking protective measures (or paternalistic ones) before collecting enough reliable information'.[141] These concerns may be valid in the Irish context when one considers the four different stages of cohabitation outlined by Kiernan:

> Simplifying, in the first stage cohabitation emerges as a deviant or avante-garde phenomenon practised by a small group of the single population, whilst the great majority of the population marry directly. In the second stage cohabitation functions as either a prelude or a probationary period where the strength of the relationship may be tested prior to committing to marriage and is predominantly a childless phase. In the third stage cohabitation becomes socially acceptable as an alternative to marriage and becoming a parent is no longer restricted to marriage. Finally, in the fourth stage, cohabitation and marriage become indistinguishable with children being born and reared within both, and the partnership transition could be said to be complete.[142]

Based on the findings outlined in Census reports, Ireland would appear to be somewhere between the second and third stages outlined by Kiernan. While Census 2011 indicated that 57.8 per cent of cohabiting couples had no children,[143] Census 2016 later demonstrated that *almost half* of all cohabiting couples have children (50.4 per cent recorded as childless)[144] and, since 2017, statute law has extended to cohabiting couples eligibility to jointly apply to adopt a child or to acquire automatic parentage of a child conceived via donor-assisted human reproduction that takes place in a clinical setting; thus, in these contexts, becoming a parent is certainly no longer restricted to marriage.[145]

---

[140] J Mee, 'A Critique of the Cohabitation Provisions of the Civil Partnership Bill 2009' (2009) 12 *Irish Journal of Family Law* 83, 90. Indeed, it is notable that although the Scottish Law Commission stated in its recent Discussion Paper on Cohabitation that responses to its Tenth Programme of Law Reform, in which cohabitation laws were proposed as a topic for review, involved 'a range of views … expressed to us by respondents to the Tenth Programme consultation, stakeholders, and Advisory Group members as to whether there is a justification for retaining different regimes for financial provision on cessation of cohabitation and on divorce or dissolution' *none* of the 49 respondents to the Tenth Programme were members of the public experiencing legal difficulties as a result of their status as cohabitants: www.scotlawcom.gov.uk/law-reform/tenth-programme-of-law-reform-consultation/respondents-to-the-scottish-law-commissions-consultation-on-topics-for-inclusion-in-its-tenth-programme-of-law-reform. See Scottish Law Commission, 'Aspects of Family Law – Discussion Paper on Cohabitation' Scottish Law Com No 170 (2020).

[141] HE Hörster, 'Does Portugal Need to Legislate on de facto Unions?' (1999) 13 *International Journal of Law, Policy and the Family* 274, 279.

[142] K Kiernan, 'The Rise of Cohabitation and Childbearing Outside Marriage in Western Europe' (2001) 15 *International Journal of Law, Policy and the Family* 1, 3.

[143] Census 2011, 'This is Ireland – Part 1' (CSO, 2012) 27.

[144] See Census 2016, 'Summary Results' (2017) 41.

[145] See the Adoption (Amendment) Act 2017, s 16, amending the Adoption Act 2010 s 3, and the Children and Family Relationships Act 2015 Pt 2, which was only commenced as recently as 4 May 2020.

Nonetheless, Ireland is not yet a country at a stage where cohabitation and marriage are virtually interchangeable, because Census 2016 reiterated an earlier finding from Census 2011 that 'cohabitation is often a precursor to marriage in Ireland' and confirmed that married couples consisting of 'husband, wife and children remained the most common family type, accounting for almost half of all families in Ireland'.[146] Therefore, a legislative approach to cohabitants' rights that does not assume that the parties to a cohabiting relationship wish for the legal rights and obligations associated with it to be synonymous with marriage remains appropriate.[147]

XII. Cohabitation Law Reform in the UK

In clear contrast to the situation in Ireland, where Mee observes that 'the idea of legislative reform seems to have gained traction simply because of an awareness of the fact that the social phenomenon of cohabitation was increasing in importance ... and of the fact that legislative reform had been implemented, or was under consideration, in cognate jurisdictions',[148] McCarthy asserts that the Scottish cohabitation provisions, enacted in 2006, had a 'somewhat elephantine gestation period', having first been proposed in a different form in the Scottish Law Commission's 'Report on Family Law', which was published back in 1992.[149] The Family Law (Scotland) Act 2006 introduced a redress scheme for cohabitants which does not require any minimum period of cohabitation before one cohabitant can seek redress from the other, irrespective of whether or not there are any children of the relationship. However, the remedies available under the Scottish cohabitation model are far more limited than those provided by its Irish counterpart. Indeed, in Scotland, 'the only tool available to judges' to provide an economically disadvantaged cohabitant with a form of redress is an order for the payment of a capital sum.[150] Nonetheless, the Scottish Law Commission published a Discussion Paper in 2020 in which it sought consultees' views on a range of options for reform of the Scottish cohabitation regime, and its final report, published in November 2022, recommended a range of remedies that could extend beyond the payment of a capital sum.[151]

In 2007, a similar scheme to the one currently operating in Scotland was recommended by the Law Commission of England and Wales in its report, 'Cohabitation: The Financial Consequences of Relationship Breakdown',[152] and while the

---

[146] ibid.

[147] ibid, 38.

[148] J Mee, 'Cohabitation Law Reform in Ireland' (2011) 23 *Child and Family Law Quarterly* 323, 326.

[149] F McCarthy, 'Cohabitation: Lessons from North of the Border?' (2011) 23 *Child and Family Law Quarterly* 277, 280.

[150] See Scottish Law Commission, 'Aspects of Family Law' (2020) 104.

[151] ibid. See Scottish Law Commission, Report on Cohabitation (2022) 112–113.

[152] See Law Commission, 'Cohabitation: The Financial Consequences of Relationship Breakdown' Law Com No 307 (2007).

Commission also recommended no minimum duration period before a cohabitant could seek redress where there is a child of the relationship, it proposed a minimum requirement of between two and five years' cohabitation for situations involving childless cohabitants, but left this for the Westminster Parliament to decide. However, to date, successive British governments have not proceeded with the Law Commission's recommendations. The Women and Equalities Committee considered the possibility of legal protections for cohabitants in England and Wales. The Committee's report was published in 2022 but its recommendation for the introduction of an 'opt out' redress scheme for cohabitants in England and Wales, as suggested by the Law Commission in 2007, was rejected by the U.K. Government for now.[153] Thus, as Miles, Wasoff and Mordaunt observe regarding cohabitation, 'while reform is not ruled out, England and Wales must continue to wait'.[154]

The cohabitation regime introduced in Ireland in 2011 appears to have 'appropriate regard to the value of autonomy of private relations while providing a safety net to address the needs of particularly vulnerable persons'[155] and may be of particular interest to those considering cohabitation law reform elsewhere. In Ireland, cohabiting relationships are only recognised for redress purposes once they have ended by means of death or dissolution. Therefore, unlike marriage or civil partnership where parties 'opt-in' at the outset, cohabitation is recognised *retrospectively, if* certain criteria are fulfilled. These criteria comprise the statutory time period(s) applicable before one cohabitant can seek redress from the other at the end of their relationship and the requirement that the applicant must be *financially dependent* on the respondent. In addition, cohabitants can choose to 'opt-out' of the statutory redress scheme by agreement. In a cohabitation context, the regulatory approach adopted in Part 15 of the 2010 Act arguably achieves an equitable balance between the competing concerns of undue State interference in private relationships and providing legislative protection for a truly vulnerable cohabitant.

XIII. Qualified Cohabitants and the Relief Available in Ireland under the 2010 Act

Section 172(1) defines a cohabitant as one of two adults (whether of the same or the opposite sex) who live together as a couple in an intimate and committed relationship and who are not related to each other within the prohibited degrees of

---

[153] See Women and Equalities Committee, *The Rights of Cohabiting Partners: Second Report of Session 2022–23* (HC 92, 2022), at https://committees.parliament.uk/publications/23321/documents/170094/default/; see also Women and Equalities Committee, *The Rights of Cohabiting Partners: Government response to the Committee's Second Report* (HC 766, 2022), at https://committees.parliament.uk/publications/31430/documents/176284/default/.

[154] J Miles, F Wasoff and E Mordaunt, 'Cohabitation: Lessons from Research North of the Border?' (2011) 23 *Child and Family Law Quarterly* 302, 322.

[155] Law Reform Commission, 'Report on the Rights and Duties of Cohabitants' (2006) 19.

relationship or married to each other or civil partners of each other. Section 172(2) provides that when determining whether or not two adults are cohabitants, a court must take into account all the circumstances of the relationship and in particular have regard to the following, including: (a) the duration of the relationship; (b) the basis on which the couple live together; (c) the degree of financial dependence of either adult on the other and any agreements in respect of their finances; (d) the degree and nature of any financial arrangements between the adults including any joint purchase of property; (e) whether there are one or more dependent children; (f) whether one of the adults cares for and supports the children of the other; and (g) the degree to which the adults present themselves to others as a couple.

This redress model of relationship recognition provides that once cohabitants who satisfy the definition in section 172 have been living together for five years, or two years where there is a dependent child of the relationship, they become 'qualified cohabitants', after which a 'financially dependent' cohabitant can apply to the court for certain types of relief upon termination of the relationship.[156] The relief available can include a lump sum or periodical payments order, a pension adjustment order or a property adjustment order.[157] While the Irish redress scheme for cohabitants *potentially* allows for a claimant to access a broader range of remedies than its Scottish counterpart, it is only where proper provision cannot be made *solely* by virtue of a lump sum or periodical payments order that the court can consider making a pension adjustment order or, if necessary, a property adjustment order.[158] This staggered approach to remedies may serve to allay fears persons in cohabiting relationships might have concerning undue state encroachment on their autonomy, their pensions and their property rights, and might be worth replicating in England and Wales, and in any reform of the Scottish regime.

Section 195 provides that an application for relief must 'save in exceptional circumstances, be instituted within two years of the time that the relationship between the cohabitants ends, whether through death or otherwise'.[159] A qualified cohabitant can also seek an order that provision be made out of the net estate of a deceased cohabitant where inadequate or no provision has been made for them

---

[156] For the purposes of s 172, a couple can be 'living together' for the requisite statutory time period(s) even when one of them has been away from home for work purposes for extended periods of time: see *GR v Regan* [2020] IEHC 89. However, the couple must have been living together for a *continuous* period of five years, or two years where there is a child of the relationship, immediately before the time that the relationship ended. Shorter, separate periods of cohabitation cannot be aggregated to satisfy the temporal requirements of s 172(5): see *XY v ZW* [2019] IEHC 259.

[157] See the Civil Partnership and Certain Rights and Obligations of Cohabitants Act 2010, ss 175, 187 and 174, respectively.

[158] See the Civil Partnership and Certain Rights and Obligations of Cohabitants Act 2010, ss 187(6) and 174(2), respectively.

[159] The Court of Appeal in Ireland has held that an extension of the two-year time limit is indeed permissible 'in exceptional circumstances': see *MW v DC* [2017] IECA 255 (Court of Appeal (civil)). In Scotland, a claim for relief must be initiated by a cohabitant no later than one year after the date of cessation of cohabitation: see the Family Law (Scotland) Act 2006, s 28(8).

in the deceased's will or under the rules of intestacy.[160] If the qualified cohabitants were in a relationship immediately prior to the death then the applicant need not establish financial dependence; otherwise this requirement is applicable. This is logical because, as Mee points out: ' This reflects the fact that, in such cases, neither party ever withdrew his or her commitment to the relationship and so there seems to be a 'qualitative difference' from those cases where the relationship ended in acrimony'.[161]

A. The Situation of the 'Married' Cohabitant

Prior to 1 December 2019, an adult could not be a qualified cohabitant if one or both of the adults is or was, at any time during the relationship concerned, married to someone else and, at the time the cohabiting relationship ended, they had not 'lived apart' from their spouse for at least four of the previous five years, which was the waiting period required by the Family Law (Divorce) Act 1996 (and Article 41.3.2 of the Constitution) before a divorce could be sought.[162] However, following a successful referendum to remove the lengthy 'living apart' requirement from Article 41.3.2 of the Constitution, legislative change was possible, and, as discussed earlier, section 3 of the Family Law Act 2019 reduced the 'living apart' requirement for divorce from four out of the previous five years to two out of the previous three years.[163]

Since the provisions of the Family Law Act 2019 entered into force on 1 December 2019, marital status is now *prospectively irrelevant* when a cohabiting relationship is dissolved. Given the reduced waiting period for divorce, this is an entirely logical approach, because a 'qualified cohabitant' can only be recognised as such after a minimum of two years of 'living with' the other cohabitant under section 172(5) of the 2010 Act, so there simply could not be a situation where a married cohabitant would satisfy this cohabitation requirement without also 'living apart' from a spouse for the requisite period of two years for a divorce. As the Minister of State at the Department of Justice and Equality, David Stanton TD, stated during Oireachtas debates when this aspect of the Family Law Bill 2019 was being debated, 'a person cannot simultaneously be living with his or her spouse *and* be a cohabitant as defined in section 172

---

[160] See the Civil Partnership and Certain Rights and Obligations of Cohabitants Act 2010, s 194. See *DR v DC* [2015] IEHC 309 and *GR v Regan* [2020] IEHC 89. For a discussion of these cases, both of which involved a qualified cohabitant claiming a proportion of the deceased cohabitant's estate where the couple were living together as cohabitants until the time of the death, see A Adanan, 'Succession Law and Cohabitation after 10 Years of the Civil Partnership and Certain Rights and Obligations of Cohabitants Act 2010' (2020) 25 *Conveyancing and Property Law Journal* 70.

[161] J Mee, 'The Property Rights of Cohabitants under the 2010 Act' (Conference on the Civil Partnership and Certain Rights and Obligations of Cohabitants Act 2010, Trinity College Dublin, 2 April 2011).

[162] See the Civil Partnership and Certain Rights and Obligations of Cohabitants Act 2010, s 172(6).

[163] Section 3 of the Family Law Act 2019 did so by amending the Family Law (Divorce) Act 1996, s 5.

[(5) of the 2010 Act]'.[164] Nonetheless, section 173 (5) of the 2010 Act still prevents a court from making an order for redress in favour of a qualified cohabitant that would affect any right of any person to whom the other cohabitant is or was married. This is most likely to comply with Article 41 of the Constitution and protect the primacy of the marital family because it is well established, as Walsh and Ryan observe, 'that any legislative arrangement which serves to give preferential treatment to de facto couples over their married counterparts is generally inconsistent with the Constitution'.[165]

B. The Financial Dependence Criterion

A qualified cohabitant will only be entitled to relief under Part 15 of the 2010 Act if they were 'financially dependent on the other cohabitant'. Mee is critical of this requirement because 'it provides no remedy for claimants who have suffered major financial loss during the relationship but have not become "financially dependent" as a result'.[166] Mee considers how a qualified cohabitant who has sacrificed a career to work in the home caring for the family would likely be 'financially dependent' and entitled to a remedy under the Act. However, such a person would be disallowed a remedy if they suffered the same economic loss but inherited from a parent and thus were not rendered financially dependent upon the termination of the cohabiting relationship. Mee believes that in the latter situation a cohabitant could be 'equally deserving' of a remedy. He argues that the financial dependency criterion: 'Attempts to restrict the scope of the scheme so that it will not go too far in creating rights for cohabitants against each other, resulting in a half-hearted approach that leads to indefensibly arbitrary results'.[167] This author fails to see how it is 'indefensibly arbitrary' to deny the claimant in the latter scenario outlined by Mee the best of both worlds (ie an inheritance *and* a statutory remedy). In a cohabitation situation this type of claimant should be disentitled to any statutory remedy, because in enacting cohabitation legislation a state's legislature must be respectful of the fact that cohabitants have not made a life-long commitment to one another as with a marriage or a civil partnership

---

[164] See Dáil debate, vol 988, no 1 (16 October 2019), available at www.oireachtas.ie/en/debates/debate/dail/2019-10-16/35. The reason s 172 (6) continues to apply to cohabiting relationships that ended prior to 1 December 2019 is that to have retrospectively aligned it with the amended temporal requirements for divorce in s 5 of the Family Law (Divorce) Act 1996 would have retrospectively converted some people who were not qualified cohabitants at the time their relationships ended into qualified cohabitants. Cases may have already been decided or settled (or not commenced) based on the understanding that dual status was not possible unless the married cohabitant had been living apart from their spouse for at least four years. Changing the law with retrospective effect may therefore have upset existing arrangements between parties and understandings on which they were based. The author wishes to thank Dr Fergus Ryan, Associate Professor, Law Department, Maynooth University, for providing me with his astute observations in this regard.
[165] Walsh and Ryan (n 25) 81.
[166] Mee, 'The Property Rights of Cohabitants' (2011).
[167] Mee, 'A Critique of the Cohabitation Provisions' (2009) 83.

and that citizens largely choose to cohabit to avoid financial obligations extending beyond the cessation of their union.

Further, when the 2010 Act was being debated, the Minister for Justice, Equality and Law Reform, Dermot Ahern, stated that the purpose of the redress scheme provided for in Part 15 is to 'protect a financially dependent person who may be left *high and dry* if a couple split up'.[168] Hence a cohabitant who has sufficient means should not be entitled to seek relief from the other cohabitant at the end of a relationship. Mee gives another example of a cohabitant who would fall foul of the financial dependency requirement because they have transferred a valuable family home into joint names and included an express declaration of the beneficial interests to ensure that their partner would acquire the intended joint beneficial interest.[169] Again, in this type of scenario the cohabitant transferor has a joint share in a 'valuable' family home to rely on once the cohabitation ends. Why should such a claimant also be entitled to statutory relief against the other cohabitant? Yes, the other cohabitant has gained a property interest because of a generous yet arguably unwise choice that was made by their partner, but that was the latter party's *choice*, and it has not left them financially dependent. In 2002, in the case of *Nova Scotia (Attorney General) v Walsh*, Justice Bastarache, speaking for the majority of the Canadian Supreme Court, stressed the importance of the concept of 'freedom of choice' in intimate relationships because 'all cohabitants are deemed to have the liberty to make fundamental choices in their lives'.[170] Thus, it is opined that the requirement of financial dependency in the 2010 Act arguably achieves as equitable a balance as possible between the competing aims of protecting a truly vulnerable party once cohabitation ends and avoiding undue interference with what is perhaps a fundamental attribute of cohabitation, 'the freedom of living according to one's own criteria'.[171] Cohabitation is a phenomenon largely synonymous with 'an individualistic outlook on intimate relations'[172] and the type of support obligations undertaken by parties who chose to formalise their relationships and later divorced or separated should not be imposed on separating cohabiting partners *unless this is truly necessary to avoid injustice*. Indeed, when proposing the redress model, the Law Reform Commission emphasised that

> the objective of reform in the particular context of ancillary relief on breakdown of the relationship is to provide a default scheme of redress that would ensure relationships, in respect of which economic dependency existed *and have resulted in some form of vulnerability on termination of the relationship*, are protected.[173]

---

[168] Dáil Deb, vol 714, col 353 (1 July 2010); emphasis added.

[169] Mee (n 140) 86.

[170] *Nova Scotia (Attorney General) v Walsh* [2002] SCJ No 84 (QL), 32 RFL (5th) 81. See the discussion of this case in Bala, 'Controversy over Couples in Canada' (2003) 51.

[171] H.E. Hörster, 'Does Portugal Need to Legislate' (1999) 274.

[172] J Lewis, 'Debates and Issues Regarding Marriage and Cohabitation in the British and American Literature' (2001) 15 *International Journal of Law, Policy and the Family* 159, 171.

[173] Law Reform Commission (n 135) 3; emphasis added.

Nonetheless, once a cohabitant satisfies the financial dependency requirement, the court may grant them relief if it is 'just and equitable' to do so. Section 173(3) enables the court to consider numerous factors in this regard. These include 'the financial circumstances, needs and obligations' of each qualified cohabitant, and 'the duration of the parties' relationship, the basis on which the parties entered into the relationship and the degree of commitment of the parties to one another', 'any physical or mental disability' of the applicant cohabitant, and 'the conduct of each of the cohabitants, if the conduct is such that, in the opinion of the court, it would be unjust to disregard it'.

C. Constitutional Concerns

Further, although Mee is (arguably unfairly) critical of the financial dependency criterion, he nonetheless concludes that it would be unworkable to simply discard it as a filter and allow the numerous factors that are listed in section 173(3) to be solely determinative of a claimant's case. This is because these factors mirror those applicable in the context of ancillary relief upon divorce or judicial separation and if a qualified cohabitant could seek relief solely by reference to them then qualified cohabitation would be akin to marriage and could possibly be declared unconstitutional as a result. If a cohabitant could seek ancillary relief upon termination of a cohabitation after as little as two years where there is a child of the relationship, without any strict filter and by reference to virtually the same criteria applicable on divorce or judicial separation, then this would place such a person in a position identical to that of a spouse, who must be living apart from the other spouse for two out of the previous three years before they can seek a divorce and the ancillary reliefs attendant upon it. Such a legislative dispensation in favour of cohabitants might very well encourage cohabitation over marriage and constitute an 'attack' on the institution of marriage, which the state 'pledges itself to guard with special care' under Article 41.3.1 of the Constitution. Thus, the financial dependency requirement ensures that the redress model 'does not attempt to create ancillary relief as it applies to spouses'.[174] Instead, it acts as a necessary springboard for only the most vulnerable cohabitants to have their case decided by reference to the 'just and equitable' requirement and the criteria outlined in section 173, and this in turn helps to maintain the balance between a 'safety net' approach and making qualified cohabitation another substantive legal institution which may not withstand constitutional scrutiny. Indeed, constitutional concerns might be part of the reason why qualified cohabitation is a concept only recognised at the end of a relationship, because in a jurisdiction where marriage enjoys special protection under the Constitution, with the type of redress scheme in the 2010 Act 'the State is effectively saying that non-marital partnerships are

---

[174] ibid, 69.

only deserving of recognition *once they are over*[175] and only in quite limited circumstances.

D. The Impact of the Statutory Time Frames for Qualified Cohabitation

In addition to the requirement of financial dependency, the Irish cohabitation regime is limited by the statutory timeframes applicable before a cohabitant can qualify to seek relief from the courts against their partner. While a cohabitant can apply for relief after two years where there is a child of the relationship, it is still the case that a thin majority of cohabiting couples in Ireland are childless family units.[176] Further, since *both* qualified cohabitants must be the parents of the 'child of the relationship' some same-sex couples would seem to be precluded from applying for relief after two years because in cases of children born through surrogacy or certain types of donor-assisted human reproduction *both* parties simply cannot be the legal parents of a child born during their cohabitation.[177] Although all other cohabitants can apply for relief after five years or more, Kiernan observes that in most European countries 'one in two cohabitations had converted into marriages by the fifth anniversary of the union'.[178] Similarly in Ireland, research indicates that there is likely to be a much smaller pool of cohabitants by this time. Halpin and O'Donoghue estimate that in Ireland, 70 per cent of cohabiting relationships last for at least two years, with the average duration of a cohabitation being a little over two years.[179] Further, the authors estimate that only 25 per cent of couples cohabit for six years or more.[180] This low statistic is possibly because for many Irish opposite-sex couples cohabitation 'is functioning increasingly as a standard route into marriage'[181] with over 40 per cent of new marriages being preceded by a period of cohabitation. Hence, the number of opposite-sex couples satisfying both the five-year timeframe *and* the financial dependency requirement is statistically unlikely to be all that significant. One is inclined to agree with Mee's observation,

---

[175] O Doyle, 'Moral Argument and the Recognition of Same-Sex Partnerships' in O Doyle and W Binchy (eds), *Committed Relationships and the Law* (Dublin, Four Courts Press, 2007) 154; emphasis added.

[176] See Census 2016 (n 137) 41.

[177] Section 172(5) of the 2010 Act makes it clear that a qualified cohabitant is an adult who was in a relationship of cohabitation with another adult and living with that adult as a couple for a period of two years or more 'in the case where *they are the parents* of one or more dependent children'. A cohabiting intended mother of a child born through surrogacy who cannot be recognised as a legal parent under Irish law would similarly appear to be excluded from the ambit of the 2010 Act, s 172(5).

[178] Kiernan, 'The Rise of Cohabitation and Childbearing' (2001) 7.

[179] B Halpin and C O'Donoghue, 'Cohabitation in Ireland: Evidence from Survey Data' Working Paper (University of Limerick, 2004-01), available at ulir.ul.ie/bitstream/handle/10344/3630/Halpin_2004_cohabitation.pdf?sequence=2.

[180] ibid.

[181] ibid, 10.

which holds particular relevance for same-sex couples, most of whom are indeed childless,[182] 'in the context of couples without dependent children, it is relatively difficult to envisage cases where one party makes himself or herself "financially dependent" on the other as a result of the relationship'.[183]

Although it is still early days, one wonders if same-sex cohabitation will now similarly begin to increasingly act as a forerunner for entry into marriage, and if such marriages will largely come about within five years of the parties' cohabitation. If so, this hypothesis, when coupled with the five-year cohabitation requirement in section 172(5)(b) and the financial dependence criterion in section 173(2), not to mention the minute number of same-sex couples listed in Census 2016, would appear to indicate that the redress model provided for in the 2010 Act is in practice likely to benefit very few same-sex cohabitants in Ireland.

XIV. Cohabitants' Agreements

A further restriction on the potential efficacy of the redress scheme is to be found in section 202 of the 2010 Act, as this allows cohabitants to enter into enforceable agreements 'to provide for financial matters during the relationship or when the relationship ends'. The upshot of this is, as Byrne and Binchy observe: 'Thus parties contemplating cohabitation may first enter a cohabitants' agreement, excluding financial implications, if they so wish, just as parties in some jurisdictions may validly enter prenuptial agreements with similar unromantic intent'.[184] One might wonder how aspiring cohabitants can validly conclude such an agreement since they surely cannot satisfy the definition of cohabitant in section 172 of the 2010 Act because they do not yet 'live together as a couple in an intimate and committed relationship'. Nonetheless, section 202(5) allays any potential anomaly by stipulating that 'an agreement that meets the other criteria of this section shall be deemed to be a cohabitant's agreement under this section even if entered into before the cohabitation has commenced'. Section 202(3) states that a cohabitants' agreement may exclude either cohabitant from seeking an order for redress under section 173 or an order for provision from the estate of their partner, although section 202(4) enables a court to set aside an agreement 'in exceptional circumstances, where its enforceability would cause serious injustice'. Therefore, cohabitants can contractually 'opt-out' of the redress scheme provided for in Part 15 and avoid being subjected to the certain rights and obligations that are associated with it.

However, in order to be valid a cohabitants' agreement must comply with certain formalities. In particular, before signing the agreement each cohabitant must receive legal advice independently of the other or, if the parties have not

---

[182] Census 2016 (n 137) 41. This Census records 6,034 same-sex couples, with only 591 of these couples raising children.
[183] Mee (n 161).
[184] Byrne and Binchy, 'Family Law' (2011) 398.

been so separately advised, they must have been advised together and waived in writing their right to independent legal advice.[185] Compliance with this particular formality should help to support a conclusion that the cohabitation agreement was entered into fairly. As the Law Reform Commission has stressed, 'agreements must limit opportunities for the exercise of undue influence on the party who potentially stands to lose more as a result of the agreement'.[186] It is arguable that the stringent criteria also ensure that an agreement is less likely to be struck down by the courts where one of the cohabitants has a change of heart and seeks to challenge the arrangement later on because 'the more criteria required, the less opportunity there should be for the courts to overturn it'.[187]

Nonetheless, irrespective of the fact that they allow couples to 'opt-out' of the redress scheme, cohabitants' agreements appear unlikely to become the norm in Ireland because contracts 'are primarily designed to regulate economically based relations and transactions where each party acts primarily in his or her own economic interest'.[188] Schrama argues that such agreements do not reflect 'the love-based nature of the relationship' which dominates the parties' financial behaviour.[189] Indeed, Sutherland points out that 'people meet, fall in love (or lust or convenience) begin to live together and life goes on' and 'new relationship optimism makes it unlikely that [the parties] will conclude a contract'.[190] Consequently, as Bala has pointed out,

> people are generally not psychologically prepared to make contracts about their personal relationships, and the evolving roles and expectations of the partners in nonmarital relationships in any event tend to make contracts problematic when dealing with familial rights and obligations.[191]

XV. Conclusion

Little over a decade ago same-sex relationships were virtually unknown to Irish law. Through the establishment of civil partnership, and a cohabitation regime for opposite-sex and same-sex couples, the 2010 Act 'definitively challenges the well-worn Irish legal tradition of treating couples outside of marriage as strangers at law',[192] though the legislation very carefully avoids any collision between the

---

[185] See the Civil Partnership and Certain Rights and Obligations of Cohabitants Act 2010, s 202. The other formalities required by this section are that the agreement must be in writing, signed by both parties, and it must comply with the general law of contract.

[186] Law Reform Commission (n 135) 41.

[187] ibid.

[188] WM Schrama, 'The Dutch Approach to Informal Lifestyles: Family Function over Family Form? (2008) 22 *International Journal of Law, Policy and the Family* 311, 321.

[189] ibid.

[190] EE Sutherland, 'From "Bidie-In" to "Cohabitant" in Scotland: The Perils of Legislative Compromise' (2013) 27 *International Journal of Law, Policy and the Family* 143, 145.

[191] Bala (n 33) 54–55.

[192] Ryan (n 22) 52.

entitlements of civil or cohabiting partners and those of the members of a marital family unit. While the availability of civil partnership in Ireland was short-lived, it served an important pragmatic function for same-sex couples seeking recipro-cal rights and duties at a time when marriage was simply unavailable to them. In Ireland, as in many jurisdictions, civil partnership was but a precursor to marriage equality. Nonetheless, in light of the success of the Marriage Referendum, the Oireachtas had no option but to disallow the registration (and recognition) of any further civil partnerships in a jurisdiction where the marital family has remained on a constitutional pedestal since 1937. The retention of same-sex civil partnership as an alternative to marriage for same-sex couples would likely have been consti-tutionally unsound. In addition, this course of action may have been subject to scrutiny under Articles 8 and 14 of the ECHR. Therefore, phasing out civil partner-ship has left Irish law both Constitutionally compliant and Convention-compliant.

However, while the subsequent introduction of marriage equality was a welcome, progressive development, it is lamentable that civil partnership, viewed by some as a modern, egalitarian alternative to marriage, was denied the oppor-tunity to coexist, develop and perhaps ultimately be assimilated into Irish culture. This is especially so when one considers both the recent evolution of civil part-nership in the UK, where the state now recognises formalised same-sex *and* opposite-sex familial unions that extend beyond Ireland's constitutional ideal, and the even more recent recommendations of the Citizens Assembly and Joint Committee on Gender Equality in Ireland, which favour a referendum to intro-duce a broader constitutional definition of the 'Family' in Article 41 beyond the marital family.

The redress scheme for cohabitants in Ireland is somewhat novel in that it potentially provides qualified cohabitants whose relationships have broken down with access to a range of remedies when compared to a similar scheme in Scotland, without unduly encroaching on an individual's pension and property rights. Further, by virtue of the financial dependency criterion, the redress scheme argua-bly manages to effectively balance the need to protect a truly vulnerable cohabitant while respecting the individual autonomy of the other cohabitant following the termination of cohabitation. This criterion also ensures that the scheme does not impinge on the constitutional protection for the married family unit as it does not equate cohabitation too closely with marriage. The autonomy associated with cohabiting relationships is also respected by allowing couples to 'opt-out' of the redress scheme by concluding a valid cohabitants' agreement, though this option appears unlikely to be popular. In any event, when coupled with the empirical evidence on cohabitation trends in Ireland, the financial dependency criterion and the statutory timeframes that must be satisfied before one can be deemed a quali-fied cohabitant who is entitled to seek a remedy before the courts indicate that the redress scheme is likely to benefit very few cohabitants in practice, whether the parties are of the same or the opposite sex.

4

Parental Rights for Same-Sex Parents of Surrogate-Born and Donor-Conceived Children

Forging a Legal Framework for Ireland

I. Introduction

This chapter will explore the various ways in which same-sex couples can acquire parental rights and responsibilities under Irish law, and examine the notable shortcomings that remain. It will begin by analysing and attempting to refute the common arguments against extending parental rights to same-sex couples, and will demonstrate clearly that same-sex parents are just as capable of responsible child-rearing as their opposite-sex counterparts. The chapter will then analyse inclusive amendments to the laws on adoption and guardianship that were made by the Children and Family Relationships Act 2015 (CFRA 2015) in order to embrace the reality of same-sex parenting. However, the chapter will mostly explore the unsatisfactory state of the law pertaining to surrogacy, which is the only means by which a male same-sex couple can engage in procreation. Although the statutory regulation of domestic surrogacy arrangements seems imminent, this chapter will propose a more balanced regulatory model, one that is compliant with international law and international best practice, and which could encourage recourse to domestic over international surrogacy. The chapter will also analyse the issues pertaining to international surrogacy arrangements. Finally, it will explore the remaining, unresolved issues associated with the law on donor-assisted human reproduction (DAHR). Although DAHR was regulated by the CFRA 2015, there is some uncertainty surrounding the legal status of reciprocal IVF under the legislation, and non-clinical DAHR procedures are excluded. Reciprocal IVF and non-clinical DAHR would appear to be practised and popular methods of procreation among female same-sex couples; thus, the chapter concludes by proposing statutory reforms that would expressly confirm the inclusion of the former under the CFRA 2015, and a potential regulatory model for the latter.

II. Same-Sex Parenting and the Welfare of the Child

The more common arguments surrounding same-sex parenting and child welfare centre on the notion that 'harm' will be caused to the child if raised by two persons of the same sex. The allegedly higher rates of dissolution associated with same-sex relationships, the potential effect on a child's adult sexual orientation and the need for a child to be raised in the 'optimal' familial environment with two parents of the opposite sex have all been proffered as arguments *against* permitting the legal recognition of parental rights for same-sex couples. However, I shall attempt to refute each of these below.

A. Rates of Dissolution in Same-Sex Relationships

It has been argued that growing up in same-sex family units is potentially harmful for a child because of the higher rate of dissolution associated with same-sex relationships when compared to their opposite-sex counterparts.[1] Indeed, there is some empirical evidence to support the argument that same-sex relationships *were* prone to greater rates of dissolution. In a study comparing same-sex and opposite-sex unions in the UK from 1974 to 2004, Lau concludes that the higher dissolution rate amongst same-sex couples is explainable because 'the lack of legal and social institutionalization of same-sex couples may lead same-sex couples to perceive fewer barriers, fewer rewards, and more alternatives to their unions, leading to higher rates of dissolution'.[2] Lau observes that in the UK during those years 'the lack of legal marriage for same-sex couples and greater difficulty having children means that there was not a logical endpoint for same-sex relationships' in the way that there was for their opposite-sex counterparts.[3] Thus, for the same-sex couples surveyed by Lau, because civil partnership, marriage equality, the ability to jointly adopt a child and legislation permitting both same-sex partners to be legally recognised as the parents of a child born through donor-assisted human reproduction or surrogacy were unavailable in the UK from 1974 to 2004, there were certainly, legally and socially, 'fewer barriers' to exiting and 'fewer rewards'

---

[1] LD Wardle, 'The Boundaries of Belonging: Allegiance, Purpose and the Definition of Marriage' (2011) 25 *Brigham Young University Journal of Public Law* 287, 309.

[2] CQ Lau, 'The Stability of Same-Sex Cohabitation, Different-Sex Cohabitation, and Marriage' (2012) 74 *Journal of Marriage and Family* 973, 984.

[3] ibid. Indeed, the authors of a study comparing dissolution rates amongst opposite-sex and same-sex married couples (and same-sex couples in registered partnerships) in Norway and Sweden concluded that 'a higher propensity for divorce in same-sex couples may not be too surprising given this group's relative non-involvement in joint parenthood and its lower exposure to normative pressure about the necessity of life-long unions': see G Andersson et al, 'The Demographics of Same-Sex Marriages in Norway and Sweden' (2006) 43 *Demography* 79.

from entering into and committing to a long-term same-sex relationship during that time.[4]

Also, the social prejudice experienced by same-sex couples at the time undoubtedly led to quite a number of LGBT+ persons deciding to discontinue their relationship and instead opt for the safer, more socially accepted alternatives such as life in an opposite-sex marital or cohabiting relationship, or life as a single person. Hence there are reasonable socio-legal explanations for the correlation between same-sex couples and higher rates of union dissolution when compared to opposite-sex couples.

In addition, Lau notes that one of the methodological 'limitations' of his study on rates of union dissolution among same-sex and opposite-sex couples is the use of 'small samples'.[5] Lau's study does not encompass same-sex couples that were raising children from 1974 to 2004, most likely because of the small sample size discussed in his study and the fact that same-sex parenting was far less common during that period. Consequently, Lau's study shows no evidence of a high rate of dissolution among same-sex couples *raising children together*. Further, Bracken points out that today, in jurisdictions 'where same-sex couples are able to have their relationships legally recognised, for example through civil partnership or marriage, the rate of relationship breakdown decreases'.[6]

B. Sexual Orientation of Children Raised by Same-Sex Parents

A further argument proffered against same-sex parenting is that the children of same-sex parents will be less likely to enter into a 'normative' sexual relationship upon maturity.[7] Pennings observes that this argument 'presupposes that being homosexual is a mental illness, a pathology or, at least, a type of harm'.[8] While the Australian Psychological Society has observed that research on the sexual orientation of children raised by same-sex parents is 'fairly scant', there is evidence to suggest that some children of same-sex parents may feel more comfortable to either have or consider the possibility of having a same-sex relationship.[9] In this regard, Golombok observes that

> the large majority of young people raised by lesbian mothers identify themselves as heterosexual, showing that the sexual orientation of parents does not influence the

---

[4] Although the Adoption and Children Act 2002 enabled same-sex couples to jointly apply to adopt a child, the requisite provisions of that legislation only entered into force on 30 December 2005.

[5] Lau, 'The Stability of Same-Sex Cohabitation' (2012) 985.

[6] L Bracken, *Same-Sex Parenting and the Best Interests Principle* (Cambridge, CUP, 2019) 74. See further, M Rosenfeld, 'Couple Longevity in the Era of Same-Sex Marriage in the United States' (2014) 76 *Journal of Marriage and Family* 905.

[7] LD Wardle, 'Form and Substance in Committed Relationships in American Law' in O Doyle and W Binchy (eds), *Committed Relationships and the Law* (Dublin, Four Courts Press, 2007) 61, 78.

[8] G Pennings, 'Evaluating the Welfare of the Child in Same-Sex Families' (2011) 26 *Human Reproduction* 1609, 1610.

[9] E Short et al, 'Lesbian, Gay, Bisexual and Transgender (LGBT) Parented Families: A Literature Review prepared for The Australian Psychological Society' (The Australian Psychological Society,

sexual orientation of their children. However, the daughters of lesbian mothers are more likely than daughters from heterosexual parent families to explore same-sex relationships as they grow up.[10]

Thus, Golombok concludes that same-sex parents' 'sexual orientation may have some influence on the sexual *experimentation* of their children' but believes that this might simply be because such parents' attitudes towards sexuality create a family environment that 'allows non-heterosexual relationships to be explored'.[11] Thus, the evidence would appear to suggest that same-sex parents may have some impact on the willingness of their children to at least explore same-sex sexual attraction and relationships. However, Golombok points out that this willingness to experiment is most likely because children from same-sex households 'may hold less rigid stereotypes about what constitutes appropriate male and female sexual behaviour than their peers from traditional families'.[12] It is submitted that parents with tolerant attitudes towards their child's individual exploration of sexuality and gender identity are acting in a supportive, child-centric manner that should not give rise to any concerns about the welfare of children being raised in same-sex unions.

C. Optimal Parenting and Child Development: Family Structure, or Family Processes?

It has been argued that same-sex parenting is detrimental to child welfare because of a child's need for parenting by parties of the opposite sex.[13] Wardle argues that because of the differences between how mothers and fathers nurture, care for and interact with their children, 'a child raised by two women or two men is deprived of extremely valuable developmental experience and the opportunity for optimal individual growth and interpersonal development'.[14] Wardle notes the more physical and tactile play between fathers and children when compared to the more gentle play between mothers and children.[15] He observes that infants whose fathers are actively involved in their lives not only have greater mental development at six months old but are more socially responsive and better able to withstand stressful situations than infants 'relatively deprived of substantial interaction with their fathers'.[16] Wardle stresses that when children are raised in same-sex family units

---

2007) 11, available at psychology.org.au/getmedia/47196902-158d-4cbb-86e6-2f3f1c71ffd1/lgbt-families-literature-review.pdf.

[10] S Golombok, *Modern Families* (Cambridge, CUP, 2015) 209.

[11] ibid; emphasis added.

[12] ibid.

[13] LD Wardle, 'The Potential Impact of Homosexual Parenting on Children' (1997) *University of Illinois Law Review* 833, 863.

[14] ibid.

[15] ibid, 857.

[16] ibid, 858.

they 'must cope with the loss of example, counsel, and experience that living with the missing-gender parent would have provided'.[17] Thus, *for Wardle* and others, the 'biological differentiation in the roles of mothers and fathers makes it rational to encourage situations in which children have one of each'.[18]

However, Walker and McGraw conclude in relation to the assertion that all children 'need' or 'deserve' the involvement of a parent of a certain gender that 'although there might be an ideological basis to this assumption, it lacks empirical support'.[19] Similarly, Biblarz and Stacey have observed that 'no research supports the widely held conviction that the gender of parents matters for child well-being'.[20] Indeed, the Australian Psychological Society has noted that an abundance of research since the 1970s has indicated that it is *family processes* that contribute to determining children's well-being and outcomes, rather than family structures per se, such as the number, gender, sexuality and co-habitation status of parents:

> Specifically, *and regardless of family structure*, children are likely to do well in a family environment characterised by an absence of conflict; high levels of co-operation, trust, ease and cohesion; high levels of warmth and care; and high levels of social connection and support.[21]

Further research suggests that these positive familial processes are as much at work in same-sex family units as in their opposite-sex counterparts. Following a comprehensive review of the literature pertaining to same-sex parenting, Tobin and McNair concluded that there is no credible evidence that same-sex parents cause harm to the development of their children by virtue of their sexual orientation and that there is in fact an overwhelming and growing body of evidence to suggest that such parents are just as capable of fulfilling their duties and responsibilities towards their children.[22] Similarly, Golombok recently concluded that

---

[17] ibid.

[18] Brief for Respondent BLAG, *United States v Windsor* No 12-307 (US, 22 January 2013) 48, available at www.clearinghouse.net/chDocs/public/PB-NY-0017-0015.pdf.

[19] AJ Walker and LA McGraw, 'Who is responsible for responsible fathering?'(2000) 62 *Journal of Marriage and Family* 563.

[20] TJ Biblarz and J Stacey, 'How does the Gender of Parents Matter?' (2010) 72 *Journal of Marriage and Family* 3.

[21] Short et al, 'Lesbian, Gay, Bisexual and Transgender (LGBT) Parented Families' (2007) 8; emphasis added. Similarly, the American Academy of Paediatrics has observed that more than 100 scientific publications over 30 years have demonstrated that children's well-being is affected much more by their relationships with their parents, their parents' sense of competence and security, and the presence of social and economic support for the family than by the gender or the sexual orientation of their parents: see E Perrin, B Siegel et al, 'Promoting the Well-being of Children whose Parents are Gay or Lesbian' (2013) 131 *Paediatrics* 1374, 1378.

[22] J Tobin and R McNair, 'Public International Law and the Regulation of Private Spaces: Does the Convention on the Rights of the Child Impose an Obligation on States to Allow Gay and Lesbian Couples to Adopt?' (2009) 23 *International Journal of Law, Policy and the Family* 110, 127.

'children are most likely to flourish in families that provide love, security and support, *whatever their family structure*'[23] and observed that

> the large research literature on two-parent lesbian mother families and the small but growing body of research on two-parent gay father families consistently shows that there are no differences in psychological adjustment or gender development between children who grow up with same-sex parents and those who are raised by two hetero-sexual parents.[24]

While the weight of available evidence clearly suggests that being raised by same-sex parents does not adversely affect a child's development, Golombok nonetheless emphasises the 'limitations to the growing body of research on new family forms that must be borne in mind'.[25] She points to, inter alia, small sample sizes and the lack of longitudinal studies focussing on children in adolescence and beyond. Further, Golombok points out that due to the stigma associated with LGBT+ families, 'parents whose children are experiencing difficulties may decide against participating in research' and those who do participate 'may play down difficulties, as they may wish to present their families in a favourable light'.[26] Despite these limitations, there is no evidence in the research carried out to date indicating that same-sex parenting is in any way harmful to children or that being raised by same-sex parents results in a child having a less 'optimal' familial environment than their peers.

III. Parental Rights for Same-Sex Couples: The Children and Family Relationships Act 2015

The CFRA 2015 was the first piece of domestic legislation to comprehensively extend many parental rights to same-sex couples. Previously, a same-sex second parent could not acquire guardianship rights in relation to their partner's child other than via a testamentary disposition, nor could they have their parentage and guardianship recognised when a child was born to the couple via donor-assisted human reproduction that took place in a clinical setting.[27] Further, same-sex

---

[23] S Golombok, *Modern Families* (2015) 214. Indeed, this finding was more recently reiterated in S Imrie and S Golombok, 'Impact of New Family Forms on Parenting and Child Development' (2020) 2 *Annual Review of Developmental Psychology* 295, 307.

[24] ibid, 198-99. Indeed, Golombok observes (at 202) that this is the case in those same-sex families where children are conceived through surrogacy or donor conception: 'the growing body of research on new family forms leads to the conclusion that family structure – including the number, gender, sexual orientation and genetic relatedness of parents, as well as their method of conception – does not play a fundamental role in children's psychological adjustment or gender development'.

[25] ibid, 210.

[26] ibid.

[27] The Guardianship of Infants Act 1964, s 7 enables the guardian of a child to appoint any person(s) to be the guardian(s) of the child *after their death*. Section 8 enables a court, on application to it by any

couples were not eligible to jointly apply to the Adoption Authority to adopt a child, and a same-sex second parent could not seek to adopt their partner's child with whom they had a pre-existing relationship. The CFRA 2015 was initially designed to remedy all of this, but due to the removal of surrogacy from early drafts of the legislation, some errors and omissions within the Act, the non-commencement of the provisions on adoption and a five-year delay before other crucial parts of the Act were commenced, its success in improving the position of many existing and prospective same-sex parents is certainly debatable.

The CFRA 2015 was enacted less than seven weeks before the Marriage Referendum, but no part of the Act was commenced prior to the referendum.[28] The timing of its enactment is indicative of a political desire to place parental rights for same-sex couples on a legislative footing in order to try to diffuse arguments against same-sex parenting made by anti-marriage equality campaigners prior to the referendum. Indeed, although same-sex couples acquired the right to marry following the success of the Marriage Referendum in 2015, their ability to acquire parental rights and privileges only began to be slowly realised from 2016 onwards, and the fight for recognition is still ongoing.[29] The following sections shall discuss the guardianship and adoption provisions of the CFRA 2015, and the non-commencement and transfer of the latter to more recent legislation. Subsequent sections shall discuss parentage for same-sex couples in surrogacy situations, something that is not covered by the CFRA 2015 nor regulated by domestic legislation at present, before returning to assess the strengths and weaknesses of the donor-assisted human reproduction provisions contained in the CFRA 2015.

A. Guardianship

The first provisions of the CFRA 2015 which extended parental rights to same-sex couples were commenced on 18 January 2016.[30] Section 49 of the CFRA 2015 inserted section 6C into the Guardianship of Infants Act 1964 and enabled a same-sex (or opposite-sex) step-parent to apply for guardianship in certain

---

person(s), to appoint a person as a guardian where a child *has no guardian*. Before the commencement of the relevant provisions of the CFRA, a same-sex step-parent had no possibility of becoming a joint guardian of their spouse or partner's child during the lifetime of that spouse or partner.

[28] Although the CFRA was signed into law by the President of Ireland on 6 April 2015, the guardianship provisions were only commenced on 18 January 2016 and the provisions concerning the parentage of children born through donor-assisted human reproduction were commenced as recently as 4 May 2020. The provisions concerning adoption were never commenced and were instead replicated in the Adoption (Amendment) Act 2017, which was commenced on 19 October 2017.

[29] In cases of non-clinical donor-assisted human reproduction only the birth mother's parentage is currently recognised under Irish law, and in domestic and international surrogacy arrangements only the genetic father's parentage is currently recognised under Irish law. Advocacy groups such as Equality for Children, Irish Families through Surrogacy, Irish Gay Dads and LGBT Ireland continue to advocate for the requisite changes in the law.

[30] See the Children and Family Relationships Act 2015 (Commencement of Certain Provisions) Order 2016 (SI 2016 No 12).

circumstances. Where a person is married to, in a civil partnership with, or has been for over three years a cohabitant of a parent of the child, and has shared with that parent responsibility for the child's day-to-day care for more than two years, the court can make an order appointing that person as a guardian of the child.[31] The consent of each existing guardian of the child is required before the court will make an order, but the court can dispense with the consent of a guardian where it is satisfied that 'the consent is unreasonably withheld and that it is in the best interests of the child to make such an order'.[32] Once appointed, a step-parent guardian acts alongside the child's existing guardians – their appointment by the court does not affect the parental rights of any existing guardians.[33]

However, acquiring guardianship only enables a step-parent to participate in decisions concerning the child's upbringing. Guardianship should not be confused with holding the legal status of 'parent' because it ends when the child reaches the age of 18. Further, a step-parent guardian may not acquire all of the same rights and duties as the child's other guardians because although the CFRA 2015 expressly outlines the various 'rights and responsibilities of a guardian', it nonetheless provides that a step-parent guardian shall only enjoy these 'where the court expressly so orders' and 'to the extent specified in the order'.[34] However, the court is required to have regard to the relationship between the step-parent guardian and the child, and the best interests of the child, in deciding whether or not to limit the rights and responsibilities of the former.[35] Later in this chapter, we shall see that guardianship may not be an adequate solution for same-sex parents of surrogate-born or donor-conceived children who cannot be recognised as a child's legal parent under Irish law.

B. Adoption

There were attempts to legislate for joint adoption for same-sex couples as far back as 2009. When the Adoption Bill 2009 was being debated, efforts were made to amend the Bill in order to enable same-sex couples to jointly adopt. Since the Adoption Bill 2009 was being debated in the Oireachtas prior to the Civil Partnership Bill 2009, it was argued in the Seanad that the Irish experience should mirror that of the UK, where the Adoption and Children Act 2002 opened up eligibility for adoption to same-sex couples prior to the enactment of the Civil Partnership Act 2004. Consequently, Senator Bacik argued that 'a precedent therefore exists for providing for eligibility for same-sex couples in adoption rather

---

[31] Guardianship of Infants Act 1964, s 6(C)(2)(a), as inserted by CFRA 2015, s 49.

[32] Guardianship of Infants Act 1964, s 6(C)(2)(a), as inserted by CFRA 2015, s 49.

[33] Guardianship of Infants Act 1964 s 6(C)(5), as inserted by CFRA 2015, s 49.

[34] The rights and responsibilities of a guardian are stipulated in the Guardianship of Infants Act 1964, s 6(C)(11), as inserted by CFRA 2015, s 49, but these can be limited by the court under the Guardianship of Infants Act 1964 s 6(C)(9), as inserted by CFRA 2015, s 49.

[35] See the Guardianship of Infants Act 1964 s 6(C)(10), as inserted by CFRA 2015, s 49.

than civil partnership law'.[36] She proposed that section 33 of the Bill should be amended to include within the definition of 'married couple' a same-sex couple that had entered into a registered civil partnership with each other.[37] However, the then Minister for Health and Children, Deputy Barry Andrews, argued that because the UK does not have a written Constitution, it was not restricted from legislating in this area. He confirmed that, given the definition of marriage in the Irish Constitution (at the time), adoption would not be made available to same-sex couples by legislation.[38]

Subsequently, the CFRA 2015 made provision in Part 11 for joint adoption by same-sex civil partners and cohabiting couples. There had been no change to the constitutional definition of marriage between the enactment of the Adoption Act 2010 and the CFRA 2015, five years later, and as seen in chapter two, there was a degree of uncertainty surrounding the potential for the Marriage Referendum to be successful, so enacting legislation providing for joint adoption by same-sex couples was arguably a bold move.[39] Part 11 of the CFRA 2015 amended the Adoption Act 2010 to provide that, inter alia, civil partners and cohabiting couples (whether same-sex or opposite-sex) were eligible to jointly apply to adopt a child. However, Part 11 of the CFRA 2015 was never commenced. The provisions of Part 11 were later transferred to the Adoption (Amendment) Act 2017, which was commenced on 19 October 2017. Section 16 of the 2017 Act finally enabled civil partners and cohabiting couples to apply to adopt by amending section 33 of the 2010 Act. By 2017, making legislative provision for same-sex civil partners and cohabiting couples to adopt was quite uncontroversial, as same-sex married couples had become eligible to apply to adopt a child almost two years previously. In 2015, following the success of the Marriage Referendum and the enactment of the requisite pieces of legislation making constitutional provision for marriage equality and giving effect to the result of the referendum, same-sex married couples automatically came within the definition of a 'married couple' in section 33 of the Adoption Act 2010. Further, as demonstrated in the last chapter, the ability to enter into a civil partnership had been discontinued, so allowing subsisting civil partners to jointly adopt was not in any way going to collide with Article 41 by discouraging same-sex couples from prospectively formalising their relationship through marriage; similarly, conditions for adoption by couples cohabiting outside of marriage or civil partnership are more stringent than those for married couples or civil partners as they must be living together for a minimum period of three years.[40]

Second-parent adoption is also provided for in the 2017 Act such that a spouse, civil partner or cohabitant of the child's parent is eligible to apply to adopt provided

---

[36] Seanad Debate (4 March 2009) vol 194, col 349.
[37] Seanad Debate (4 March 2009) vol 194, col 348.
[38] Seanad Debate (4 March 2009) vol 194, col 361.
[39] See pp 31–33 of ch 2.
[40] See the Adoption (Amendment) Act 2017 s 3, amending the Adoption Act 2010, s 3(1).

that they have lived with the child and the legal parent for a continuous period of not less than two years.[41] Once adopted by a step-parent, the child is deemed to be the child of that step-parent and the step-parent's spouse, civil partner or cohabitant, who is the child's existing legal parent in this type of adoption situation. The child's legal relationship with their existing legal parent remains intact, but they acquire an additional legal parent and guardian by virtue of the step-parent adoption. Article 42A.4.1 of the Constitution requires that 'provision shall be made by law' for the best interests of the child to be the 'paramount consideration' in the resolution of, inter alia, adoption proceedings, and therefore, legislation stipulates that in all adoption matters, applications or proceedings, the Adoption Authority (or the court) shall regard the best interests of the child as the paramount consideration and must take into account 'all of the factors or circumstances that it considers relevant to the child' who is the subject of the matter, application or proceedings.[42]

C. Adoption in the Context of Surrogacy

While joint or second-parent adoption is potentially an option for the intended parents of a surrogate-born child to acquire parentage, neither is appropriate in the context of surrogacy. Joint adoption usually involves adoption of a child by a couple who are strangers to that child, in circumstances where the child's parents find themselves unable or unwilling to care for them. Thus, a 'surrogacy-related' joint adoption would involve intended parents, at least one and often both of whom are genetically related to the child (in opposite-sex couples), and who planned for the birth of the child and to provide for their wellbeing, having to avail of a mechanism neither intended nor conceptually suitable for their particular familial situation. Further, the New Zealand Law Commission observes that 'the difference between surrogacy and adoption calls into question whether the suitability of intended parents to care for and raise the child should be assessed in the same way as prospective adoptive parents'.[43]

Similarly, second-parent adoption of a surrogate-born child by its intended mother or non-genetic intended father is unsuitable because in the case of a *genetic* intended mother, she would be adopting her own genetic child, and in the case of a

---

[41] See the Adoption Act 2010, s 37, as amended by the Adoption (Amendment) Act 2017, s 18. To be eligible for step-parent adoption, a cohabiting couple must have been living together as cohabitants for a continuous period of not less than three years: see the Adoption (Amendment) Act 2017, s 3.

[42] A list of relevant factors or circumstances to be taken into account is contained in the Adoption Act 2010, s 19(2), as amended by the Adoption (Amendment) Act 2017, s 9. However, as Harding points out: 'Article 42A.4.1 does not create a constitutional best interests principle. It merely requires that statutory provision is made to ensure that the best interests of children is the paramount consideration' in the resolution of, inter alia, adoption proceedings: see M Harding, '"Best Interests" as a Limited Constitutional Imperative' in *International Survey of Family Law 2019* (Cambridge, Intersentia, 2019) 139, 149.

[43] New Zealand Law Commission, 'Review of Surrogacy' NZLC R146 (2022) 171.

non-genetic intended mother or father, they would be adopting the very child that they helped bring into the world. In addition, an intended mother or non-genetic intended father has to wait two years before they can apply for second-parent adoption under the existing adoption legislation, and it is costly, inconvenient and stressful to have to initiate two separate legal processes at different points in the child's early formative years. The child's genetic father would acquire a declaration of parentage and guardianship in the courts after their birth, whereas the child's intended mother or non-genetic intended father would only acquire these rights years later via a different, lengthier, less suitable process. Therefore, a regulatory model for establishing parentage that is specific to surrogacy arrangements would be a more appropriate solution.

IV. Towards Regulating Domestic Surrogacy Arrangements under Irish Law

Male same-sex couples who wish to procreate must do so with the assistance of a surrogate.[44] However, there is no domestic legislation which specifically regulates any form of surrogacy, and this has a significant impact on the ability of male same-sex couples to establish legal parentage and guardianship rights under Irish law in respect of their surrogate-born children. This section will examine Part 7 of the Health (Assisted Human Reproduction) Bill 2022 (the '2022 Bill'), which contains proposals to regulate domestic surrogacy, and assess whether these are likely to meet the needs of intended parents, in particular male same-sex couples, and their surrogate-born children. The section will begin by outlining the somewhat tortuous journey towards establishing a statutory regime for the regulation of surrogacy in Ireland. It will then critique the proposed, complex 'hybrid model' for regulating surrogacy arrangements, and discuss the potential policy reasons that may have led to this type of regulatory model being proposed. The section will continue by advocating for an alternative model for regulating domestic surrogacy arrangements, one that better reflects the intentions of the parties while respecting the state's international law obligations. Further, this section will consider measures designed to protect the child's right to knowledge of genetic identity in surrogacy arrangements. Since the Bill only proposes to regulate surrogacy arrangements that will be carried out in Ireland, the section will briefly discuss the prevailing status quo in law for male same-sex couples who avail of international surrogacy arrangements, and explore potential pathways which might enable such couples to establish legal parentage for *both* intended parents under Irish law. Much of the analysis in this section is also of relevance to opposite-sex intended parents who engage in surrogacy arrangements.

---

[44] It is also possible that a female same-sex couple might need to procreate with the assistance of a surrogate, but in practice this is likely to be an extremely rare occurrence.

The statutory regulation of surrogacy arrangements was first recommended by the Commission on Assisted Human Reproduction in its report in 2005.[45] At the time, the Commission noted that no Irish fertility clinic appeared to be providing surrogacy treatment. The members of the Commission favoured the regulation of *altruistic* surrogacy in Ireland, and strongly opposed 'commercialisation of the practice'.[46] However, it was almost eight years before the political will to regulate surrogacy gained any impetus. On 12 February 2013, the then Minister for Justice and Equality, Alan Shatter, announced that he was 'reviewing existing legislation worldwide addressing the issues of parentage, assisted human reproduction and surrogacy and considering the recommendations contained in the Report of the Commission on Assisted Human Reproduction published by the Department of Health in 2005'.[47] Less than a year later, on 30 January 2014, the Minister published the General Scheme of the Children and Family Relationships Bill, and proposals to place the regulation of domestic, altruistic, gestational surrogacy *and* 'pre-commencement' international surrogacy arrangements on a statutory footing were included therein. However, Ireland's 'premier' surrogacy proposals were met with heavy criticism and were never enacted.[48] Indeed, by the time a revised version of the General Scheme of the Children and Family Relationships Bill was published later that year, on 25 September 2014, the surrogacy provisions had been deleted in their entirety.[49] A new Minister for Justice and Equality, Frances Fitzgerald, had succeeded Alan Shatter, and she stated that the surrogacy provisions had been removed because the Supreme Court's decision in the 'surrogacy case' of *MR and Another v An tArd Chláraitheoir*[50] was pending and because there were very critical issues relating to the rights of children born through surrogacy.[51] The Minister acknowledged

[45] In March 2000 the Commission on Assisted Human Reproduction was established by the then Minister for Health and Children, Micheál Martin. Its role was to examine how assisted human reproduction, including surrogacy, might be regulated in Ireland. 'The Report of the Commission on Assisted Human Reproduction' was published in 2005. Among its 40 recommendations was a proposal that assisted human reproduction, including surrogacy, should be regulated by a regulatory body established by the Oireachtas.

[46] 'Report of the Commission on Assisted Human Reproduction' (Department of Health, 2005) 52 and 54, available at www.dohc.ie/publications/pdf/cahr.pdf.

[47] Joint Committee on Justice, Defence and Equality, 'Report on hearings in relation to the Scheme of the Children and Family Relationships Bill' (2014) [3.1].

[48] See B Tobin, 'The Revised General Scheme of the Children and Family Relationships Bill 2014: Cognisant of the Donor-conceived Child's Constitutional Rights?' (2014) 52 *Irish Jurist* 153; see also the comments from Professor Deirdre Madden, School of Law, UCC, in the 'Report on hearings in relation to the Scheme of the Children and Family Relationships Bill' (ibid).

[49] When signed into law by the President on 6 April 2015, Pts 2 and 3 of the CFRA 2015 purported to regulate, inter alia, parentage in cases of DAHR *other than surrogacy*. For an analysis of this legislation, see G Shannon, *Children and Family Relationships Law in Ireland: Practice and Procedure* (Dublin, Clarus Press, 2016).

[50] *MR and Another v An tArd Chláraitheoir* [2013] IEHC 91.

[51] Department of Justice and Equality, 'Minister Fitzgerald publishes General Scheme of Children and Family Relationships Bill' (Department of Justice and Equality, 2014), available at www.justice.ie/en/JELR/Pages/PR14000257.

that surrogacy legislation was indeed 'very complex' and raised 'many questions of balancing constitutional rights'.[52]

As this author has stressed elsewhere, it is ironic that the Minister showed such deference to the Supreme Court's pending decision in *MR and Another v An tArd Chláraitheoir*[53] because, in its decision, released in November 2014, the Supreme Court *largely*[54] deferred to the Oireachtas[55] as regards the regulation of surrogacy, and invited it to take 'urgent action'.[56] Subsequently, on 17 February 2015, the then Fine Gael/Labour coalition Government approved the drafting by the Department of Health of the General Scheme of a Bill on Assisted Human Reproduction. The Government decided that surrogacy was one of the areas to be included in this Scheme. The General Scheme of the Assisted Human Reproduction Bill 2017 was approved by the subsequent Fine Gael/Fianna Fáil minority Government on 3 October 2017, and despite languishing in something of a 'development hell' for almost five years, it was finally succeeded in March 2022 by the Health (Assisted Human Reproduction) Bill 2022. If enacted, the 2022 Bill will regulate many matters pertaining to assisted human reproduction, such as gamete and embryo donation and embryo and stem cell research, and it will lead to the establishment of a regulatory body known as the Assisted Human Reproduction Regulatory Authority (AHRRA). Part 7 of the Bill contains detailed proposals for the regulation of domestic, altruistic, gestational surrogacy arrangements, but not international surrogacy, although the myriad issues surrounding these complex transnational arrangements were recently considered by the Oireachtas Joint Committee on International Surrogacy.[57]

V. A Critique of the Hybrid Model for Regulating Domestic Surrogacy in Part 7 of the Health (Assisted Human Reproduction) Bill 2022

Part 7 of the 2022 Bill provides for the regulation of surrogacy in Ireland through what would appear to be a 'hybrid' model. The proposed regulatory model

---

[52] ibid.

[53] *MR v An tArd Chláraitheoir* [2014] IESC 60.

[54] The Supreme Court did not give the Oireachtas free reign in relation to the regulation of surrogacy because in his judgment Clarke J frequently referred to 'constitutionally permissible' legislation: see *MR v An tArd Chláraitheoir* [2014] IESC 60 [8.7] (Clarke J). As Mulligan points out, 'as well as failing to show sufficient regard for the Constitution, a framework that did not give enough weight to constitutional rights would be vulnerable to constitutional challenge': see A Mulligan, 'From *Murray v Ireland* to *Roche v Roche*: Re-Evaluating the Constitutional Right to Procreate in the Context of Assisted Reproduction' (2012) *Dublin University Law Journal* 261, 262.

[55] Oireachtas is the word for Parliament in the Irish language.

[56] See B Tobin, 'Forging a Surrogacy Framework for Ireland: the Constitutionality of the Post-birth Parental Order and Pre-birth Judicial Approval Models of Regulation' (2017) 29 *Child and Family Law Quarterly* 133,142.

[57] Section 54 of the Bill expressly prohibits commercial surrogacy. However, s 55 permits the payment of 'reasonable expenses' to the gestational surrogate.

contains elements of both the 'pre-conception state approval' and 'post-birth Parental Order' models.[58] In Part 8, the Bill provides for the setting up of the AHRRA, a state body that must, among its many functions, approve a surrogacy agreement *prior to treatment*. This regulatory oversight is similar to that which exists in other jurisdictions – Greece, South Africa, Israel, New Zealand, and the Australian States of Victoria and Western Australia, require a court or a regulatory body to 'pre-authorise' a surrogacy agreement before any treatment can go ahead. This form of pre-surrogacy state oversight might help to assuage the fears of those who are uncomfortable with surrogacy being practiced in Ireland. Indeed, in 2013 a nationally representative sample survey carried out by the Royal College of Surgeons in Ireland found that only 52 per cent of those surveyed were in favour of domestic surrogacy.[59]

In any event, if Part 7 is ultimately enacted, the AHRRA's 'pre-authorisation' of the surrogacy agreement between the intended parents[60] and the surrogate will be limited to the approval of treatment, *not parentage of the surrogate-born child*. Part 7 does not propose to sanction any 'pre-conception state approval' of parentage. Instead, the surrogate will be the legal mother and guardian at birth and the intended parents must go through a 'post-birth Parental Order' process in court to establish their parentage.[61]

The 2022 Bill's approach to legal parentage is quite remarkable for a variety of reasons. First, according to section 52 of the Bill, before the surrogacy agreement can be submitted to the AHRRA for this 'pre-authorisation' process, the surrogate must be 'assessed and approved as suitable to act as a surrogate by a registered medical practitioner'.[62] This process should help to ensure that, inter alia, the surrogate has the legal capacity to consent to the surrogacy agreement. Further, to ensure that her consent to the agreement is a free and fully informed one, the surrogate is required to receive independent legal advice, that is, legal advice separate and independent from that received by the intended parents, and she must also receive 'AHR counselling'.[63] Therefore, if the medical assessment is sound and

---

[58] For a discussion of these models see generally B Tobin, 'Forging a Surrogacy Framework for Ireland' (2017).

[59] See DJ Walsh, 'Irish Public Opinion on Assisted Human Reproduction Services: Contemporary Assessments from a National Sample' (RCSI, 2013): available at www.ncbi.nlm.nih.gov/pmc/articles/PMC3913896.

[60] The intended parents (or commissioning couple) are the couple that commissions the surrogacy arrangement. Section 53 of the Health (Assisted Human Reproduction) Bill 2022 also allows for there to be a single intended parent in a domestic surrogacy arrangement.

[61] However, following the birth, the surrogate will be able to make a statutory declaration agreeing to the appointment of the intended parents as guardians of the child: see the Health (Assisted Human Reproduction) Bill 2022, s 156, which proposes to insert s 6BA into the Guardianship of Infants Act 1964.

[62] Section 53(5) requires each intended parent who is providing a gamete that will be used to create the embryo to undergo the medical screening required for donors of reproductive cells: see European Communities (Quality and Safety of Human Tissues and Cells) Regulations 2006 (SI 2006 No 158), Reg 11.

[63] See s 58 and s 17 of the Health (Assisted Human Reproduction) Bill 2022. These sections of the Bill also require the intended parents to receive independent legal advice and AHR counselling, respectively.

the surrogate has received the requisite independent legal advice and implications counselling, and is content to proceed with the arrangement, surely she should be deemed capable of consenting to a clause in the surrogacy agreement which stipulates that immediately upon the birth of the child, legal parentage rests with the intended parent(s) by operation of law? In other words, given the *significant pre-surrogacy safeguards* that are contained in the Bill, the surrogate should be able to consent to, and Part 7 of the Bill should enable the AHRRA to approve, as part of the 'pre-conception state approval' process, legal parentage arising in favour of the intended parents by operation of law *at birth*.[64]

Second, the General Scheme only proposes to regulate gestational surrogacy in Ireland, where the surrogate does not use her own genetic material in the arrangement but instead carries an embryo formed from the genetic material of others. Having had the benefit of medical assessments, legal advice and counselling, the gestational surrogate is likely to fully understand, and freely agree to, her role as a 'carrier'.[65] In the UK, where the surrogate is also regarded as the legal mother at birth under existing law, the Law Commission of England and Wales and the Scottish Law Commission (hereafter the Law Commissions) published a joint consultation paper on surrogacy law reform in 2019, in which they pointed out that the view that has been expressed to them by surrogates is that

> by making them the legal mother at birth, the current law goes directly against their wishes. They do not consider themselves to be the mother of the child they have gestated for the intended parents, and do not want to be held legally responsible for a child whom they have never considered to be theirs.[66]

Indeed, *intention-based status* is a fundamental aspect of all surrogacy arrangements.[67] The gestational surrogate should not be viewed as the legal mother at birth not merely because she is genetically unrelated to the child, but because, in a well-regulated surrogacy system, this clearly reflects her free and informed intention, as well as that of the intended parents. The intention of the parties is also what justifies according legal parentage at birth to intended parents, genetically related and otherwise.[68] As noted by the Law Commissions in 2019, 'the intention

---

[64] However, as discussed later in this chapter, this would be subject to the surrogate's right to object to this within a defined period after birth, which appears to be required by international law.

[65] The most 'surrogacy-friendly' states in the US – California, New Hampshire, Nevada, Connecticut, Delaware and Maine – have all only legislated for gestational surrogacy. Greece, Portugal and Israel similarly recognise only gestational surrogacy in their respective assisted human reproduction legislation.

[66] Law Commission, 'Building Families through Surrogacy: A New Law' Law Com No 244 (HMSO, 2019) 182, available at www.lawcom.gov.uk/project/surrogacy.

[67] Horsey has long-since advocated that the notion of '"intention" should operate as the pre-birth determinant in "awarding" parental status when a child is born following surrogacy or assisted conception' as this 'would more precisely reflect the expected outcome for *all* parties concerned'. See K Horsey, 'Challenging Presumptions: Legal Parenthood and Surrogacy Arrangements' (2010) 22 *Child and Family Law Quarterly* 449, 455 and 472.

[68] See V Jadva, 'Surrogacy: Issues, Concerns and Complexities' in S Golombok et al (eds), *Regulating Reproductive Donation* (Cambridge, CUP, 2016) 126, 128.

of all the parties to the arrangement that the surrogate will have a child which the intended parents will then raise as their own is the very core of what a surrogacy arrangement is'.[69]

Thus, it is unclear as to why Part 7 does not propose to settle the issue of parentage in favour of the intending parent(s) at the 'pre-conception state approval' stage, especially when one considers that, in addition to the intentions of the parties, according to section 53(3), at least one of the intended parents is required to contribute a gamete to the formation of the embryo. Thus, in all domestic, gestational surrogacies, *unlike the surrogate*, one of the intended parents will always be genetically related to the child. Indeed, in practice, it appears that it is not unusual for both intending parents who are of the opposite sex to contribute their genetic material to the formation of the embryo(s).[70]

A. *MR & Another v An tArd Chláraitheoir*

Further, in the 'surrogacy case' of *MR & Another v An tArd Chláraitheoir* the Supreme Court established that it is for the Oireachtas to determine motherhood in surrogacy arrangements. The case involved an amicable, altruistic surrogacy arrangement between family members. The gestational surrogate gave birth to twins on behalf of her sister and her sister's husband, the intended *and* genetic parents of the children. However, in line with existing legislation, the registrar would only allow the birth mother and the genetic father to be recorded as the parents on the twins' birth certificates. The genetic parents applied to the Registrar General to have the twins' birth certificates amended to reflect the genetic reality of their familial situation, but were denied a remedy. The genetic parents then applied to the High Court for a declaration that the genetic mother was the legal mother.[71] In the High Court, Abbott J granted a declaration that the genetic mother was the legal mother of the twins and was entitled to be recorded as such on their birth certificates. However, the state appealed this finding to the Supreme Court, which reversed the High Court decision and quashed the declaration that the twins' genetic mother was entitled to be registered as their

---

[69] Law Commission, 'Building Families through Surrogacy' (2019) 25. Indeed, Douglas argues that a law which makes a gestational surrogate the legal mother of the child at birth when she has no wish to be is 'a deliberate measure designed to discourage people from entering into surrogacy arrangements': see G Douglas, 'The Intention to be a Parent and the Making of Mothers' (1994) 57 *Modern Law Review* 636, 637.

[70] See M Crawshaw, E Blyth and O van den Akker, 'The Changing Profile of Surrogacy in the UK – Implications for National and International Policy and Practice' (2012) 34 *Journal of Social Welfare and Family Law* 267; C Coulter, 'Why surrogacy has nothing to do with same-sex marriage' *Irish Times* (27 April 2015), available at www.irishtimes.com/opinion/why-surrogacy-has-nothing-to-do-with-same-sex-marriage-1.2189717.

[71] See the Status of Children Act 1987, s 35, which allows a person to apply to the court for a declaration that the person named in the application is their mother/father.

'mother' on their birth certificates, because existing legislation did not permit this outcome.

The case has been interpreted by the Department of Health as requiring the surrogate to be recognised as the legal mother of a surrogate-born child at birth. Indeed, when the predecessor to the current Bill, the General Scheme of the Assisted Human Reproduction Bill 2017 (the 'General Scheme') was being drafted, department officials claimed that 'the proposed legislation will take cognisance of the 2014 Supreme Court judgment in the *MR & Another v An tArd Chláraitheoir* (surrogacy) case, which found that the birth mother, rather than the genetic mother, is the legal mother'.[72] However, this appears to be a misreading by the Department of the judgment in the *MR* case. *The Supreme Court did not find that the birth mother must always be the legal mother.* Denham CJ actually found that the principle of *mater semper certa est* – 'mother is always certain' – is not part of the common law of Ireland:

> It appears to me that in fact the maxim *mater semper certa est* was not part of the common law of Ireland. It was a statement which recognised the medical and scientific fact that a birth mother was the mother of the child. The common law of Ireland has not addressed the issue of motherhood in a surrogacy situation.

More significantly, Denham CJ held that the legal definition of 'mother' in the context of surrogacy was a matter for the Oireachtas to determine through appropriate legislation, as

> such lacuna should be addressed in legislation and not by this Court … Under the current legislative framework it is not possible to address issues arising on surrogacy, including the issue of who is the mother for the purpose of registration of the birth. *The issues raised in this case are important, complex and social, which are matters of public policy for the Oireachtas.*[73]

On this analysis, it would appear that it was entirely open to the Department of Health to draft legislation allowing for pre-conception approval of parentage in surrogacy situations. Given this, and the pre-surrogacy safeguards contained in Part 7, and the fact that it is proposed that only altruistic, gestational surrogacy will be regulated, it seems bizarre that intended parents, at least one of whom must have a genetic link to the child, will be unable to avail of 'pre-conception state approval' of their legal parentage if Part 7 is enacted.[74]

---

[72] Email from Paul Ivory, Bioethics Unit, Department of Health, to author (16 November 2016).

[73] [2014] IESC 60 [116]–[118].

[74] Indeed, during oral evidence sessions at the Houses of Parliament in Westminster in 2018, the UK All-Party Parliamentary Group on Surrogacy (APPG Surrogacy) was impressed by the same safeguards in the direct predecessor to the 2022 Bill, the General Scheme of the Assisted Human Reproduction Bill 2017, and expressly commented on these safeguards in its report. See All-Party Parliamentary Group on Surrogacy, 'Report on Understandings of the Law and Practice of Surrogacy' (APPG, 2021) 12, available at www.andrewpercy.org/storage/app/media/appgs/Surrogacy%20APPG%204.pdf.

B. The Safety of Surrogate-Born Children – Section 16 of the Bill

In order to prevent a situation like that which arose in the 'baby Gammy' case, where the genetic father of twins born to a Thai surrogate was found to have child sex convictions, this author previously suggested that Irish law should require intended parents to disclose any previous convictions/undergo a form of Garda[75] vetting prior to treatment being approved.[76] Permission for treatment could be refused by the AHRRA only where the nature of any relevant previous convictions indicates that allowing a child to be born via surrogacy and ultimately parented by the intending parents (or the surrogate, and her spouse/partner, if any) may be contrary to the best interests of the child. Indeed, in the 'Report of the Commission on Assisted Human Reproduction' in 2005, the Commission recommended that if 'there is objective evidence of a risk of harm to any child that may be conceived through AHR, there should be a presumption against treatment'.[77]

While provisions concerning the safety of surrogate-born children were absent from previous legislative attempts to regulate surrogacy, section 16 of the Bill provides that an AHR treatment provider shall not provide AHR treatment unless it is satisfied that the intending parents, and the surrogate and her partner, if any, do not present a potential significant risk of harm to *any child*, surrogate-born or otherwise.[78] The parties will be required to complete a 'section 16' assessment form for the AHR treatment provider, but section 16(2)(b) of the Bill states that the information to be provided in such a form is to be determined by the Minister via ministerial regulations after commencement. However, section 16(2)(c) provides guidance to the Minister by stating that 'in determining the information to be specified, *the paramount consideration is the safety of any child*'.[79] Thus, it appears that, at a minimum, in order to achieve this child-centred objective, the ministerial regulations will have to require, as part of a 'section 16' assessment, the disclosure of previous convictions related to children which are relevant to

---

[75] 'Garda' is the word for police in the Irish language.

[76] See B Tobin, 'An Appraisal of Ireland's Current Legislative Proposals for Regulating Domestic Surrogacy Arrangements' (2019) 41 *Journal of Social Welfare and Family Law* 205, 212. Such cases are likely to be very rare, but there is research detailing several cases where Australians used surrogacy to gain access to children to abuse or exploit: S Allan, 'The Review of the Western Australian Human Reproductive Technology Act 1991 and the Surrogacy Act 2008' (Report: Part 2) (Dept of Health, 2019) 91.

[77] 'Report of the Commission on Assisted Human Reproduction' (2005) 16.

[78] The requirement for the surrogate and her spouse/partner (if any) to also undergo a criminal record check is crucial in a jurisdiction like Ireland, where it is proposed that the surrogate will be the legal mother at birth and can refuse to consent to a transfer of parentage/guardianship. A similar requirement has been suggested by the Law Commissions in the UK in order to ensure that there are no risks to the child of harm or neglect if the child remains in the surrogate's care after birth: see Law Commission (n 66) 314–16.

[79] Emphasis added.

a decision-making process concerning the granting of permission for treatment that might lead to the birth of a child. The requirement for the surrogate and her spouse/partner (if any) to also undergo a 'section 16' assessment is crucial because the Bill proposes that the surrogate will be the legal mother at birth and can refuse to consent to a transfer of parentage/guardianship.[80] Thus, the 'section 16' assessment will at least help to limit any potential risks to the child of harm or neglect if they must remain in the surrogate's care following their birth.

Since the 'baby Gammy' case in 2014, pre-conception screening of intended parents for criminal offences has also found favour elsewhere. In Israel, the Surrogate Motherhood Agreements (Approval of Agreement and Status of Newborn Law) (Amendment No 2) Law 2018 provides that the intended parents must not have been convicted of an offence which, in light of its severity or circumstances, constitutes a risk to the welfare of the child, and criminal proceedings are not pending against them in relation to such an offence.[81] Further, in 2019, the Law Commissions also favoured introducing into UK law a requirement that the intended parents and the surrogate and her partner, if any, should be screened for 'criminal offences or behaviour that amount to a risk of harm to a child'.[82] The Commission recommended that all parties should be required to obtain an 'enhanced criminal record certificate' to be reviewed by whoever is overseeing their arrangement.[83]

C. Post-Birth Parental Orders and the Surrogate's Consent

The requirement in Part 7 of the Bill that, at birth, the surrogate will be the child's legal mother, is not unusual – it is replicated in, inter alia, the UK, New Zealand, Portugal, and the Australian States of Victoria and Western Australia.[84] However, despite the rather selfless, admirable role she undertakes, a gestational surrogate has no genetic connection to the child, and designating her the child's legal parent at birth does not accord with her intention.[85] Nonetheless, akin to the UK,[86] Part 7 provides that the intended parents must go through a 'post-birth Parental Order' process to establish their parentage. The intended parents will have to apply to the

---

[80] See the Health (Assisted Human Reproduction) Bill 2022, ss 63 and 156.

[81] See R Schuz, 'Surrogacy in Israel' in JM Scherpe, C Fenton-Glynn and T Kaan (eds), *Eastern and Western Perspectives on Surrogacy* (Cambridge, Intersentia, 2019) 176.

[82] See Law Commission (n 66) 314–16.

[83] ibid.

[84] However, the New Zealand Law Commission recently suggested that where a surrogacy agreement is approved at the pre-conception stage by the Ethics Committee on Assisted Reproductive Technology (ECART) the intended parents could be recognised as the legal parents *after birth*, simply by the surrogate completing a statutory declaration seven days after the birth confirming her consent to this. See New Zealand Law Commission, 'Review of Surrogacy' (2022) 194–95. A similar recommendation for law reform has been made by the Law Commissions in the UK: see Law Commission (n 66) 156–59.

[85] See Law Commission (n 66) 182.

[86] See the Human Fertilisation and Embryology Act 2008, s 54.

court seeking a Parental Order transferring legal parentage from the surrogate to them a minimum of 28 days after the birth of the child, and the surrogate will need to consent to the granting of the order by the court.[87]

Mirroring the UK legislation, Part 7 affords remarkable post-birth leeway to the surrogate, which makes more sense in the UK context where traditional surrogacy is permitted and the surrogate can be the genetic mother, but makes little sense in an Irish context where only the regulation of gestational surrogacy is proposed.[88] Significantly, Part 7 of the Bill mirrors the current UK law surrounding the surrogate's consent to a Parental Order, such that this can only be dispensed with by the court where she is either deceased or cannot be located after reasonable efforts have been made to find her.[89] This is a significant retrograde step when compared to the Bill's immediate predecessor, the General Scheme, because at least there was a provision in that draft piece of legislation which provided some potential relief for intended parents should the surrogate refuse to consent to a Parental Order. The General Scheme enabled the court to waive the requirement for the surrogate's consent in a wider variety of circumstances, including where she is deceased; lacks the capacity to provide consent; cannot be located after reasonable efforts have been made to find her; or, importantly, 'for any other reason the court considers to be relevant'.[90]

This would have offered a potential lifeline to intended parents in this particular predicament and might in practice have prevented the kind of outcome that occurred in the recent case of *Re AB (Surrogacy: Consent)*[91] in the UK. Indeed, in 2018, during oral evidence sessions at Westminster to consider reform of the law on surrogacy in the UK, the All-Party Parliamentary Group on Surrogacy ('APPG Surrogacy') was impressed that in Ireland, the General Scheme was 'responding to some of the thorny issues that have arisen in the English courts, by planning

---

[87] See the Health (Assisted Human Reproduction) Bill 2022, ss 62(4) and 63(1)(a)(iii).

[88] Indeed, in South Africa, where traditional surrogacy is permitted, the surrogate has a cooling-off period up to 60 days after the birth of the child, during which she has the right to terminate the surrogacy agreement with the intended parents and keep the child: see M Slabbert and C Roodt, 'South Africa' in K Trimmings and P Beaumont (eds), *International Surrogacy Arrangements: Legal Regulation at the International Level* (London, Bloomsbury, 2013) 325–45.

[89] See the Health (Assisted Human Reproduction) Bill 2022, s 63(2). The equivalent provision in the UK is the Human Fertilisation and Embryology Act 2008, s 54(7), which provides that the surrogate's consent to a parental order is not required *only* when she cannot be found or is incapable of giving agreement. There is no opportunity for the court to otherwise dispense with the surrogate's consent, as observed by Theis J in *Re AB (Surrogacy: Consent)* [2016] EWHC 2643 (Fam).

[90] See Head 48 of the General Scheme of the Assisted Human Reproduction Bill 2017. Indeed, elsewhere I have questioned 'whether this provision was intentionally removed from the Bill to make domestic surrogacy as perilous an undertaking as possible for Irish intended parents': see B Tobin, 'Proposed Laws Discourage Surrogacy Arrangements Here' *Irish Examiner* (16 March 2022) 11.

[91] [2016] EWHC 2643 (Fam). In this case the surrogate and her husband refused to consent to a Parental Order in favour of the intended parents, and there was no possibility for the court to waive their consent as the UK Human Fertilisation and Embryology Act 2008 does not make provision for this, except in limited circumstances. For an analysis of this case, see B Tobin, 'A Critique of *Re AB (Surrogacy: Consent)*: Can Ireland learn from the UK Experience?' (2017) 20 *Irish Journal of Family Law* 3. See also G Douglas, 'Case Report: *Re AB (Surrogacy: Consent)* [2016] EWHC 2643 Fam' (2017) *Family Law* 57.

to remove the aspect of the law that means the surrogate's consent could not be dispensed with if unreasonably withheld'.[92] Nonetheless, Part 7 of the Bill has reverted to a provision identical to that contained in Ireland's premier legislative proposals on surrogacy, which were scrapped back in 2014. In Part 3 of the General Scheme of the Children and Family Relationships Bill 2014, Head 13(12) only allowed for the surrogate's consent to a Parental Order to be waived by the court if she was deceased or could not be located after reasonable efforts had been made to locate her.

Given that children's rights are expressly protected in Article 42A of the Irish Constitution, I would prefer to see the restoration of the court's ability to dispense with the surrogate's consent if it is unreasonably withheld where the resulting situation would be contrary to the best interests of the child.[93] A provision equivalent to that contained in section 31 of the Adoption Act 2010, as amended by section 14 of the Adoption (Amendment) Act 2017, would be a worthwhile addition to the Bill.[94] In the context of an adoption, section 31 of the 2010 Act allows the High Court to dispense with the need for the natural mother's consent where she fails, neglects or refuses to give her consent to the making of an adoption order. However, before doing so the High Court must have regard to 'the rights, whether under the Constitution or otherwise, of the persons concerned (including the natural and imprescriptible rights of the child)'.[95]

D. Restrictive Domestic Surrogacy Laws: Encouraging International Commercial Surrogacy?

If the 'post-birth Parental Order' model provided for in the Bill becomes law, intended parents will continue to have recourse to international surrogacy. A model where the surrogate will be the legal mother at birth and can arbitrarily refuse to consent to a Parental Order, with no possibility for the court to resolve the situation in favour of the intended parents if she does so, will discourage domestic

---

[92] See All-Party Parliamentary Group on Surrogacy, 'Report' (2021) 13.

[93] The Law Commissions have suggested that the law in the UK could be amended to enable a court to dispense with the need for the surrogate to consent to a Parental Order, *but only* in situations where the surrogate has consented to the child living with the intended parents, or where a court determines that the child's primary residence should be with the intended parents, and the child's welfare should be the paramount consideration for the court: see Law Commission (n 66) 266–67.

[94] O'Mahony also appears to be in favour of this approach: see C O'Mahony, 'A Review of Children's Rights and Best Interests in the Context of Donor-Assisted Human Reproduction and Surrogacy in Irish Law' (Department, of Children, Equality, Disability, Integration and Youth, 2021) 24, available at www.gov.ie.

[95] See the Adoption Act 2010, s 31(4)(a)(iv), as amended. In any event, should the surrogate refuse to consent to a parental order, the genetic intended father will still be able to apply for a Declaration of Parentage and guardianship in the courts because the 2022 Bill recognises him as a parent. Section 14(2)(c) of the 2022 Bill provides that the intended parents will not 'without a parental order, be the parents of any child born as a result of AHR treatment provided pursuant to the agreement *other than in the case of an intending parent who provided the sperm used in such treatment*'.

surrogacy arrangements. Where there is uncertainty regarding legal parentage under a domestic surrogacy regime, intended parents are inclined to go abroad. This has been highlighted in very recent literature from New Zealand and the UK. As the New Zealand Law Commission clearly emphasised in its recent 'Review of Surrogacy',

> while disputes over legal parenthood are rare, their potential and the lack of any process to resolve disputes can 'create an atmosphere of fear and mistrust' in surrogacy arrangements. This may deter some intended parents from pursuing a domestic surrogacy arrangement in favour of an international surrogacy arrangement in a jurisdiction where they have clearer legal rights and responsibilities in relation to the child.[96]

The New Zealand Law Commission has observed that, when preparing its 'Review of Surrogacy', 'several intended parents we spoke with told us that the legal uncertainty in Aotearoa New Zealand was a factor in them deciding to pursue surrogacy offshore',[97] while in the UK a recent survey of international surrogacy arrangements published by the Cambridge Family Law Centre, reveals that, for intended parents, 'legal considerations were key to their decision-making process' and 'the existence of pre-birth orders in some jurisdictions was seen as a significant benefit' by intended parents.[98]

VI. The Pre-Conception State Approval Model for Regulating Surrogacy

As demonstrated, a 'pre-conception state approval' model would be a logical means of regulating surrogacy in Ireland, given that a regulatory body is being established and there are many appropriate pre-surrogacy safeguards in place to protect the surrogate's interests.[99] This type of approach can be found in Greece, which operates a *fully* 'pre-conception state approval' model for regulating surrogacy. Akin to what is currently proposed in Ireland, the Greek model allows for gestational, altruistic surrogacy and necessitates approval (albeit by a court, not a regulatory authority) of the parties' arrangement *prior* to any treatment being permitted to take place.[100] However, once the court has approved the surrogacy arrangement and given permission for treatment, *unlike Ireland*, in Greece the *intended mother* is the child's legal mother at birth. Further, if she is married or in a civil partnership, her spouse or civil partner is presumed to be the legal father at

---

[96] New Zealand Law Commission (n 43) [7.34].

[97] ibid, [7.35].

[98] C Fenton-Glynn, 'International Surrogacy Arrangements: A Survey' (Cambridge Family Law, 2022) 8. There were 168 participants involved in this survey.

[99] Indeed, the 2022 Bill contains sound 'pre-authorisation' safeguards for *all* of the parties to the arrangement.

[100] See E Zervogianni, 'Greece' in JM Scherpe, C Fenton-Glynn and T Kaan (eds), *Eastern and Western Perspectives on Surrogacy* (Cambridge, Intersentia, 2019) 149.

birth, and this presumption cannot be contested. If the intended mother is neither married nor in a civil partnership, then the prior consent of her partner to the surrogacy arrangement serves as an 'acknowledgement' of the child. The intended mother's consent to the surrogacy is equally regarded as consent to her partner's 'acknowledgement', and his paternity is thus established. The father's 'acknowledgement' cannot be challenged. Although the Greek model currently only embraces opposite-sex intended parents, if a similar model was established in Ireland it could encompass same-sex intended parents who are married, in a civil partnership or cohabiting. Provided that the parties provide the requisite consents as to each other's parentage, it is submitted that, subject to the requirements of international law, and international best practice as suggested by the Verona Principles, a statutory presumption of 'parentage' could arise in their favour as soon as the child is born.[101]

As I shall discuss later in this chapter, a *fully* 'pre-conception state approval' model like the one operating in Greece is no longer an option for other states that are moving to either enact or reform laws pertaining to surrogacy. Since 2018, it has become clear that where the surrogate is not a legal parent at birth, international law and best practice require her to be able to freely and expeditiously confirm or revoke her consent, *post-birth*, to the intended parents having exclusive legal parentage. The Greek model does not allow this. Nonetheless, while it might now need to be reconsidered in light of the above, the 'pre-conception state approval' surrogacy regime has been in operation in Greece for 20 years, since the Civil Code was amended by Law 3089/2002 on Medically Assisted Human Reproduction, and, as Rokas has observed, 'the almost complete non-existence of judicial controversies in relation to surrogacy in past years constitutes an indication that this new institution is functioning well in the country'.[102]

A. Equitably Balancing the Rights of the Parties to Surrogacy Arrangements

A fully pre-conception state approval model has much to recommend it, given the balance it achieves between the rights of all parties. From the intended

---

[101] A similar pre-conception model operates in South Africa, where a surrogacy agreement is confirmed by the High Court at pre-conception stage and the intended parents are the child's legal parents from the time of birth. The surrogate does not acquire parental status at birth. However, South Africa permits both gestational *and* traditional surrogacy and, consequently, where the latter is availed of and the surrogate is the genetic mother of the child she can seek to terminate the surrogacy agreement for up to 60 days after the birth of the child. However, contrary to Greece, surrogacy is available to both opposite-sex *and* same-sex couples in South Africa. See further, J Sloth Nielsen, 'South Africa' in JM Scherpe, C Fenton-Glynn and T Kaan (eds), *Eastern and Western Perspectives on Surrogacy* (Cambridge, Intersentia, 2019) 186 and 191.

[102] K Rokas, 'Greece' in K Trimmings and P Beaumont (eds), *International Surrogacy Arrangements: Legal Regulation at the International Level* (London, Bloomsbury, 2013) 165.

parents' perspective, it provides them with a strong incentive to choose domestic surrogacy over international surrogacy, as their parental rights in relation to the surrogate-born child can be established in their own jurisdiction very early on in the process.[103] Thus, there is no need to worry about any time-consuming, costly and stressful post-birth court application and a parental order being made subject to the surrogate's consent. From the surrogate-born child's perspective, their intended (opposite-sex or same-sex) family structure is recognised by domestic law *at birth*. The child would only ever have one legal mother or set of legal parents, and again there would be no need for post-birth court proceedings to transfer legal parentage from the surrogate. The gestational surrogate will have availed of significant pre-surrogacy safeguards in the form of medical assessments, AHR counselling and independent legal advice, and establishing the intended parents' parental rights and the child's familial rights pre-conception would not conflict with her right to manage her pregnancy in the same way as any other pregnant woman,[104] because it is proposed that the statutory presumption of parentage should only commence at the time of the child's birth, and not before. The 'pre-conception state approval' model achieves an equitable balance between the rights of the gestational surrogate, intended parents and, most importantly, the child, and there is no apparent reason why it could not operate effectively in Ireland, with some modifications to reflect the requirements of international law, and international best practice as suggested by the Verona Principles, all of which will be discussed further below.

VII. The Child's Right to Knowledge of Identity – A Comparison between the Post-Birth Parental Order and Pre-Conception State Approval Models

Kilkelly succinctly explains why respecting the child's right to knowledge of identity is imperative to any legislation pertaining to surrogacy and donor-assisted human reproduction:

> Supported by considerable research and the development of best practice across the world, the strong consensus emerging is that it is without a doubt not only in children's interests to know the full details of their history (and indeed that of their

---

[103] B Tobin, 'Surrogacy Proposals would make Process Costly, Time consuming and Frustrating', *TheJournal.ie* (27 October 2017), available at www.thejournal.ie/readme/opinionsurrogacy-proposals-would-make-process-costly-time-consuming-and-frustrating-3666377-Oct2017. While intended parents' parental rights can be established pre-conception, this must be subject to the surrogate's post-birth right to object, as required by international law.

[104] Indeed, the Health (Assisted Human Reproduction) Bill 2022, s 56(2) provides that the surrogate has 'the right to manage all aspects of her health during the pregnancy and, in that regard, to freely seek and obtain medical services in relation to the pregnancy'.

family) but that an overwhelming number of them request, want and need that information.[105]

Similarly, Cowden emphasises the importance that a child can attach to their origins and that 'the evidence is growing that access to identifying information regarding one's genetic parents is essential to a child's mental health'.[106] In *McD v L*, the Supreme Court recognised that 'there is natural human curiosity about parentage'.[107] Further, the ECtHR has recognised 'the importance to children of accessing information about their identity'[108] and it appears to require some positive state intervention to facilitate this.[109] Indeed, I have suggested elsewhere that the right to knowledge of one's identity is possibly a 'natural' constitutional right of the child under the Children's Amendment, Article 42A, a corollary of the right to know the identity of one's natural mother that was identified by the Supreme Court in *I'OT v B*[110] as a personal right of the child under Article 40.3 (prior to the introduction of Article 42A).[111]

Part 7 of the 2022 Bill provides, in section 65, that the AHRRA must establish and maintain the National Surrogacy Register, wherein an entry must be made regarding each child born via a domestic surrogacy agreement. The entry shall include details of the child, the surrogate, the relevant intending parents, and the relevant donor, if any. The entry shall also include details as to whether a court application for a Parental Order was made and whether such application was successful. Once established, the National Surrogacy Register will interact with the Register of Births because the AHRRA will link in with *an tArd Chláraitheoir* (the Registrar General), who will be required to note in the entry in the Register of Births that the child was born via a surrogacy agreement and that further information in relation to the child is available from the National Surrogacy Register. However, such note will only be released to a surrogate-born person once they apply for a copy of their birth certificate upon reaching the age of 16, which is the

---

[105] U Kilkelly, 'Complicated Childhood: the Rights of Children in Committed Relationships' in O Doyle and W Binchy (eds), *Committed Relationships and the Law* (Dublin, Four Courts Press 2007) 215, 234.

[106] M Cowden, '"No Harm, No Foul": A Child's Right to Know their Genetic Parents' (2012) 26 *International Journal of Law, Policy and the Family* 102, 110–11. As authority for this statement, the author cites JE Scheib, M Riordan and S Rubiri, 'Choosing Identity – Release Sperm Donors: The Parents' Perspective 13-18 Years Later' (2003) 18 *Human Reproduction* 1115.

[107] *McD v L* [2010] 1 ILRM 461, 524.

[108] See Kilkelly, 'Complicated Childhood' (2007) 237.

[109] *Gaskin v United Kingdom* (1989) 12 EHRR 36; *Mikulic v Croatia* App No 53176/99 (ECHR, 7 February 2002); *SH v Austria* App No 57813/00 (ECHR, 1 April 2010). As Brown and Wade have emphasised, 'it is clear that information about genetic progenitors is seen as important to a person's identity, as an aspect of private life under Article 8' of the European Convention on Human Rights: see A Brown and K Wade, 'The Incoherent Role of the Child's Identity in the Construction and Allocation of Legal Parenthood' (2022) 42 *Legal Studies* 1, 5–6.

[110] *I'OT v B* [1998] 2 IR 321, 328 (Hamilton CJ).

[111] B Tobin, 'The Revised General Scheme' (2014) 161.

age at which a child born via AHR is designated an adult under the provisions of the Bill.[112]

When one considers the importance of the child's right to knowledge of their genetic identity, the establishment of a National Surrogacy Register that is linked to the Register of Births seems like a rather innovative and pragmatic course of action when a jurisdiction is moving to regulate surrogacy for the first time.[113] Section 157 of the Bill requires an tArd Chláraitheoir to establish and maintain a Register of Parental Orders and to establish and maintain an index to make traceable the connection between each entry therein and the corresponding entry in the Register of Births. Any legal requirement for the production of a birth certificate shall instead be satisfied by the production of a certified copy of a Parental Order. While the Bill's proposed establishment of the National Surrogacy Register and its interaction with the Register of Births seems well intentioned from a children's rights perspective, the system is undoubtedly complex. However, there is an identifiable policy goal. By providing that a certified copy of a Parental Order supplants a birth certificate for legal purposes, section 157 of the Bill encourages intended parents to *complete* the 'post-birth Parental Order' process to establish their legal parentage and acquire and duly register a document that can be presented for various legal purposes on behalf of their child.[114] Such encouragement to establish legal parentage is arguably necessary because in the UK, evidence from Surrogacy UK suggests that not all intended parents apply to the court for a Parental Order after the birth of the child, or even intend to do so.[115] Similarly, the New Zealand Law Commission has observed that it is also common for intended parents in that jurisdiction to forego the formal process of establishing a legal relationship with their surrogate-born child after birth, because

> a common scenario seems to be that the surrogate mother enters her own name and the intending father's name on the birth certificate without any other steps being taken to transfer or establish the intending parents' legal status in relation to the child. They simply take custody of the child and care for it on a day-to-day basis.[116]

The pre-conception state approval model is preferable to what is proposed by the Bill because it can simply allow for the intended parents to be named on the

---

[112] See the Health (Assisted Human Reproduction) Bill 2022, s 2(1). Section 159 of the Bill amends CFRA 2015, ss 34-38 of the such that a person conceived via DAHR will now also be able to access identifying/non-identifying information about their gamete donor at the age of 16. Previously, a DAHR-conceived person had to be 18 to access such information.

[113] On this right of the child, see Cowden, "No Harm, No Foul" (2012); see also K Wade, 'The Regulation of Surrogacy: a Children's Rights Perspective' (2017) 29 *Child and Family Law Quarterly* 113.

[114] The Health (Assisted Human Reproduction) Bill 2022, s 157 proposes to insert Pt 4A into the Civil Registration Act 2004.

[115] Surrogacy UK, 'Surrogacy in the UK: Myth Busting and Reform – Report of the Surrogacy UK Working Group on Surrogacy Law Reform' (Surrogacy UK, 2015) 23.

[116] New Zealand Law Commission, 'New Issues in Legal Parenthood' NZLC R88 (2005) [7.7]. In New Zealand, there is currently no equivalent of the 'post-birth Parental Order' process and the intended parents must jointly adopt the child in order to establish the legal parent-child relationship.

child's birth certificate without the need for a birth certificate naming the surrogate as the mother, a post-birth Parental Order that names the intended parents as parents and, subsequently, a certified copy of such an order that can supplant the original birth certificate for legal purposes. Under a pre-conception state approval model, legislation could provide that every entry in the Register of Births concerning a surrogate-born child should be linked to the National Surrogacy Register in order to safeguard the child's right to knowledge of genetic identity. The intended parents could present the registrar with their pre-authorised surrogacy agreement confirming their details and those of the surrogate, as well as evidence from the clinic confirming that they engaged in surrogacy treatment, that gametes from at least one of the intended parents were used in the treatment, the details of the other gamete donor, if any, and the details of the woman who had the resulting embryo implanted in her uterus. The birth notification form sent to the Registrar by the hospital would confirm that the child whose birth is being registered was indeed born to the woman confirmed as the surrogate in both the pre-authorised agreement *and* evidence from the clinic regarding implantation.[117] When registering the birth, the Registrar could make a note in the register of births that the child was born as a result of AHR treatment provided pursuant to an approved surrogacy agreement and that additional information is available from the National Surrogacy Register. Following registration of the birth the Registrar could be required to furnish the AHRRA with the details and evidence of all parties involved in the surrogacy arrangement. The AHRRA could cross-check these details with the surrogacy arrangement it pre-authorised and, once verified, it could proceed to record the intended parents, surrogate and any donor involved in the National Surrogacy Register. To reflect the intention of all parties to a surrogacy, the National Surrogacy Register is the appropriate repository for the surrogate's details.

However, in the case of male same-sex parents, the type of birth certificate I propose would not record the child's 'mother', thus the child will have no legal mother at birth. However, speaking in the context of the UK, the Law Commissions believe that the establishment of 'a national register of surrogacy arrangements which would record the identity of the surrogate … addresses any issue of the "erasure" of the surrogate'.[118] Indeed, as demonstrated, the surrogate's details would be readily available to the child from the National Surrogacy Register once they become an adult, while their intended same-sex family structure would be recognised on their birth certificate.

Nonetheless, there is a potential obstacle which *somewhat* inhibits Ireland from introducing a *fully* pre-conception domestic surrogacy model. In 2018, the UN

---

[117] Depending on which option was availed of in legislation to comply with international law (ie allowing the surrogate to freely confirm *or* revoke consent post-birth), the intended parents could be obliged to present the Registrar with written evidence from the surrogate confirming her consent, or be restricted from registering the birth until the period during which the surrogate can revoke her consent has passed.

[118] Law Commission (n 66) 182.

Special Rapporteur published a report which stipulated that *all surrogacy regimes* should regard the surrogate as the legal mother of the child at birth, subject to her post-birth ability to transfer parentage and parental responsibility (guardianship) in relation to the child *if she chooses*, and it is now prudent to consider these recommendations and the state's international law obligations.

VIII. The UN Special Rapporteur's Position on Surrogacy Arrangements

In 2018, the then UN Special Rapporteur on the Sale and Sexual Exploitation of Children (the 'UN Special Rapporteur') published a report that was highly critical of states that permit the practice of *commercial surrogacy*.[119] Echoing the earlier findings of the UN Committee on the Rights of the Child, the UN Special Rapporteur's main concern appears to be that in jurisdictions that permit commercial surrogacy, parentage is decided by virtue of a contract at pre-conception stage, where 'intending parent(s) pay the surrogate mother to release and transfer legal parentage and parental responsibility, as well as to physically transfer the child' after birth, and the contract is often enforceable against the surrogate.[120] The UN Special Rapporteur stated that under the Optional Protocol to the Convention on the Rights of the Child on the Sale of Children, Child Prostitution and Child Pornography, surrogacy arrangements constitute the sale of children whenever the surrogate receives 'remuneration or any other consideration' in exchange for the legal and physical transfer of a child.[121] Fenton-Glynn and Scherpe observe that this is a 'powerful argument from an influential source, and cannot be dismissed lightly'.[122]

In order that a commercial surrogacy arrangement does not constitute sale of children, the UN Special Rapporteur stated that the surrogate must be accorded the status of mother at birth, and must be under no legal obligation to participate in transferring the child. All payments must be made to the surrogate prior to the post-birth transfer of the child, and all such payments must be non-refundable. On this analysis, the surrogate would be viewed as having been remunerated for

---

[119] See UNHRC, 'Report of the Special Rapporteur on the Sale and Sexual Exploitation of Children' (UNHRC, 2018), available at digitallibrary.un.org/record/1473378?ln=en.

[120] As Scherpe and Fenton-Glynn point out, in the commercial surrogacy jurisdiction of California 'the obligation to hand over the child is unconditionally enforceable': see JM Scherpe and C Fenton-Glynn, 'Surrogacy in a Globalised World: Comparative Analysis and Thoughts on Regulation' in JM Scherpe, C Fenton-Glynn and T Kaan (eds), *Eastern and Western Perspectives on Surrogacy* (Cambridge, Intersentia, 2019) 526.

[121] UNHRC, 'Report of the Special Rapporteur' (2018) 12. Ireland ratified the UN Convention on the Rights of the Child in 1992, but this international human rights instrument has not yet been incorporated into domestic law. The Optional Protocol on the Sale of Children, Child Prostitution and Child Pornography has not yet been ratified by Ireland.

[122] JM Scherpe and C Fenton-Glynn, 'Surrogacy in a Globalised World' (2019) 585.

the acts of gestation and childbirth and would have satisfied her legal and contractual obligations in that regard *at the time of birth*. Therefore, her choice after the birth to legally and physically transfer the child to the intending parent(s) would be a gratuitous act, based on her own post-birth intentions, rather than on any legal or contractual obligation to make the transfer.[123] This ensures that there is no 'sale' of a child.

IX. Altruistic Surrogacy Arrangements in the UK and Ireland: In Principle *and* in Practice?

One might counterargue that Ireland is proposing to introduce an altruistic surrogacy regime, and O'Mahony rightly observes that, in the 2018 report, the UN Special Rapporteur's 'concerns regarding sale of children were *primarily* directed towards commercial surrogacy'.[124] Indeed, in the UK, the Law Commissions are of the opinion that

> in the context of an arrangement from which the surrogate is not profiting, there may be scope to query the Rapporteur's view that not recognising the surrogate as a legal parent at birth means that there is a breach of the Optional Protocol.[125]

Similarly, O'Mahony argues that 'the UN Special Rapporteur appears to have allowed legitimate concerns relating to international surrogacy to spill over into the very different context of domestic altruistic surrogacy'.[126] However, it is open to debate as to whether, in practice, domestic altruistic surrogacy truly differs from international commercial surrogacy. The UN Special Rapporteur made it clear in her report that 'a truly "altruistic" surrogacy does not constitute sale of children, since altruistic surrogacy is understood as a gratuitous act, often between family members or friends with pre-existing relationships'.[127] The UN Special Rapporteur cautioned that 'labelling surrogacy arrangements or surrogacy systems as "altruistic" does not automatically avoid the reach of the Optional Protocol' because altruistic surrogacy arrangements can involve substantial reimbursements to surrogates that exceed reasonable expenses, thus blurring the lines between commercial and altruistic surrogacy.[128] The UN Special Rapporteur seemed to be aware that altruistic surrogacy regimes do not always operate as such in practice, and consequently she advised nations that 'to prevent the sale of children in the context of altruistic surrogacy' the surrogate must, as in the context of commercial surrogacy arrangements, 'retain parentage and parental

---

[123] UNHRC (n 119) 17–18.
[124] O'Mahony, 'A Review of Children's Rights' (2021) 21; emphasis added.
[125] Law Commission (n 66) 155.
[126] O'Mahony (n 94) 22.
[127] UNHRC (n 119) 16.
[128] ibid.

responsibility at birth'.[129] Indeed, in states where altruistic surrogacy is regulated, evidence suggests that, in practice, it is rarely of the truly altruistic variety. In the UK, despite operating an altruistic domestic surrogacy regime, the law allows for the very broad and undefined payment of 'expenses reasonably incurred' to the surrogate and, as Fenton-Glynn and Scherpe observe, 'payment for services of surrogates is being hidden behind the shield of undefined and unmonitored "expenses"'.[130] Indeed, as far back as 1998, the Brazier Report pointed out that in the UK, 'in many cases a component of the amount paid to the surrogate mother is a direct payment for services rendered rather than the reimbursement of actual expenses'.[131]

Nonetheless, the UN Special Rapporteur provided some regulatory guidance for states operating (or contemplating) altruistic surrogacy regimes which, *in principle*, seeks to ensure that altruistic surrogacy regimes operate as such

> it is necessary to appropriately regulate altruistic surrogacy to avoid the sale of children. Courts or other competent authorities must require all 'reimbursements' to surrogate mothers to be reasonable and itemized, as otherwise 'reimbursements' may be disguised payments for transfer of the child.[132]

Ireland's proposed, strict legislative approach to the payment of 'reasonable expenses' is very much in line with the approach suggested by the UN Special Rapporteur when compared to the current approach to expenses in the UK. In Ireland, section 55 of the 2022 Bill proposes to tightly control the reasonable expenses that can be paid to the surrogate by the intended parents by providing that these must be 'verified by receipts or other documentation' and, therefore, altruistic surrogacy *as contemplated by* the Bill would not be in breach of the Optional Protocol.[133] However, despite the different legislative approaches to expenses in the UK and Ireland, neither jurisdiction can really ensure that altruistic surrogacy is taking place *in practice* because the surrogate's 'expenses' will only come to be properly scrutinised by a court during a post-birth application for a Parental Order.[134] Irrespective of the payment of expenses or beyond, Fenton-Glynn and Scherpe observe that 'when presented with the "result" of a commercial surrogacy, i.e. the child, the courts will virtually always be compelled

---

[129] ibid, 19.

[130] Scherpe and Fenton-Glynn (n 120) 580.

[131] In 1997, the Labour Government asked Margaret Brazier to chair a group that would review surrogacy laws. This resulted in the publication of the Brazier Report in 1998. See M Brazier, A Campbell and S Golombok, 'Surrogacy: Review for Health Ministers of current Arrangements for Payments and Regulation – Report of the Review Team' (HMSO, 1998) 43.

[132] UNHRC (n 119) 16.

[133] O'Mahony made the same astute observation about altruistic surrogacy as contemplated by the Bill's predecessor, the General Scheme: see O'Mahony (n 94) 21.

[134] Law Commission (n 66) 363-64. As noted by the Law Commissions, 'there is no effective means to enforce the limitation on payments to reasonable expenses' in the UK, because all 'expenses reasonably incurred' are only considered by a court during a post-birth application for a Parental Order. At that stage, as pointed out by the Law Commissions 'the paramount consideration of the welfare of the child will point to the award of a Parental Order in all but the most egregious case'.

to make the Parental Order'.[135] Thus, Fenton-Glynn and Scherpe outline the 'futility' of the UK's current 'post-birth Parental Order' approach to surrogacy, because

> once the child is in existence, and has been handed over to the commissioning parents, it is rarely going to be in the child's best interests not to legally recognise that factual tie – no matter what the conduct of the commissioning parents has been.[136]

The authors conclude that 'the interests of the child – who is an innocent party in all this – must dictate the outcome, meaning that other policy considerations give way to legal certainty regarding parenthood and identity'.[137] Indeed, Fenton-Glynn observes that in the UK, no application for a Parental Order has been refused by the courts on the grounds of payments going beyond reasonable expenses.[138]

In Ireland, section 63 of the Bill states that a court may grant a post-birth Parental Order if the surrogacy met all of the requirements in section 50, one of which is that the surrogacy arrangement must be *non-commercial*. In order to determine this the court would most likely seek to review the verified expenses. Nonetheless, akin to the UK at present, it is submitted that it is extremely unlikely that parental orders would be refused by the courts in Ireland on the basis of excessive payments to the surrogate, because in a majority of cases this would not be in the best interests of the child. Indeed, where the surrogate-born child is in the care of its intended parents, refusing a post-birth Parental Order may even impinge on its constitutional right to family life in Article 42A.[139] Thus, in practice, 'altruistic' surrogacy in Ireland may prove to be similar to other jurisdictions and involve compensation that goes far beyond reasonable expenses, rendering the Bill's ban on domestic, commercial (or at the very least, compensated) surrogacy largely ineffective. Indeed, O'Mahony seems to be acutely aware that although the type of altruistic surrogacy model contemplated by the Bill does not amount to the sale of children, *in practice* 'post-birth court proceedings are not an effective vehicle for preventing illicit payments being made to surrogates'.[140]

---

[135] Scherpe and Fenton-Glynn (n 120) 570.

[136] ibid, 554.

[137] ibid, 569.

[138] C Fenton-Glynn, 'The Regulation and Recognition of Surrogacy under English Law: an Overview of the Case Law (2015) 27 *Child and Family Law Quarterly* 83, 87. Indeed, Emily Jackson has argued that because of this judicial approach, 'the UK's prohibition on commercial surrogacy is, therefore, completely ineffective'. See E Jackson, 'Assisted Conception and Surrogacy in the United Kingdom' in J Eekelaar and R George (eds), *Routledge Handbook of Family Law and Policy* (London, Routledge, 2014) 189, 198.

[139] G Shannon, *Child Law*, 2nd edn (Dublin, Thomson Round Hall, 2010) 36. Shannon has suggested that a child may enjoy a 'natural constitutional right to family life pursuant to Article 42A.1'.

[140] O' Mahony (n 94) 23. However, there is evidence from Greece indicating that pre-conception court proceedings approving surrogacy agreements and the transfer of parentage are equally as ineffective as post-birth court proceedings at preventing any illicit payments being made to surrogates. Despite commercial surrogacy being prohibited by the relevant part of the Greek Civil Code, and the requirement for surrogacy agreements to be pre-authorised by a court before the parties can proceed with any treatment, Zervogianni observes that in Greece 'it is doubtful if parties actually comply with the prohibition of remuneration' and that 'practice has shown that the provisions on altruistic surrogacy are

X. Proposals for Allocating Parentage via Pre-Conception Authorisation in the UK and Ireland

Despite the above observations by the UN Special Rapporteur regarding the allocation of legal parentage at birth in altruistic surrogacy regimes, proposals for the allocation of parentage in cases of domestic, altruistic surrogacy by the Law Commissions in the UK and the Special Rapporteur for Child Protection in Ireland, Professor Conor O'Mahony, respectively, still favour the pre-conception allocation of parentage in favour of intended parents by either administrative (UK) or judicial means (Ireland). However, these proposals enable the surrogate to dispute legal parentage post-birth, and are thus mindful of the need to avoid a breach of the Optional Protocol on the sale of children.

A. Proposals Regarding Legal Parentage in Surrogacy Arrangements in the UK

As demonstrated, in Ireland the Bill's proposal to allocate parentage via a 'post-birth Parental Order' model mirrors the current UK legislation on surrogacy; however, this proposal is completely out of sync with the proposal for law reform previously made by the Law Commissions in their consultation paper in 2019. In the UK, the Law Commissions propose a 'new pathway' to parentage involving the 'pre-authorisation' of a domestic surrogacy agreement by a regulatory body prior to conception. The parties to the agreement must comply with certain procedural safeguards, including implications counselling, independent legal advice and criminal record checks.[141] Following 'pre-authorisation' of their agreement, *by operation of law* the intended parents will be the legal parents of the child *at birth*.[142] However, this is subject to the surrogate's right to object to the intended parents' legal parentage for a certain period after the birth. If the surrogate objects, the Law Commissions propose that the surrogacy arrangement will exit the 'new pathway' and fall under the existing law – the surrogate will automatically be the

---

rather unenforceable'. In Greece, a surrogate can be compensated for lost profits due to the pregnancy, to a maximum value of €10,000, but there is evidence to suggest that, *in practice*, the remuneration of surrogates there is between €20,000-€40,000: see Zervogianni, 'Greece' (2019) 151.

[141] All of these pre-surrogacy safeguards are contained in the Health (Assisted Human Reproduction) Bill 2022.

[142] Parentage will arise by operation of law rather than via enforcement of the parties' surrogacy agreement. Indeed, in 2015, the Surrogacy UK Working Group on Surrogacy Law Reform advocated in its report for a move away from the 'post-birth Parental Order' model, and for the law to instead move towards the pre-authorisation of surrogacy arrangements so that legal parenthood can be conferred on intending parents at birth: see Surrogacy UK, 'Surrogacy in the UK' (2015) 39. Academic commentators in the UK also favour a pre-conception model of surrogacy regulation: see A Alghrani and D Griffiths, 'The Regulation of Surrogacy in the United Kingdom: The Case for Reform' (2017) 29 *Child and Family Law Quarterly* 165.

legal parent of the child and the intended parents will have to apply for a Parental Order in order to establish their legal parentage.[143]

The Law Commissions' proposal that a surrogate should have a right to object after the birth appears to be heavily influenced by the UN Special Rapporteur's recommendations. The Law Commissions wish to 'ensure that the law respects the autonomy of women who become surrogates to make their own decisions',[144] and they are very much of the view that 'The right for the surrogate to object to the intended parents acquiring legal parenthood automatically, on the birth of the child, ensures respect for the surrogate's wishes and intentions *at that stage*'.[145] The Law Commissions' reasoning in the consultation paper is remarkably similar to that of the UN Special Rapporteur in her report because the latter spoke of the need to respect the surrogate's 'post-birth intentions' as regards parentage. Indeed, the Law Commissions emphasise that under their proposed 'new pathway', the surrogate's right to object to the allocation of parentage in favour of the intended parents is 'in order for the new pathway to respect the rights of the surrogate *and international law*'.[146]

This is not to suggest that the Law Commissions' proposal is not to be welcomed – it represents something of a balance between the competing concerns of avoiding the sale of children and potentially breaching international law, and respecting the actual intentions of the parties to the surrogacy arrangement as regards parentage of the surrogate-born child. In fact, it could be argued that in light of the UN Special Rapporteur's recommendations, the Law Commissions' proposal is rather bold because it makes the intended parents, rather than the surrogate, the child's legal parents at birth. Nonetheless, by respecting a potential change in the surrogate's post-birth intentions and allowing her the right to object to the allocation of parentage in favour of the intended parents, the spirit of the UN Special Rapporteur's recommendations is arguably being complied with. Indeed, the Law Commissions' reason for this divergence is logical in light of the pre-surrogacy legislative safeguards that will have been complied with by the 'pre-authorisation' stage, because

> given that the surrogate will have been involved in a regulated process, where she is aware of her right to object, we do not believe that a situation where a surrogate must positively raise an objection, rather than positively consent, infringes her rights.[147]

---

[143] Law Commission (n 66) 164.

[144] The Law Commissions' reasoning here is somewhat incongruous given that, elsewhere in their paper, they stated that 'the views of surrogates', that they do not consider themselves to be the legal mother of the child at birth, were a 'powerful and persuasive factor' in their provisional proposal of a 'new pathway' to parentage. However, enabling the surrogate to seek to be a legal parent of the child after birth indicates that surrogates' own views as to *their* preferred legal status at birth were not nearly as 'powerful and persuasive' as the UN Special Rapporteur's view concerning their post-birth status, it seems: see Law Commission (n 66) 182.

[145] ibid, 181.

[146] ibid, 162.

[147] Law Commission (n 66) 163.

B. Proposals Regarding Legal Parentage in Surrogacy Arrangements in Ireland

Although the 2022 Bill does not propose to allocate parentage in favour of the intended parents at the pre-conception stage, O'Mahony argues in favour of pre-conception authorisation of surrogacy arrangements in Ireland, akin to what is being proposed in the UK

However, O'Mahony proposes that the pre-conception transfer of legal parentage could instead be effected by a court order and, consequently 'pre-conception authorisation and transfer of parentage in properly regulated domestic altruistic surrogacy arrangements does not amount to sale of children'.[148] To further comply with the UN Special Rapporteur's recommendations, O'Mahony suggests that provision could be made in Irish law for the surrogate to raise an objection to the pre-conception judicial transfer of parentage within a defined period following the child's birth, 'in which case it would be for a court to decide whether the child's best interests require that the transfer of parentage be reversed'.[149] Therefore, akin to the Law Commissions', O'Mahony is also mindful of the Special Rapporteur's interpretation of the Optional Protocol and his proposal is somewhat sensitive to the need for Ireland's proposed altruistic surrogacy regime to respect international law.

However, there are notable differences between O'Mahony's proposal and that of the Law Commissions, and it is submitted that the latter proposal is preferable and more likely to be in compliance with international law obligations. While both proposals recognise the surrogate's right to object to the allocation of parentage, under the Law Commissions' proposal, the surrogate can object after birth simply by writing to the intended parents and the body responsible for overseeing the surrogacy agreement.[150] Legal parentage of the child *automatically* reverts to the surrogate and the onus is on the intended parents to initiate court proceedings for a parental order in respect of the child.[151] Under O'Mahony's proposal, the surrogate can object post-birth, but the pre-conception, *court ordered* transfer of parentage would appear to remain in place unless and until the court decides that the best interests of the child require this to be reversed.[152] Thus, it appears that the onus is on the surrogate to make an objection by initiating costly court proceedings *and* she must then demonstrate in court that the pre-conception order allocating parentage should be quashed. The upshot of O'Mahony's proposal is that not only is the surrogate not a legal parent at birth, but a lot of affirmative action is required on her part to try to acquire that status, and the added expense of initiating court proceedings might disproportionately infringe her ability to actually *exercise* her

---

[148] O'Mahony (n 94) 23.
[149] ibid.
[150] Law Commission (n 66) 163.
[151] ibid, 164
[152] O'Mahony (n 94) 23.

post-birth right to object. This might not be in keeping with the spirit of the UN Special Rapporteur's recommendations.[153]

XI. The AHRRA – An Administrative Route to Legal Parentage

I agree with O'Mahony's suggestion that parentage in altruistic surrogacy cases should be regulated at the pre-conception stage.[154] However, whereas O'Mahony proposes that the surrogacy arrangement between the parties should be approved, and legal parentage transferred by the District Court prior to the conception of the child, I believe that these functions would be more suited to the AHRRA, or a legal and ethical division thereof, pre-conception, but understand that O'Mahony's proposal might be based on the simple fact that the AHRRA has not yet been established.[155] Nonetheless, once it is established, I believe that it should carry out these functions, because all surrogacy arrangements could then be approved by a single body with relevant expertise in the area of assisted human reproduction. In Israel, for example, the Approvals Committee that is responsible for the 'pre-authorisation' of surrogacy arrangements consists of, inter alia, doctors with expertise in gynaecology and obstetrics and internal medicine; a clinical psychologist; a social worker and a lawyer. In New Zealand, the Ethics Committee on Assisted Reproductive Technology (ECART) 'comprises of members with expertise in assisted reproductive procedures, human reproductive research, ethics and law, as well as members with the ability to articulate issues from a consumer perspective and a disability perspective'.[156] It is submitted that the AHRRA could form a similar approvals committee that could meet on a quarterly basis, or more frequently if necessary, to evaluate any domestic surrogacy arrangements that are submitted to it.[157]

---

[153] O'Mahony does however offer an alternative proposal based partly on the models of surrogacy regulation that operate in Ontario and British Columbia. O'Mahony argues that pre-conception authorisation of a surrogacy agreement and a Parental Order for the intended parents could be made by the court at the same time, *but with* the surrogate retaining parentage and guardianship at birth such that the child would have three parents/guardians until such time as the surrogate consents to relinquishing her parental rights through a post-birth administrative process. It is submitted that this model, which appears to involve both court-based *and* administrative processes, is complex and unlikely to encourage intended parents, most of whom seek legal certainty, to avail of domestic surrogacy arrangements. However, it would appear to be very much in compliance with the UN Special Rapporteur's recommendations which do not envisage intended parents having exclusive legal parentage of the child at birth in any event: see O'Mahony (n 94) 24.

[154] This author has long-since favoured the pre-conception/pre-birth model for regulating domestic surrogacy: see Tobin (n 56) above: B Tobin, 'An Appraisal of Ireland's Current Legislative Proposals' (2019). Bracken also favours pre-conception authorisation of domestic surrogacy arrangements in Ireland: see Bracken, *Same-Sex Parenting* (2019) 232.

[155] However, the Health (Assisted Human Reproduction) Bill 2022, Pt 8 provides for the establishment of the AHRRA, and the Bill is currently being debated in the Oireachtas.

[156] See New Zealand Law Commission (n 43) 69.

[157] It is submitted that home-insemination agreements could also be approved at such meetings; see pp 134–135 of this chapter.

A. Recent Recommendations of the New Zealand Law Commission

At present, this might seem like a somewhat novel suggestion – in those jurisdictions where an administrative body is responsible for *pre-authorising* a surrogacy arrangement, an affirmative decision from that body does not result in the allocation of legal parentage in favour of the intended parents at birth. In New Zealand, Israel and the Australian States of Victoria and Western Australia, all of which have administrative bodies that pre-authorise surrogacy arrangements, the intended parents must currently apply to the court to have their parentage confirmed after the birth of the child. However, in the UK, the Law Commissions have proposed that the 'new pathway' to parentage should enable a medical or administrative body such as a regulated clinic or a regulated surrogacy organisation to pre-authorise a surrogacy agreement, after which the intended parents will become the legal parents at birth by operation of law.[158]

Similarly, in May 2022, the New Zealand Law Commission recommended, in its ultimate report on surrogacy, that the law in that jurisdiction could be changed such that legal parentage in domestic surrogacy situations might be determined by a fully administrative process overseen by the ECART, a body that is New Zealand's equivalent of the AHRRA.[159] Under these proposals, there would be no need for the intended parents to apply to the court for a post-birth parental order transferring parentage. Essentially, for domestic surrogacy arrangements that have been ECART-approved, the surrogate will be the legal mother at birth, and the intended parents will be additional legal guardians of the child until the surrogate consents to the transfer of parentage via a standard form statutory declaration.[160] The surrogate cannot consent until the child is at least seven days old, and her consent must be witnessed by her lawyer, who would be required to certify on the standard form that they have explained the effect and implications of the statutory declaration to the surrogate.[161] Nonetheless, once the surrogate provides valid consent, the transfer of parentage to the intended parents by operation of law is complete.[162]

The New Zealand Law Commission favours an administrative route to legal parentage in domestic surrogacy arrangements that is likely to be attractive to intended parents because it removes the need for a post-birth court process. However, by proposing that the surrogate will be a legal parent and guardian at birth and must *confirm* her consent to the transfer of parentage, the New Zealand Law Commission errs more on the side of caution as regards compliance with

---

[158] Law Commission (n 66) 156–58.
[159] See New Zealand Law Commission (n 43) 194–95.
[160] In New Zealand, the parties are required to have received counselling and independent legal advice before the ECART can approve their gestational surrogacy agreement: see New Zealand Law Commission (n 43) 99–100.
[161] ibid, 194–95.
[162] The intended parents must have taken the child into their care in order for the administrative route to the transfer of parentage by operation of law to be effective.

international law obligations when compared to the earlier proposals by the Law Commissions in the UK, where the surrogate would not be a legal parent at birth and would be required to *revoke* her pre-conception consent to the transfer of parentage, albeit that she can do so rather swiftly and easily.[163]

It is opined that Ireland could follow suit by realising the potential of the AHRRA and enabling it to 'pre-authorise' surrogacy arrangements; subsequently, by operation of law, parentage could similarly be established in favour of the intended parents at or after birth, subject to the surrogate's confirmation (or revocation) of consent after a 'cooling off' period. It is submitted that a fully administrative route to legal parentage, with an AHRRA that ensures robust pre-surrogacy safeguards for the parties are complied with, would make domestic surrogacy more attractive than the current proposals in Part 7 of the 2022 Bill.

B. Pre-Birth Court Orders Establishing Legal Parentage

There may be a preference in some quarters for legal parentage to be decided by a court, rather than a regulatory body, pre-conception. However, the Law Commissions were 'concerned about the ability of the court to make an order before birth in respect of a child not yet born', and this author agrees.[164] Permitting the AHRRA to approve surrogacy arrangements and for legal parentage to subsequently arise in favour of the intended parents simply by operation of law at birth is arguably more appealing in a jurisdiction that is legislating for surrogacy for the first time. Where parentage arises at birth by virtue of a court order (even though parentage also arises in this instance by operation of law) it might create the sense among the general public that women who act as surrogates are *bound* to hand over the child because this is what has been dictated by a court at the pre-conception stage. Further, a surrogate might be less willing to invoke her post-birth right to object in a situation where a court order has previously allocated parentage, and it would appear to be difficult in practice to *exercise* the right to object in this context.

In addition, the District Court is by far the busiest tier of the court system, 'having handled 82% of the work of the courts system' in 2021.[165] Indeed, the District Court's 'increasing caseloads have not been met with greater investment in judges and staff', thus one wonders whether a timely hearing to approve the surrogacy arrangement and approve parentage at the pre-conception stage might

---

[163] However, it should be noted that either approach to legal parentage would appear to be in compliance with international best practice as outlined in the Verona Principles. See Principles for the Protection of the Rights of the Child born through Surrogacy (Verona Principles), Principle 10, available at www.iss-ssi.org/images/Surrogacy/VeronaPrinciples_25February2021.pdf.

[164] Law Commission (n 66) 149.

[165] See 'The Irish Times View on The District Court: Ripe for Reform' *Irish Times* (21 January 2022), available at www.irishtimes.com/opinion/editorial/the-irish-times-view-on-the-district-court-ripe-for-reform-1.4782642.

even be a possibility.[166] O'Mahony appears to be very much aware of this dilemma, adding that if his recommendation for a 'judicial model' was legislated for, then 'provision will need to be made to avoid undue delay in the hearing of court applications relating to surrogacy arrangements'.[167] However, it is arguable that it is neither possible nor desirable to make such special provision in respect of matters pertaining to a child that has not even been conceived yet, when the Irish Human Rights and Equality Commission (IHREC) has observed that the current Irish system of family law proceedings is 'marked by chronic delays in court proceedings, repeat adjournments, crowded lists, excessive caseloads, delays in conducting assessments of children and adults'.[168] IHREC has also raised concern about 'the unsuitability of the physical facilities in a number of courts for children and families due to issues including inadequate separation from other court proceedings, such as criminal proceedings'.[169]

Thus, once established, the AHRRA is the appropriate body to carry out the pre-authorisation of surrogacy arrangements *in tandem* with pre-authorisation of the child's legal parentage. Further, the surrogate should be able to exercise her right to object to the allocation of parentage within a certain period after the birth of the child simply by writing to the AHRRA, and the latter should duly notify the intended parents, who should in turn be able to apply to the court for a Parental Order in respect of the child. This process would easily facilitate the surrogate's right to object should she wish to exercise it, is consistent with a similar proposal in the UK, and is likely to be compliant with the spirit of the UN Special Rapporteur's recommendations, as well as the Verona Principles.[170] Alternatively, the somewhat similar administrative approach to parentage recommended by the New Zealand Law Commission could be adopted in Ireland.

XII. The Verona Principles

The Hague Conference on Private International Law is currently examining private international law issues in relation to legal parentage, including the issues arising from international surrogacy arrangements. In 2015, an Experts' Group was convened and is currently focused on developing a general private international law instrument on legal parentage, as well as a separate protocol on legal parentage established as a result of international surrogacy arrangements. The Experts'

---

[166] ibid.

[167] O'Mahony (n 94) 17.

[168] IHREC, 'Submission on the General Scheme of the Family Court Bill 2020' (IHREC, 2021) 3–4, available at www.ihrec.ie/app/uploads/2021/08/Submission-on-the-General-Scheme-of-the-Family-Court-Bill-2020-Final.pdf.

[169] ibid. The General Scheme of the Family Court Bill 2020 provides for the establishment of a District Family Court, a Circuit Family Court, and a Family High Court as divisions within the existing court structures, and these 'family courts', if established, will have specialist judges.

[170] See Verona Principles (n 163), Principle 10.

Group is expected to submit its final report to the Hague Conference in 2023.[171] In the absence of an international treaty or convention that deals with legal parentage and surrogacy, states must decide how best to regulate domestic and international surrogacy arrangements under their own domestic laws, and the Verona Principles are instructive in that regard.

In her 2018 report, the UN Special Rapporteur urged the international community to 'support the work of the International Social Service in developing international principles and standards governing surrogacy arrangements'.[172] The Verona Principles, a set of non-binding international principles which, in the words of the UN Committee on the Rights of the Child, are designed to contribute 'to developing normative guidance for the protection of the rights of children born through surrogacy' and 'may serve as an important tool that will help identify appropriate legislative responses to the new challenge related to the protection of children's rights' in the context of surrogacy',[173] were published by the International Social Service (ISS) in 2021. The Principles contemplate that states can provide intended parents with exclusive legal parentage and parental responsibility by operation of law at birth, but only if the following two conditions are met: the surrogate must confirm consent post-birth; and a post-birth best interests of the child determination must not be required.[174] According to the principles, the main reasons why a post-birth best interests of the child determination might be necessary are where there 'have not been adequate pre-surrogacy arrangements' or 'if the surrogate mother either revokes consent or fails to confirm consent', or where the surrogacy arrangement is an *international* one. Thus, it would appear that pre-conception authorisations of domestic surrogacy arrangements and legal parentage with built-in pre-surrogacy safeguards for the parties, coupled with a process that easily facilitates the surrogate's post-birth right to object to (or confirm) the earlier determination of parentage, is in compliance with the Verona Principles. Although only recently published, the Verona Principles are already having a notable impact on national surrogacy law reform efforts.[175]

However, the Verona Principles are non-binding guiding principles to which states may have recourse when enacting or amending surrogacy laws. The Optional Protocol is also non-binding in Ireland as it has not yet been ratified, but the Oireachtas is likely to be cognisant of any potential future international law obligations when legislating for domestic surrogacy. Ironically, the UN Special Rapporteur's interpretation of the Optional Protocol could arguably justify a

---

[171] See www.hcch.net/en/projects/legislative-projects/parentage-surrogacy.

[172] See UNHRC (n 119) 20.

[173] See Verona Principles (n 163) 3.

[174] The Verona Principles seem to envisage that states can provide for the surrogate to either expressly confirm consent after birth, akin to what is proposed in New Zealand, or tacitly confirm consent after birth by not exercising her right to revoke consent within a specified time period, akin to what is proposed in the UK. See Verona Principles, Principles 10.5 and 10.6 (n 163).

[175] See generally, New Zealand Law Commission (n 43).

decision by the state to forge ahead with the 'post-birth parental order' model for establishing parentage in altruistic surrogacy cases. Indeed, upon the publication of the Bill's predecessor, the General Scheme, officials from the Department of Health, which is responsible for the drafting of both documents, were wedded to the notion that the surrogate should be recognised as the child's mother at birth. In 2018, Department of Health officials were invited to address the Oireachtas Joint Committee on Health as regards the provisions of the Bill's predecessor, the General Scheme, and it was stated by Geraldine Luddy that 'in this country, the birth mother is the mother. That is not changed in surrogacy cases in the scheme. The surrogate must transfer her right. If she does not do so, she remains the mother'.[176]

The Department of Health's Dr Tony Holohan also reinforced this stance when questioned:

> The scheme clearly provides that at the point of birth, the Latin principle is *mater semper certa est*, or motherhood is always certain. The birth mother is the mother until such time as she goes through or consents to the parental order process through the courts.[177]

This policy position was not in any way based on the UN Special Rapporteur's report, as it had not been published at the time, but rather, as discussed earlier in this chapter, a somewhat flawed interpretation of the Supreme Court's judgment in *MR v An t-Ard Chláratheoir*.[178] Nonetheless, as evident from Part 7 of the Bill, this approach to parentage in surrogacy is still favoured by the Department of Health and, ironically, it is arguably now supported by the UN Special Rapporteur's interpretation of the Optional Protocol, and the Verona Principles also contemplate that states can choose to make the surrogate the legal mother at birth.[179]

XIII. International Surrogacy

The majority of Irish couples who need to have a child through surrogacy avail themselves of such services internationally in countries such as the US, Canada and the Ukraine. However, for those intended parents who have gone and will continue to go abroad for surrogacy, Part 7 does not propose to establish any legal mechanism whereby an intended mother or, in a same-sex relationship, a non-genetic intended father, can establish parentage in relation to the child upon their return to Ireland. This means that the current status quo will prevail and Irish

---

[176] Committee Debates, Joint Committee on Health, 17 January 2018, available at www.oireachtas.ie/en/debates/debate/joint_committee_on_health/2018-01-17/3.
[177] ibid.
[178] *MR v An t-Ard Chláraitheoir* [2014] IESC 60.
[179] See Verona Principles, Principle 10 (n 163).

law will continue to recognise the surrogate – the woman who gives birth to the child – as its mother.[180] An intended father can be recognised as a parent and guardian following a successful court application, but only where he is the genetic father of the child.[181] A child born through international surrogacy is unable to have their intended mother recognised as their legal mother under Irish law, even where she has provided the ova used to help form the embryo(s) carried by the surrogate. Similarly, a non-genetic intended father cannot be recognised as a parent of a child born via an international surrogacy arrangement. The intended mother or non-genetic intended father can apply for second-parent adoption, but only a minimum of two years after the birth of the child.[182] They can also apply to be appointed as a guardian of the child by a court, but again they can only do so a minimum of two years after the child's birth if they are either married to, in a civil partnership with, or cohabiting with the genetic parent of the child.[183] However, unlike parentage, guardianship rights end when the child reaches the age of 18.[184] As outlined in the next chapter, the two-year waiting period before second-parent adoption or guardianship can be applied for in surrogacy situations may be contrary to the child's rights under Article 8 ECHR.

The Joint Committee on Health carried out pre-legislative scrutiny of the General Scheme, the predecessor to the Bill and, in July 2019, published its 'Report on Pre-Legislative Scrutiny of the General Scheme of the Assisted Human Reproduction Bill', in which it merely recommended that 'further consideration' be given to the surrogacy provisions therein, in particular to parentage issues which may arise for children born via international surrogacy.[185] Nonetheless, Part 7 of the Bill, which recently succeeded the General Scheme, does not contain any provisions relating to international surrogacy.

---

[180] *MR v An t-Ard Chláraitheoir* [2014] IESC 60.

[181] See the Status of Children Act 1987, s 35, and the Guardianship of Infants Act 1964, s 6, as inserted by the Status of Children Act 1987, s 11.

[182] See the Adoption Act 2010, s 37, as inserted by the Adoption (Amendment) Act 2017, s 18.

[183] See CFRA 2015, s 49, which inserted s 6C into the Guardianship of Infants Act 1964. This lengthy waiting period could have significant consequences where the genetic father and the intended mother/intended father are in disagreement about important decisions that need to be made in relation to the child's welfare before the intended mother/intended father acquires guardianship, because only a guardian can make decisions about the most crucial and important aspects of a child's upbringing, and the genetic father will be the child's sole guardian.

[184] While few parentage rights extend into adulthood in any event, the legal status of 'parent' can hold significant symbolic importance for many persons and couples.

[185] See Joint Committee on Health, 'Report on Pre-Legislative Scrutiny of the General Scheme of the Assisted Human Reproduction Bill' (July 2019) 22, available at: data.oireachtas.ie/ie/oireachtas/committee/dail/32/joint_committee_on_health/reports/2019/2019-07-10_report-on-pre-legislative-scrutiny-of-the-general-scheme-of-the-assisted-human-reproduction-bill_en.pdf. During pre-legislative scrutiny, officials from the Department of Health were not questioned by the members of the Joint Committee on Health as to why international surrogacy arrangements were excluded from the General Scheme, and they provided no explanation as to why the General Scheme ignores such arrangements: see www.oireachtas.ie/en/debates/debate/joint_committee_on_health/2018-01-17/3/?highlight%5B0%5D=legislation&highlight%5B1%5D=ahr&highlight%5B2%5D=ahr&highlight%5B3%5D=legislation&highlight%5B4%5D=ahr&highlight%5B5%5D=legislation&highlight%5B6%5D=legislation&highlight%5B7%5D=ahr&highlight%5B8%5D=legislation.

A. Legislating for Pre-Commencement International Surrogacy Arrangements

However, the Oireachtas had previously given some consideration to this issue, because the surrogacy provisions deleted from the original General Scheme of the Children and Family Relationships Bill, published in January 2014, proposed to regulate domestic surrogacy and *some* international surrogacy arrangements. These provisions stipulated that, provided they were married to or in a civil partnership or cohabiting with the child's genetic male parent, an intended parent of a child born through a 'pre-commencement surrogacy arrangement' could apply to the court to be recognised as a legal parent.[186] The surrogate's consent to the declaration of parentage would have been essential. In addition, the provisions would have applied only if the surrogate was a gestational surrogate and an application would have had to be made within two years of commencement. The provisions would have applied to 'pre-commencement surrogacy agreements' where the child was born either within or outside of the state, but if the child was born outside of Ireland the intended parent would have needed to be an Irish citizen or ordinarily resident in the State for the court to exercise jurisdiction.[187] The provisions clearly envisaged the regulation of *international commercial* pre-commencement surrogacy arrangements by purporting to recognise the parentage of children born outside of the state, even in cases where the surrogate received a fee, because they stipulated that the court would only refuse to grant a declaration of parentage where a payment was made in respect of an arrangement entered into *after commencement*. However, there is nothing in Part 7 of the 2022 Bill that resembles these provisions to regulate parentage in the context of international pre-commencement surrogacy arrangements.

B. Legislating for International Surrogacy: Legally and Ethically Complex

The failure in Part 7 of the Bill to provide a legal mechanism by which an intended parent of a child born through international surrogacy can have their parentage recognised under Irish law could also be regarded as being *somewhat* inconsistent with sections 20-21 of the CFRA 2015, which enable the legal recognition of the parentage of a child conceived via a DAHR procedure carried out abroad *pre-commencement*. Indeed, in February 2019, LGBT Ireland argued before the Joint Committee on Health that in the Bill's predecessor, the General Scheme, 'a similar

---

[186] See General Scheme of the Children and Family Relationships Bill 2014, available at: www.justice.ie/en/JELR/General%20Scheme%20of%20a%20Children%20and%20Family%20Relationships%20Bill.pdf/Files/General%20Scheme%20of%20a%20Children%20and%20Family%20Relationships%20Bill.pdf.
[187] ibid.

process to that which applies in cases of DAHR should be allowed for cases of surrogacy' to 'create parity in our legislation'.[188] However, international DAHR procedures and international surrogacy are rather different. A child conceived through a DAHR procedure abroad will usually be born in Ireland. Indeed, the provisions in the 2015 Act stipulate that while the child can be conceived abroad, they *must* have been born in Ireland.[189] A child conceived with the assistance of a foreign surrogate will almost indubitably not have been born in Ireland, so the legislation would have to differ in that respect and allow for the child to be born abroad. Further, those countries that regulate surrogacy can differ remarkably and children born to Irish parents via international surrogacy are often born in countries that permit commercial surrogacy arrangements to take place.[190] As Zervogianni observes, 'in many countries there is a correlation between exploitation of women and commercial surrogacy. This has been the case in Thailand and India, and both ended up prohibiting international surrogacy agreements'.[191] The Law Commission of England and Wales notes that there have also been concerning reports about the treatment of surrogates in the Ukraine, a commercial surrogacy destination that has proven hugely popular with Irish intended parents in particular.[192] In light of these ethical concerns, it is more difficult to critique the state's willingness under the 2015 Act to regulate the parentage of a child born in Ireland following a DAHR procedure that was carried out abroad, and its silence in the 2022 Bill on the parentage of children who were born abroad pursuant to international commercial surrogacy arrangements.

If the guidance provided in the Verona Principles is followed, international surrogacy arrangements where 'the specific arrangement' is not permitted by 'at least one State' should be regulated via post-birth proceedings before a court or a competent authority of the state where the intended parents intend to reside with the child. In Ireland, since commercial surrogacy arrangements are not permitted, the principles would undoubtedly require that a post-birth best interests of the child determination should be made by a court in these cases. Indeed, O'Mahony argues that international surrogacy arrangements could be decided by

---

[188] See Joint Committee on Health Debate (27 February 2019), available at: www.oireachtas.ie/en/debates/debate/joint_committee_on_health/2019-02-27/2/?highlight%5B0%5D=general&highlight%5B1%5D=scheme&highlight%5B2%5D=assisted&highlight%5B3%5D=human&highlight%5B4%5D=reproduction&highlight%5B5%5D=bill.

[189] CFRA 2015, s 20(1)(b).

[190] See B Tobin, 'Long-Awaited Surrogacy Laws Still Won't Recognise Many Parents' *TheJournal.ie* (4 March 2019), available at www.thejournal.ie/readme/opinion-long-awaited-surrogacy-laws-still-wont-recognise-many-parents-4513551-Mar2019.

[191] E Zervogianni, 'Lessons Drawn from the Regulation of Surrogacy in Greece, Cyprus and Portugal, or a Plea for the Regulation of Commercial Gestational Surrogacy' (2019) 33 *International Journal of Law, Policy and the Family* 160, 164. In 2015, Golombok noted that 'Indian surrogates often live in "surrogacy houses" away from their family during the pregnancy': see Golombok (n 10) 121.

[192] See Law Commission (n 66) 35-36. 68% of surrogacies for Irish intended parents are estimated to take place in the Ukraine: see B Tobin, 'Ireland's Approach to Surrogacy Law needs a Rebirth' *Irish Examiner* (28 April 2021), available at www.irishexaminer.com/opinion/commentanalysis/arid-40275641.html.

way of 'post-birth judicial proceedings' to be heard by the High Court before the child enters Ireland. O'Mahony proposes that legislation could permit the High Court to grant a Parental Order in favour of the intended parents, and nationality and citizenship to the child, where the court is satisfied that a range of prescribed criteria have been complied with. The criteria are that the surrogacy arrangement was in full compliance with the law of the state in which it was concluded and that all parties gave a free and informed consent to the arrangement; that at least one intended parent has a genetic link to the child; that the intended parents are suitable parents for the child; that the arrangement did not amount to sale or trafficking of children, and; that it is in the best interests of the child to recognise the arrangement. O'Mahony also proposes that those international surrogacy arrangements that were concluded before any Irish legislation regulating surrogacy comes into effect could be retrospectively recognised via largely the same criteria.[193]

While post-birth best interests of the child determinations and the making of parental orders by a court are a logical means of attempting to regulate international surrogacy situations, and are indeed also favoured in the UK and New Zealand,[194] there are some legal and practical difficulties associated with aspects of O'Mahony's specific proposal for Ireland. Requiring the proceedings to be heard at High Court level before the child can even enter Ireland, while perhaps designed to make international surrogacy less attractive than domestic surrogacy, seems unduly onerous and, as noted by Department of Justice officials at a recent meeting of the Joint Oireachtas Committee on International Surrogacy, could present 'practical and logistical difficulties' where, for example, the family's visa might be running out, or they could be running up accommodation and other costs abroad while awaiting a hearing.[195] Further, in respect of retrospective and prospective international surrogacy arrangements, O'Mahony believes that the court should be satisfied that the surrogacy arrangement *does not amount to sale or trafficking of children*.[196] This criteria appears difficult to satisfy in many cases because the UN Special Rapporteur has indicated that, to avoid a breach of the Optional Protocol on the sale of children, the surrogate's legal and physical transfer of the child after birth must be a gratuitous act rather than one based on a legal

---

[193] The Joint Oireachtas Committee on International Surrogacy published its Final report in July 2022, in which it also recommends accommodating international surrogacy arrangements within a judicial post-birth Parental Order mechanism for establishing parentage, and this would apply to prospective or retrospective arrangements: see Joint Committee on International Surrogacy, 'Final Report of the Joint Committee on International Surrogacy' (Joint Committee on International Surrogacy, 2022), available at data.oireachtas.ie/ie/oireachtas/committee/dail/33/joint_committee_on_international_surrogacy/reports/2022/2022-07-06_final-report-of-the-joint-committee-on-international-surrogacy_en.pdf. At the time of writing, it is uncertain as to whether the Committee's proposals will even be incorporated into the Health (Assisted Human Reproduction) Bill 2022. Hence, consideration of the Committee's proposals is beyond the scope of this work.

[194] ibid, 389. See New Zealand Law Commission (n 96) 7.37–7.40.

[195] See Joint Committee on International Surrogacy debate (7 April 2022), available at www.oireachtas.ie/en/debates/debate/joint_committee_on_international_surrogacy/2022-04-07/3.

[196] O' Mahony (n 94) 37 and 43.

or contractual obligation.[197] However, in 2018, a survey carried out by Families through Surrogacy (now Growing Families), estimated that up to 68 per cent of all surrogacies for Irish couples take place in the Ukraine, a commercial surrogacy destination.[198] Article 123(2) of the Ukrainian Family Code provides that from the moment an ovum conceived by the intended parents is implanted in the gestational surrogate, the intended parents are regarded as the parents of the child.[199] There are no limits on surrogacy-related payments in the Ukraine and the surrogacy contract between the parties is fully enforceable.[200] The surrogate has no post-birth right to object to the allocation of parentage by either Article 123 of the Ukrainian Family code *or* the contract. Thus, it is difficult to see how Ukrainian commercial surrogacy arrangements that have been entered into by a considerable number of Irish intended parents could not be regarded by an Irish court as constituting the sale of children, thus violating the UN Optional Protocol.

While the legal situation in the Ukraine may not be of any concern to same-sex intended parents given that surrogacy there is restricted to opposite-sex married couples, the Family Code of California also allows for properly executed commercial surrogacy contracts to be enforced and for a court order that 'shall terminate any parental rights of the surrogate' to be granted prior to the birth of the child.[201] California is a commercial surrogacy destination that is popular with same-sex couples from Ireland, and surrogacy arrangements entered into there would also appear difficult for an Irish court to reconcile with the Optional Protocol. Indeed, Fenton-Glynn and Scherpe have observed that, in California, 'the obligation to hand over the child is unconditionally enforceable'.[202]

XIV. Should Ireland Follow the Approach to Surrogacy Law Reform in the UK?

Although somewhat understandable in light of the aforementioned legal and ethical concerns, Ireland's unwillingness in both the 2015 Act and the 2022 Bill to regulate the parentage of children who were born through international surrogacy arrangements is dissatisfying from a child-centric perspective. This author has previously called for an equitable and pragmatic solution to this legal and ethical dilemma to be actively pursued.[203]

---

[197] UNHRC (n 119) 17–18.

[198] See B Tobin, 'Long-Awaited Surrogacy Laws Still Won't Recognise Many Parents' (4 March 2019), available at www.thejournal.ie/readme/opinion-long-awaited-surrogacy-laws-still-wont-recognise-many-parents-4513551-Mar2019.

[199] See Family Code of Ukraine, Art 123(2).

[200] www.mondaq.com/family-law/205832/ukrainian-surrogacy-laws.

[201] Family Code, 7962(f)(2) and 7962(i).

[202] See Fenton-Glynn and Scherpe (n 120) 526.

[203] See B Tobin, 'Assisted Reproductive Techniques and Irish Law: No Child left Behind?' (2020) 64 *Irish Jurist* 138, 149. It should be noted that, in its current form, second-parent adoption is not a suitable solution for children who may prospectively be conceived through surrogacy or reciprocal IVF to

On 9 February 2022, a time-limited Oireachtas Joint Committee on International Surrogacy was established in order to consider and make recommendations on measures to address issues arising from international surrogacy arrangements, and it published its Final Report in July 2022, in which it recommended accommodating international surrogacy arrangements within the judicial post-birth Parental Order system.[204]

Nonetheless, the Irish approach to regulating surrogacy has *largely* been characterised by a serious lack of consultation and collaboration when compared to a similar process in the UK. In the UK, the Law Commission of England and Wales included surrogacy as a law reform project in its 13th Programme of Law Reform and, following discussions between the two bodies, the Department of Health and Social Care (DHSC) agreed to support this project. On 6 June 2019, the Law Commission published its aforementioned, detailed Consultation Paper, 'Building Families through Surrogacy: A New Law', which was a joint Consultation Paper in collaboration with the Scottish Law Commission. In preparing this document, the Law Commissions engaged with representatives from the DHSC, relevant government departments and NGOs, and also had discussions with many academics, practitioners and other stakeholders. Following the publication of the Consultation Paper, the Law Commissions invited a broad range of stakeholders and all other interested parties to respond to the recommendations for law reform contained therein. The Law Commissions are currently reviewing these responses and aim to publish a report in late 2022 that will contain recommendations to reform the law on surrogacy in the UK, and a draft standalone Surrogacy Bill for consideration by the UK Government.

In contrast, the Irish Law Reform Commission published its Fifth Programme of Law Reform on 5 June 2019 and, again, surrogacy and DAHR, were nowhere to be found on the reform agenda.[205] It is ironic that the latter Programme was published one day before the UK Law Commissions' comprehensive Consultation Paper on surrogacy.[206] Further, although the Department of Health engaged with the Office of the Attorney General while drafting the General Scheme in 2017,[207] it frustrated a range of stakeholders in Ireland by failing to engage with

---

have their intended parent recognised by law because the child must have lived with the person who is legally recognised as a parent and the intended parent for a minimum period of two years: see the Adoption Act 2010, s 37(b), as amended by the Adoption (Amendment) Act 2017, s 18.

[204] See Joint Committee on International Surrogacy, 'Final Report' (2022).

[205] Law Reform Commission, 'Fifth Programme of Law Reform' (LRC 120-2019), available at: www.lawreform.ie/_fileupload/Programmes%20of%20Law%20Reform/LRC%20120-2019%20-%20 Fifth%20Programme%20of%20Law%20Reform.pdf. The LRC has never included surrogacy and DAHR on any of its Programmes of Law Reform, despite the complex legal issues raised.

[206] For a critique see B Tobin, 'Ireland Should Follow Britain's Lead in Surrogacy Law Reform' *Irish Examiner* (20 June 2019) 11, available at www.irishexaminer.com/breakingnews/views/analysis/ ireland-should-follow-britains-lead-in-surrogacy-law-reform-931778.html.

[207] This was confirmed by Dr Tony Holohan on 27 January 2018 at the Joint Committee on Health's pre-legislative scrutiny session on the General Scheme of the Assisted Human Reproduction Bill 2017, available at www.oireachtas.ie/en/debates/debate/joint_committee_on_health/2018-01-17/3/?highlight %5B0%5D=legislation&highlight%5B1%5D=ahr&highlight%5B2%5D=ahr&highlight%5B3%5D= legislation&highlight%5B4%5D=ahr&highlight%5B5%5D=legislation&highlight%5B6%5D=legislation &highlight%5B7%5D=ahr&highlight%5B8%5D=legislation.

them in any meaningful sense.[208] Subsequently, the Special Rapporteur on Child Protection was engaged to write a review in 2020, but most of the detailed recommendations contained therein were largely ignored. The Health (Assisted Human Reproduction) Bill 2022 does not incorporate the most significant recommendations made by the Special Rapporteur. However, to facilitate its work, the Joint Oireachtas Committee on International Surrogacy was furnished with an Issues Paper relating to international surrogacy, which was jointly prepared by the Departments of Justice, Health, and Children, Equality, Disability, Integration and Youth, which is indicative of a more collaborative approach to the issue by Government.

Nonetheless, it is submitted that, in light of the ongoing, collaborative, robust surrogacy law reform process in the UK, Ireland should consider a similar process. Part 7 of the 2022 Bill should be deleted, allowing the Bill to proceed to enactment so that the AHRRA can finally be established without haste, and other important AHR matters can be regulated. Consideration should be given to formulating a new, standalone Surrogacy Bill for Ireland, which could result from the input of, inter alia, the report of the Special Rapporteur, the abovementioned government departments, the findings of the Oireachtas Joint Committee on International Surrogacy, and engagement by the state with all other relevant stakeholders. A standalone Surrogacy Bill could provide for a more favourable domestic surrogacy regime and a means of addressing the legal parentage of children born via international surrogacy. To my mind greater research, and collaboration between relevant state bodies and actors, NGOs and stakeholders, as well as a thorough appreciation of law reform initiatives that have come or are coming to fruition elsewhere, is essential before legislation regulating an area as complex as surrogacy is advanced in the Oireachtas.[209]

XV. Donor-Assisted Human Reproduction

Parts 2 and 3 of the CFRA 2015 regulate parentage in cases of donor-assisted human reproduction, other than surrogacy. However, home-insemination is not encompassed by these parts of the CFRA 2015, and reciprocal IVF appears

---

[208] At the Joint Committee on Health's pre-legislative scrutiny session on the General Scheme of the Assisted Human Reproduction Bill 2017 on 28 February 2018, Professor Mary Wingfield, Clinical Director at the Merrion Fertility Clinic, stated that 'I think it is fair to say that we are totally frustrated by the lack of common sense in the engagement between the people who are formulating the legislation … and us, the guys at the coalface, who know what the problems are because we are dealing with it day to day. We have asked [the Department of Health] repeatedly to please talk to us. It is a small country. We ask why we cannot have a chat. We do not want to dictate the legislation but we at least want to provide some useful insights. There has been no meaningful interaction at all' (emphasis added). Available at: www.oireachtas.ie/en/debates/debate/joint_committee_on_health/2018-02-28/3/?highlight%5B0%5D=general&highlight%5B1%5D=scheme&highlight%5B2%5D=assisted&highlight%5B3%5D=human&highlight%5B4%5D=reproduction&highlight%5B5%5D=bill.

[209] Tobin, 'Assisted Reproductive Techniques and Irish Law' (2020) 152.

to be excluded. Regarding Parts 2 and 3, the journey from enactment in 2015 to commencement in 2020, is notable. The CFRA 2015 was enacted on 6 April 2015, and at the time the then Minister for Justice and Equality, Frances Fitzgerald, and the then Minister for Health, Leo Varadkar, agreed that Parts 2 and 3 would not be commenced for a minimum period of one year post-enactment.[210] The rationale for this delay was to allow those couples undergoing fertility treatments with anonymous donor gametes to complete their treatment because, once commenced, Part 3 of the Act would prohibit the use of anonymous donor gametes in Irish fertility clinics in order to protect the child's right to knowledge of genetic identity. Minister Fitzgerald believed that this 'transitional period' of a minimum of one year would allow 'for an orderly transition to the new arrangements'.[211]

Nonetheless, more than three years passed before the Oireachtas revisited the matter in 2018, despite much public criticism of the reluctance of successive Ministers for Health to commence Parts 2 and 3 of the CFRA 2015 along the way.[212] In June 2018, the then Minister for Health, Simon Harris, announced that the Oireachtas needed to enact a short piece of amending legislation to correct a number of technical errors contained in the 2015 Act before Parts 2 and 3 could be commenced by ministerial order.[213] Thus, the Children and Family Relationships (Amendment) Act 2018 was enacted in July 2018. However, Parts 2 and 3 of the CFRA 2015 were still not commenced thereafter because, in order for these Parts to be fully effective, Part 9 had to be commenced, and the Minister for Social Protection was responsible for commencing that Part of the CFRA 2015. Essentially, Part 9 enables the persons recognised as the parents of a donor-conceived child by virtue of Parts 2 and 3 to both be registered on the child's birth certificate – it complements those Parts.[214] However, amending legislation was also required to facilitate the commencement of Part 9. Consequently, when the Civil Registration Act 2019 was enacted in May 2019, it made the

---

[210] See comments made by Minister Fitzgerald as the Bill was making its passage through the Oireachtas on 24 March 2015, at www.oireachtas.ie/en/debates/debate/seanad/2015-03-24/13.

[211] ibid.

[212] N Baker, 'Same-Sex Parents 'In Legal Quagmire'' *Irish Examiner* (19 May 2016) 5; B Tobin, 'We Still Don't Have Crucial Parental Rights for Same-Sex Married Couples' *TheJournal.ie* (29 May 2017), available at www.thejournal.ie/readme/opinion-we-still-dont-have-crucial-parental-rights-for-same-sex-married-couples-3410543-May2017;

B Tobin, 'Women in Same-Sex Marriages Still Not Both Officially Parents', *Irish Examiner* (26 June 2018) 11; B Tobin, 'Donor-Conceived Children: It's Time To Ban Anonymous Sperm Donation' *TheJournal. ie* (26 June 2018), available at www.thejournal.ie/readme/donor-conceived-children-its-time-to-ban-anonymous-sperm-donation-4083400-Jun2018.

[213] See 'Ministers Harris and Zappone welcome move to close loophole and allow same-sex couples to legally declare parentage' MerrionStreet.ie (26 June 2018), available at merrionstreet.ie/en/news-room/releases/ministers_harris_and_zappone_welcome_move_to_close_loophole_and_allow_same-sex_couples_to_legally_declare_parentage.html.

[214] The persons recognised as the child's parents by virtue of Pts 2 and 3 are the birth mother and her spouse, civil partner or cohabiting partner of three years or more. Such persons are referred to as the 'intended parents' or the 'commissioning couple' because it is they who 'commission' the DAHR arrangement with the DAHR facility/fertility clinic.

requisite amendments to the CFRA 2015.[215] Section 12 of the 2019 Act inserted section 1(7) into the CFRA 2015 to provide that Part 9 of the CFRA 2015 would be commenced 54 months from the date of enactment, and so Part 9 came into operation in October 2019.[216] In November 2019, the then Minister for Health, Simon Harris, signed the Children and Family Relationships Act (Parts 2 and 3) (Commencement) Order 2019, appointing 4 May 2020 as the date on which Parts 2 and 3 would finally be commenced.[217] Thus, following a lengthy, complex process, Parts 2 and 3 of the CFRA 2015 entered into force on 4 May 2020, more than five years after they were enacted.

A. DAHR and the Recognition of Parentage under the CFRA 2015

Parts 2 and 3 of the CFRA 2015 prospectively regulate DAHR that takes place in a DAHR facility *in Ireland*. These Parts enable an intended parent of a donor-conceived child to be recognised as a second legal parent if certain criteria are fulfilled. An intended parent of a donor-conceived child can now be recognised as a second legal parent at birth once he or she and the child's mother have consented to this outcome by signing the requisite consent forms at the DAHR facility prior to any procedure taking place there.[218] The child must have been born in the state.[219] In addition, only the use of gametes from a non-anonymous donor is permitted so as to protect the child's right to knowledge of identity.[220] Previously, donor gametes used in DAHR procedures in Irish fertility clinics were often imported from countries that permit anonymous gamete donation, but the commencement of Parts 2 and 3 of the legislation means that only identifiable donor gametes can now be imported and used in procedures.

However, sections 20-23 of the CFRA 2015 also encompass retrospective recognition of parentage. An intended parent and the child's mother can make a joint application to the District Court seeking a declaration that the intended parent is a parent of a child conceived via a DAHR procedure performed in a clinic *in Ireland or abroad* before the commencement of Part 2.[221] The child's birth must

---

[215] See the Civil Registration Act 2019, ss 12 and 13, inserting s 1(7) into the CFRA 2015 and amending CFRA 2015, s 27(5)(c)(i), respectively.

[216] 6 October 2019 was 54 months from the date of the enactment of the CFRA on 6 April 2015.

[217] See the Children and Family Relationships Act 2015 (Parts 2 and 3) (Commencement) Order 2019 (SI 2019 No 541).

[218] See CFRA 2015, ss 9 and 11.

[219] See CFRA 2015, s 4.

[220] CFRA 2015, Pt 3 provides for the establishment of the National Donor-Conceived Person Register, from which a donor-conceived child will be permitted to access his or her donor's identifying/non-identifying information at the age of 18'

[221] CFRA 2015, s 22 provides that the non-birth intended parent *or* the child's mother can make a sole application to the Circuit Court for the intended parent to be recognised as a parent of a donor-conceived child who was born in Ireland, and conceived via a DAHR procedure performed in a clinic

have taken place in Ireland either before or after the commencement of Part 2: an intended parent and the child's mother cannot make a joint court application for a declaration of parentage in respect of a child conceived as a result of a DAHR procedure abroad *after* the commencement of Part 2.[222] The gamete donor(s) must be unknown to the parties, so the use of gametes from either an anonymous or a non-anonymous donor would appear to suffice where a declaration of parentage in relation to a child conceived pre-commencement is sought.[223]

Regarding the provisions on retrospective recognition, the requirement that the gamete donor must be unknown to the parties appears to be an attempt to respect the decision in *McD v L* where the Supreme Court held that a known donor has rights akin to a natural parent.[224] However, this case involved a child conceived via 'home-insemination' outside of a clinical setting so the known donor could not formally waive his parental rights in an informed way.[225] In the regulated setting of a DAHR facility a known donor would, like any donor, be fully informed before signing a consent form that he would not be the legal parent of a child born as a result of the DAHR procedure. Thus, it is difficult to understand why obtaining a declaration of parentage is not possible for a non-birth intended parent of a child conceived pre-commencement via the use of gametes provided by a known donor in a formal, controlled clinical setting, either in Ireland or abroad. Indeed, section 6(4) of the 2015 Act seems to prospectively permit a 'known donor' to donate gametes for DAHR procedures at Irish clinics. This section allows a donor to limit their written consent to the use of their gametes only to a DAHR procedure requested by an intended mother or intended parents specified by them in the written statement of consent. Thus, this section envisages a donor who can solely agree to make a gamete donation to facilitate only certain persons identified by them in writing – they are indubitably a 'known' donor.[226]

---

in Ireland or abroad before the commencement of Pt 2 of the Act. By allowing a court application by only one of the parties, this section provides for situations where the relationship between the mother and the intended parent has broken down following the conception/birth of the donor-conceived child.

[222] CFRA 2015, s 20(1)(b). Further, a sole application to the Circuit Court cannot be made by the mother or the intended parent in respect of a child conceived as a result of a DAHR procedure abroad *after* the date of commencement of Pt 2.

[223] Section 20(1)(d) (i) provides that the gamete donor must be unknown to the mother of the child and its intended parent, and they cannot be an intended parent. A known sperm donor is a man known to the child's natural mother and its non-genetic intended parent. He may be a friend, neighbour, colleague, acquaintance, etc, and the Supreme Court judgment in *McD v L* [2009] IESC 81 recognises such a man as having statutory rights akin to those of a natural father, which is most likely why the provisions on retrospective parentage require that the gamete donor must be unknown to the child's intended parents, even though the *McD* case involved non-clinical DAHR as opposed to the physician-assisted DAHR provided for under the 2015 Act.

[224] [2009] IESC 81. This decision is discussed further below.

[225] There was a private sperm donation agreement between the parties which stipulated that the female same-sex couple were to be regarded as the child's 'parents', but the Supreme Court held that this was unenforceable.

[226] This would appear contrary to the recommendation made by the Commission on Assisted Human Reproduction, which recommended that 'In general, donors should not be permitted to attach conditions to donation, except in situations of intra-familial donation or the use of donated gametes/embryos for research'. See 'Report of the Commission on Assisted Human Reproduction' (n 46) XVI.

In any event, both anonymous and non-anonymous gamete donors would appear to qualify as unknown donors for the purposes of retrospective recognition under the CFRA 2015. An anonymous gamete donor is a person who is unknown to the child's mother and its intended parent, and no identifying or non-identifying information about this person will be made available to them or the child. A non-anonymous gamete donor is a person who is not known to the child's mother and its intended parent, but identifying and non-identifying information about this person will be recorded by a DAHR facility when they donate gametes. The donor's information may be accessed by the child once they reach the age of 18.[227]

By allowing the use of unknown gamete donors, the provisions on retrospective recognition acknowledge that clinical practice in Ireland prior to the commencement of Parts 2 and 3 of the CFRA 2015 was mainly to use anonymous donor sperm in DAHR procedures, so it would be unfair to exclude intended parents from obtaining retrospective recognition of parentage on the basis of a common practice that was not prohibited at the time of the child's conception. As aforementioned, unlike the prospective provisions, the provisions on retrospective recognition apply to a child that was conceived in either an Irish clinic or a foreign clinic but, akin to the prospective provisions, they stipulate that the child must have been born in Ireland. This can cause difficulty where the child was born outside the state and the birth mother is not an Irish citizen; even if the child's other intended parent is an Irish citizen, because the parentage of the child cannot be recognised under the provisions of the 2015 Act. In such a scenario, the child will not be eligible to acquire Irish citizenship after birth.[228]

B. Reciprocal IVF

Once the requirements under the CFRA 2015 are satisfied in either of the instances above, an intended parent can now be recognised as a parent, and they can be registered on the child's birth certificate as a result of changes to Irish law made by Parts 2, 3 and 9 of the Act. However, this legislative arrangement would unfortunately appear to exclude a certain form of treatment, namely, 'reciprocal IVF', or 'shared motherhood' which is practised and popular among female same-sex couples as it allows one woman to be the gestational mother and the other woman to be the genetic mother, and vice versa where a subsequent child is conceived by the couple in this manner. In this form of IVF treatment, the embryo is formed from an egg donated by the gestational mother's same-sex partner and donor sperm,

---

[227] See the CFRA 2015, Pt 3. However, the 2022 Bill proposes to amend the 2015 Act to reduce the age at which a child can access information to sixteen. See n 112.

[228] See S Pollak, 'Getting IVF Abroad: "Our Daughter is Stateless, She Doesn't Exist"' *Irish Times* (14 October 2019), available at www.irishtimes.com/news/social-affairs/getting-ivf-abroad-our-daughter-is-stateless-she-doesn-t-exist-1.4049263. In this situation the non-birth intended parent was an Irish citizen but because Irish law does not recognise such a person as a parent other than where the provisions of Pt 2 of the 2015 Act apply, and because the 2015 Act did not apply to this situation since the child was born abroad, the child could not acquire Irish citizenship.

and transferred to the uterus of the gestational mother. However, this method of reproduction does not appear to be covered by the recently commenced legislation, so the child cannot have their genetic mother recognised as their parent. In Part 2 of the Act, a gamete donor and an intended parent cannot be one and the same person, and because the intended parent or genetic mother in a reciprocal IVF scenario is in fact also the egg donor, she cannot be recognised as a parent of the child under the provisions of Part 2.[229] In such a scenario, it would appear that only the gestational or birth mother can be recognised as the child's mother and can be registered as such on the child's birth certificate.

It appears unlikely that the Oireachtas intended to exclude reciprocal IVF from the 2015 Act: the issue was not referred to during the Joint Committee on Justice, Defence and Equality's pre-legislative scrutiny of the draft legislation in 2014 or in its subsequent report, or any of the debates in the Houses of the Oireachtas.[230] The issue might not have been considered because it appears that reciprocal IVF was not offered by any Irish fertility clinic at the time.[231] By providing that the gamete donor must be unknown to the child's mother and its intended parent, the Oireachtas was not only mindful of the Supreme Court's judgment in the *McD v L* case in 2009, but it was also most likely trying to protect those who would be legally recognised as the parents of a child born through donor conception from future interference by a known donor seeking to assert their parental rights. However, the irony is that in a reciprocal IVF scenario, the child's birth mother and her same-sex partner (the known egg donor/genetic intended parent) would both *want* the latter to be recognised as having all the legal parental rights enjoyed by a genetic parent of the child.

Not surprisingly, the exclusion of this form of IVF is a source of frustration for female same-sex couples who availed of reciprocal IVF abroad before commencement of the Act and would otherwise fall within the ambit of sections 20-23.[232] Bracken has suggested a number of useful amendments that could be made to the CFRA 2015 that would potentially resolve the dilemma faced by female same-sex couples who avail of reciprocal IVF so as to enable the child to have its intended same-sex family structure recognised by statute.[233] These include the suggestion that the words 'unless the donor of the gamete or embryo is the spouse, civil

---

[229] See ss 5(5) and (7), 6(3)(d), 7(b)(1), 9(3)(c) (i), 11(3)(d)(1), and 20(d) and (e).

[230] See Joint Committee on Justice, Defence and Equality, 'Report on Hearings' (2014).

[231] See E O'Regan, 'Irish Fertility Clinic Offers "Shared Motherhood" Service' *Irish Independent* (8 November 2019) 15, available at www.independent.ie/irish-news/irish-fertility-clinic-offers-shared-motherhood-service-38672682.html. Further, at the Joint Committee on Health's pre-legislative scrutiny session on 27 February 2019 concerning the General Scheme of the Assisted Human Reproduction Bill 2017, Paula Fagan, CEO of LGBT Ireland, acknowledged that 'reciprocal IVF is a way of conceiving that has emerged relatively recently': see Joint Committee on Health Debate (27 February 2019), available at www.oireachtas.ie/en/debates/debate/joint_committee_on_health/2019-02-27/2.

[232] See CFRA 2015, s 20(1)(d)(i). See R Lavelle, 'Winners and Losers under New Law on Parental Rights for Same Sex Couples' *Irish Independent* (8 November 2019) 14, available at www.independent.ie/irish-news/step-in-right-direction-but-not-all-same-sex-couples-are-covered-by-parental-rights-law-38672680.html.

[233] L Bracken, 'Pathways to Parenting: Proposals for Reform' (LGBT Ireland, 2019) 7–8, available at: lgbt.ie/wp-content/uploads/2018/10/LGBT-Pathways-to-Parenthood-Proposals-for-Reform.pdf.

partner or cohabitant of the mother' could be added to all sections of the 2015 Act that currently stipulate that 'a donor of a gamete [or embryo] that is used in a DAHR procedure is not the parent of a child born as a result of that procedure'.[234] I would further recommend that the provisions on retrospective recognition of parentage in section 20(1)(d) and (e), which require that the gamete donor be, and remain, unknown to the child's mother and its intending parent could similarly be amended with the same wording. Such amendments would thus enable the genetic, intended parent of a donor-conceived child in a reciprocal IVF scenario to have their parentage recognised under the 2015 Act, while respecting the Supreme Court's judgment in *McD v L*[235] regarding known donors in *non-clinical DAHR* procedures.[236] Unfortunately, however, the Oireachtas has shown no real interest in revisiting the provisions of the 2015 Act, preferring instead to do all that is necessary to simply commence the Act in its current form, as evident from the fact that these amendments were not included in the Children and Family Relationships (Amendment) Act 2018.[237] Further, the Department of Health did not include provisions relating to reciprocal IVF in the subsequent, more comprehensive General Scheme of the Assisted Human Reproduction Bill 2017 or its recent successor, the Health (Assisted Human Reproduction) Bill 2022.

C. The Attorney General's Advice on Reciprocal IVF and the CFRA 2015

It is interesting to note that female same-sex couples who are raising children born via reciprocal IVF have recently been able to have the genetic parent's parentage retrospectively recognised by a court under the relevant provisions of the CFRA 2015. Recently, it has been reported that the Office of the Attorney General has issued legal advice to the effect that it is the state's view that reciprocal IVF *is* encompassed by the CFRA 2015.[238] To date, it has been reported that two female same-sex couples have obtained a Declaration of Parentage in respect of the genetic intended parent, in courts in Bray and Dublin, respectively.[239]

---

[234] ibid. Bracken suggests amending ss. 5(5) and 5(7), 6(3)(d), 7(b)(1), 9(3)(c)(i), 11(3)(d)(1) and 'any other section' where the phrase 'a donor of a gamete [or embryo] that is used in a DAHR procedure is not the parent of a child born as a result of that procedure' the words 'unless the donor of the gamete or embryo is the spouse, civil partner or cohabitant of the mother'.

[235] [2009] IESC 81.

[236] Of course, a known donor can prospectively contribute to a clinical DAHR procedure by consenting to the type of restricted gamete donation that is in accordance with CFRA 2015, s 6(4).

[237] A Moore, 'Order Signed to let Same-Sex Couples Register Both Names on Birth Certificate' *Irish Independent* (4 November 2019), available at www.independent.ie/breaking-news/irish-news/order-signed-to-let-same-sex-couples-register-both-names-on-birth-certificate-38659393.html.

[238] See 'Irish LGBTQ+ Couple Who Conceived Through IVF Receive Declaration of Parentage' *GCN* (7 October 2020), available at gcn.ie/irish-lgbtq-ivf-declaration-parentage.

[239] See 'Same-Sex Couple Both Recognised as Parents of their Children after Lengthy Campaign' *Irish Times* (20 October 2021), at www.irishtimes.com/news/ireland/irish-news/same-sex-couple-both-recognised-as-parents-of-their-children-after-lengthy-campaign-1.4706046.

As stated in chapter one, the Attorney General's advice is not published, so there is no way of scrutinising the advice. While I fail to see how the CFRA 2015 can literally encompass reciprocal IVF arrangements in the absence of the amendments discussed above, a finding that the legislation should be read as intending to include this practice appears logical, because otherwise a man who contributes gametes to be used in a DAHR procedure with his wife or cohabiting opposite-sex partner would equally be viewed as a 'donor' and would be unable to be recognised as the child's father under the provisions of the CFRA 2015.[240] Nonetheless, the best course of action would be for the Oireachtas to enact a piece of amending legislation clarifying the parental rights of gamete donors who are spouses, civil partners or cohabitants of the child's birth mother, especially in light of a recent Bill which indicates that in a domestic AHR scenario, a *female* intended parent whose gametes were used to create the embryo cannot be recognised as a legal parent of the child.

In a surrogacy context, section 14(2)(d) of the 2022 Bill prevents a female donor whose gametes were used to create the embryo to be transferred to the surrogate mother from being recognised as a parent of the child. This prima facie implies that a genetic intended mother cannot be recognised as a parent of their surrogate-born child where they provided the gametes used in embryo formation, and indicates that the intent of the legislature, even seven years subsequent to the CFRA 2015, is that female intended parents and donors *still* cannot be one and the same person in AHR situations.

However, there is an obvious policy goal here, which is to prevent genetic intended mothers from *automatically* being recognised as the mother of a surrogate-born child, because the clear objective of the Bill is for the surrogate to be the only legal mother at birth, and she must freely consent to a *transfer* of parentage. Indeed, the previous section 14(2)(c) states that intended parents 'will not, *without a parental order*, be the parents' of the child, 'other than in the case of an intending parent who provided the sperm', so this appears to clarify that the intention in subsection (d) is that an intended genetic mother who provided the gametes used in embryo formation can be recognised as a legal mother once

---

[240] However, the situations are not entirely the same. If the parties are husband and wife, the presumption of paternity would automatically apply to the husband at birth and the parties could easily register the birth in the ordinary way without the registrar ever knowing that the child was conceived via a DAHR procedure. Similarly, an opposite-sex cohabiting couple could register the birth of the child in the ordinary way and the Registrar would most likely be none the wiser as to the child having been conceived via a DAHR procedure. In this situation, registration of the father's name on the birth certificate would lead to the presumption of paternity arising in favour of the male cohabitant. However, it should be noted that since the commencement of CFRA 2015, Pt 9 in October 2019, the birth of a donor-conceived child should be registered in compliance with the Civil Registration Act 2004, s 19A, as inserted by the CFRA 2015, s 93. This requires the parents of a donor-conceived child to give to the Registrar a certificate provided by the DAHR facility under CFRA 2015, s 27(5) confirming, *inter alia*, their consent to being the parents of the donor-conceived child, and a statutory declaration stating that they consented to being the parents of a donor-conceived child in accordance with the provisions of CFRA 2015, Pt 2.

the surrogate has consented to the transfer of motherhood via the parental order process.

Surrogacy and reciprocal IVF are different in that the birth 'mother' in the former situation will always be the surrogate, whereas in the latter situation it will always be the wife, civil or cohabiting partner of the genetic mother. Thus, prospectively making provision for the genetic intended mother of a child born via a domestic reciprocal IVF procedure to have their *parentage* automatically recognised under the 2015 Act would be very different from allowing a genetic intended mother to have their *motherhood* automatically recognised in a domestic surrogacy context where the state is enacting a post-birth parental order model that requires the surrogate to be recognised as the only legal mother at birth and to choose to consent to a transfer of their legal motherhood.

XVI. Non-Clinical DAHR Procedures

Non-clinical DAHR that occurs (or occurred) by means of 'home insemination' (outside the clinical setting) is not covered under Parts 2 and 3 of the 2015 Act. There may be a number of reasons for this, and the most obvious one is that the Oireachtas chose to exclude couples who engaged in non-clinical DAHR because of the Supreme Court's decision in *McD v L*.[241] This case involved a known donor[242] who entered into an agreement with a female same-sex couple to provide them with sperm that would enable them to have a child together. It was expressly agreed between the parties that the female same-sex couple would be the child's 'parents', with the known donor acting in the more limited role of a 'favourite Uncle'. Subsequently, the known donor supplied sperm, and this was used by the couple to conceive via home insemination. Following the birth of the child the parties were in dispute and the known donor, as the natural father, sought guardianship of and access to the child in the courts under the provisions of the Guardianship of Infants Act 1964.[243] There had been limited contact between the known donor and the child since the birth and so a limited bond had been established between them.

Previous judgments of the superior courts had indicated that such a limited bond between an unmarried father and his child was likely to be anathema to a ruling in his favour in a guardianship application before the courts.[244] Indeed, in

---

[241] [2009] IESC 81.

[242] A known sperm donor is a man known to the child's birth mother and its non-biological intended parent. He may be a friend, neighbour, colleague, acquaintance, etc. A non-anonymous sperm donor is a man who is not known to the child's natural mother and its non-biological intended parent. However, identifying and non-identifying information about this man will be recorded by a DAHR facility when he donates sperm and such information may be accessed by the child upon reaching adulthood.

[243] See Guardianship of Infants Act 1964, s 6A (as inserted by the Status of Children Act 1987, s 12), and s 11.

[244] See *JK v VW* [1990] 2 IR 437; *WO'R v EH* [1996] 2 IR 248.

the High Court, Hedigan J denied the known donor both guardianship and access rights but, on appeal, the Supreme Court granted him access to the child and even embraced the possibility of his applying to be appointed a guardian of the child in changed circumstances in the future. The Supreme Court declared the parties' private 'sperm donation' agreement unenforceable, and the members of the court clearly regarded the known donor as akin to any unmarried father because throughout the judgment the appellant, Mr McD, was referred to as 'the father' and, as Fennelly J. acknowledged, 'it is not suggested, in the present case, that the father is *any less* the biological father of the child by reason of being a sperm donor'.[245] Denham J (as she then was) also recognised the known donor as 'the biological father' and stated that 'there is benefit to a child, in general, to have the society of its father'.[246] The Supreme Court accorded significant weight to the genetic link between the known donor and the child, and Denham J. made it clear that 'the father, who was a sperm donor, *has rights as a natural father*, as provided for in s.6A of the Guardianship of Infants Act 1964, as amended, to apply to be appointed guardian of the child'.[247]

Although the Supreme Court refused the known donor's appeal on the issue of guardianship, the appeal was allowed in relation to access rights and the case was remitted back to the High Court to determine the level of access to be granted.[248] While it is notable that the appeal was dismissed insofar as it related to guardianship, the members of the Supreme Court made it clear that the known donor in this case stood every chance of being granted guardianship by the courts at a later date should the evolution of his relationship with the child warrant it. Denham J felt that 'there should be no order of guardianship made in relation to the father *at this time*. As in all family law matters, issues may be re-addressed in changed circumstances'.[249] Fennelly J also held that 'it is, of course, possible that a time will come when [a guardianship] application might be renewed in the High Court in different circumstances'.[250] Hence, the Supreme Court seemed to envisage that, if the access arrangements put in place resulted in the child establishing a strong attachment to its father over time, then an application for guardianship might be approved by the High Court one day.[251] Leonard-Kane argued that the Supreme Court's decision in *McD v L* 'completely undermined the stability and autonomy

---

[245] [2010] 1 ILRM 461, 523 (emphasis added).
[246] [2010] 1 ILRM 461, 494.
[247] [2010] 1 ILRM 461, 493 (emphasis added).
[248] [2010] IEHC 120 (Hedigan J).
[249] [2010] 1 ILRM 461, 494 (emphasis added).
[250] [2010] 1 ILRM 461, 533.
[251] In *A v B and C* [2012] EWCA Civ 285, a case in England and Wales involving a known sperm donor seeking access to a child being raised by a female same-sex couple, Black LJ at [48] recognised that 'the role of the father in the child's life will depend on what is in the child's best interests at each stage of the child's childhood and adolescence. As with any other child, the father/child relationship may turn out to be close and fulfilling for both sides, it may be no more than nominal, or it may be something in between'.

of lesbian families conceived using donor sperm'.[252] The Supreme Court's decision makes it clear that if a female same-sex couple uses sperm from a known donor to conceive a child at home, then the known donor will be treated in law as being akin to any other unmarried father, with all of the rights accompanying that status.

One should not be too critical of the Supreme Court's judgment in *McD v L* given that the court was operating in a very different legal landscape. In 2009, despite the recommendations contained in the 'Report of the Commission on Assisted Human Reproduction' in 2005, the Oireachtas had not enacted any legislation allocating parental rights in the context of DAHR.[253] Further, same-sex relationships had not yet been recognised under statute,[254] the Constitution,[255] or the European Convention on Human Rights (ECHR),[256] so the female same-sex couple had no legally recognised relationship status with which to try to counter the known donor's statutory parental rights. The law remains the same to this day and the same-sex second parent of a child conceived via home-insemination cannot be legally recognised as a parent following the child's birth. Further, the sperm donor in these situations is entitled to assert his rights as the child's natural father.

A. Regulating Non-Clinical DAHR – A Way Forward?

The Supreme Court's decision in *McD v L* seems to have precluded retrospective recognition of parentage for an intended parent of a child conceived via home insemination with sperm from a known donor within Part 2 of the CFRA 2015. Indeed, the decision may arguably preclude legislative reform allowing even prospective recognition of parentage for an intended second parent of a child conceived in this manner, but this author believes that statutory regulation of home insemination involving some *state oversight* would not be contrary to *McD v L*.[257] As stated, at the time of its judgment in *McD v L*, the Supreme Court

---

[252] M Leonard-Kane, 'Lesbian Co-Parenting and Assisted Reproduction: In an Age of Increasing Alternative Family Forms, Can Ireland Continue to Ignore the Need for Legislative Boundaries to be Placed on "Fertile" Ground?' (2010) 13 *Trinity College Law Review* 5, 23.

[253] The Commission recommended that laws be enacted by the Oireachtas to regulate legal parentage in cases of DAHR and surrogacy, although the Commission was referring to the legal regulation of procedures carried out in a clinical setting: see 'Report of the Commission on Assisted Human Reproduction' (n 46) 46.

[254] The Bill that would ultimately become the Civil Partnership and Certain Rights and Obligations of Cohabitants Act 2010 was only being debated in the Houses of the Oireachtas at the time.

[255] Same-sex *married couples* were only granted constitutional and statutory recognition following a successful constitutional referendum almost six years later, in 2015.

[256] Six months after the Supreme Court's judgment, childless same-sex couples were recognised as having a right to respect for 'family life' under Art 8 of the ECHR: see *Schalk and Kopf v Austria* (2011) 53 EHRR 20. In 2012, a same-sex couple *with children* was first recognised as having a right to respect for 'family life' in *Gas and Dubois v France*, App No 25951/07 (ECHR, 15 March 2012).

[257] In the UK, the Human Fertilisation and Embryology Act 2008, s 42 simply provides that if a female same-sex couple who are married or civil partners of each other conceive a child via home

was operating in a legislative vacuum as regards DAHR – that is why the known donor was regarded as the child's father and could benefit from existing legislation. However, if the Oireachtas prospectively legislated for home insemination in a manner that ensured that the position of intended parents, known donors and donor-conceived children was adequately protected, the courts may respect the legislature's judgment on such a complex issue.[258] As stated in chapter one, the Irish superior courts are most deferential to the Oireachtas when it comes to matters of social policy, including the regulation of assisted human reproduction and surrogacy.[259] This is quite clear from the 'surrogacy case' of *MR v An tArd Chláraitheoir*, discussed earlier.[260]

The Supreme Court does not feel that judges should 'legislate' in the area of surrogacy and DAHR where a lacuna in the law exists – that is why existing legislation was applied by the court in both the *McD* and *MR* cases. Any gap in legislative protection for intended parents and others should be addressed by the Oireachtas, and not by the courts. The upshot of this approach is that the Supreme Court also largely appears to be willing to defer to the Oireachtas as regards the balancing of the parties' constitutional rights in any legislation addressing these complex sociolegal matters.[261] Consequently, the Irish superior courts would most likely defer to the Oireachtas if it enacted a balanced model for regulating 'home insemination',

insemination, the spouse or civil partner who is not the birth mother of the child will automatically be recognised as a second female parent. Legislating for this type of model in Ireland might be difficult given the status accorded to the known donor by the Supreme Court in *McD v L* [2010] 1 ILRM 461. The UK 'home insemination' model does not ensure adequate protection for the known donor's interests because it does not require him to be counselled or to receive independent legal advice prior to providing his gametes to the couple. Further, the child's right to knowledge of genetic identity is not adequately protected because s 42 seems to allow for the use of sperm from a known donor *or an anonymous donor* in the 'home insemination' context. This could possibly be unconstitutional in Ireland in light of Art 42A, the Children's Amendment. As this author has observed previously, the child's right to knowledge of their genetic identity 'is possibly a constitutional right of the child, a corollary of the right to know the identity of one's natural mother that was identified by the Supreme Court in *I'OT v B* as a personal right of the child under Art.40.3': see B Tobin, 'The Revised General Scheme of the Children and Family Relationships Bill 2014: Cognisant of the Donor-Conceived Child's Constitutional Rights?' (2014) 52 *Irish Jurist* 153, 161.

[258] Indeed, the decision in *Ennis v Butterly* [1996] 1 IR 426 indicated that cohabitation contracts might be constitutionally infirm but in 2010 the Oireachtas legislated for these types of contract in a measured way that protects the parties before entering into the contract. See the Civil Partnerships and Certain Rights and Obligations of Cohabitants Act 2010, s 202. This legislation has not been the subject of a constitutional challenge.

[259] *Roche v Roche* [2009] IESC 82; *MR v An tArd Chláraitheoir* [2014] IESC 60.

[260] [2014] IESC 60.

[261] The Irish courts have been *largely* willing to defer to the legislature on matters of social policy and the appropriate balancing of constitutional rights for many decades. *Tuohy v Courtney* [1994] 3 IR 1 at 47 indicates that the courts will defer *unless* a party's constitutional rights have been breached by legislation in a way that is 'so contrary to reason and fairness'. Similarly, in *MR v An tArd Chláraitheoir* [2014] IESC 60 the Supreme Court was willing to accord the Oireachtas a wide margin in relation to the regulation of surrogacy, but not an entirely free reign on the issue. In his judgment Clarke J (as he then was) frequently referred to 'constitutionally permissible' legislation and cautioned that '[w]*ithin constitutional bounds* it is *largely* a question of policy for the Oireachtas to determine the precise parameters of [surrogacy] regulation' (emphasis added): see [2014] IESC 60 [8.7].

and therefore the various proposals that have been put forward to achieve workable legislation in this area shall now be explored.

B. A Proposal for Regulating Non-Clinical DAHR

I have previously proposed a mechanism for prospectively regulating the parentage of children conceived via home insemination with the use of sperm from a known donor.[262] In part, the solution to prospectively regulating home insemination with a known donor lies in the Health (Assisted Human Reproduction) Bill 2022 and its pre-surrogacy safeguards. As discussed, the Bill provides for the setting up of the AHRRA, a state regulatory body that could have tremendous potential, *if fully realised*. As suggested, the AHRRA should be able to approve treatment *and* parentage when presented with a domestic surrogacy agreement. The AHRRA could similarly approve home-insemination agreements that comply with *robust* pre-insemination safeguards identical to those contained in Part 7 of the 2022 Bill before any home-insemination technique is engaged in. Intended parents and the known donor could be required to submit to medical assessments, AHR counselling and a 'section 16' assessment.[263] The parties could also be required to receive independent legal advice related to the agreement. These statutory requirements would help to ensure that the parties' consent to the home-insemination agreement is a free and fully informed one. The AHRRA could then approve such agreements, allowing the parties to proceed with the conception through home insemination. The agreement could have a shelf life of two years; if a child is not conceived within that timeframe the parties could be required to seek a renewal of their agreement in order to proceed. This time limit would ensure parity with the expiration date for approved surrogacy agreements in section 51(4)(a) of the 2022 Bill.

---

[262] B Tobin, 'Regulating Non-Clinical Donor Assisted Human Reproduction in Ireland' (2018) 60 *Irish Jurist* 179.

[263] It could perhaps be provided in legislation that the known donor's GP could arrange for a sample of his gametes to undergo the medical screening required for donors of reproductive cells under the European Communities (Quality and Safety of Human Tissues and Cells) Regulations 2006 (SI 2006 No 158), Reg 11. The Health (Assisted Human Reproduction) Bill 2022, s 36 requires the AHR treatment provider to ensure that the potential relevant donor has undergone such medical screening before the relevant donation is made. Where the results of the screening indicate that the donation does not meet the standards of quality and safety set out by the Regulations of 2006 the AHR treatment provider must inform the potential relevant donor that they cannot accept the donation. It is submitted that the AHRRA should not pre-authorise *any* home-insemination agreement where the parties have not undergone the testing required by the Regulations of 2006 because this is imperative to protect the best interests of the child. The recent case in England and Wales of *MacDougall v SW & Ors* [2022] EWFC 50, highlights the considerable risk that can be associated with unregulated private home-insemination procedures. Mr MacDougall claimed to have fathered 15 children via private sperm donation arrangements with female same-sex couples and lesbian individuals *without disclosing* his Fragile X syndrome, a genetic condition that causes a range of developmental problems including learning difficulties and cognitive impairment, and which would have prevented him from acting as a sperm donor through a clinic. Lieven J observed that he 'took advantage of these young women's vulnerability and their strong desire to have children': see [2022] EWFC 50 at [80].

This 'pre-conception' approval of parentage as part of the sperm donation agreement would provide legal certainty for all – the intended parents would have their legal parental status in relation to the child established before its conception and the known donor will have validly waived all of his legal parental rights. Home insemination with a known donor is a cost-effective method of assisted human reproduction that is practised and popular among female same-sex couples, and it is submitted that the Oireachtas should consider this type of balanced regulatory approach in the future.[264]

C. A Known Donor's Right to Object?

It is submitted that the reasons for allowing a surrogate to object to the allocation of parentage post-birth do not apply in the case of a known donor. The known donor merely provides gametes on a once-off basis, rather than gestating a child for nine months, and will not receive payment in the form of reasonable expenses or beyond. Unlike commercial surrogacy, in particular, known donor arrangements do not involve binding contracts, gestational labour and significant payment for the transfer of a child post-birth.

However, if the Oireachtas was to enact legislation providing for the 'pre-conception state approval' surrogacy regime outlined previously, *and* a 'pre-conception state approval' model for regulating home-insemination arrangements, it might prefer parity between the post-birth legal position of the gestational surrogate and the known donor, and wish to allow the known donor a right to object to the allocation of parentage within a certain timeframe after birth. Indeed, as Fennelly J remarked in *McD v L*,

> the blood link, as a matter of almost universal experience, exerts a powerful influence on people. The father, in the present case, stands as proof that participation in the limited role of sperm donor under the terms of a restrictive agreement does not prevent the development of unforeseen but powerful paternal instincts.[265]

Given this, and because the known donor is, like a traditional surrogate, genetically related to the child, it is arguable that he should be accorded a post-birth

---

[264] Obviously, those couples and known donors who would engage in home insemination but fail to comply with the proposed regulatory model would be subject to existing law, whereby the known donor would be the child's legal father, entitled to all the rights accompanying that status. Further, those couples who import anonymous/non-anonymous donor sperm to be used in home insemination would not fall under the proposed regulatory model. In particular, couples who use imported sperm from an anonymous donor in home insemination would not only fall outside the ambit of the proposed regulatory model, but would also frustrate the possibility of respecting the child's right to knowledge of its genetic identity.

[265] *McD v L* [2009] IESC 81 [81]. Further, Wallbank and Dietz have emphasised that 'emotions can run high once a child is born and what was intended before conception can seem completely inappropriate afterwards': see J Wallbank and C Dietz, 'Lesbian Mothers, Fathers and Other Animals: Is the Political Personal in Multiple Parent Families?' (2013) 25 *Child and Family Law Quarterly* 451,467.

cooling-off period, during which time he may decide to exercise a right to object to the pre-conception allocation of parentage in favour of the intended parents. His right to object could be facilitated by writing to the AHRRA, quoting the number of the home-insemination agreement, and the AHRRA could duly inform the intended parents, who could apply to the court for a Parental Order. While this author does not believe that this approach is necessitated under international law, it would create parity in legislation between the pre-conception state approval domestic surrogacy and non-clinical donor-assisted human reproduction models that I am proposing.

D. Respecting the Child's Right to Knowledge of Genetic Identity in the Context of Non-Clinical DAHR

The child's right to knowledge of genetic identity could be easily protected because legislation could require that the known donor's identifying and non-identifying information be included in the home-insemination agreement. Following the birth of the child, the intended parents would automatically be the legal parents and could easily register the birth by producing two pieces of evidence for the Registrar. First, their state-approved home-insemination agreement could be presented as proof of legal parentage, and second, the results of a DNA test, confirmed by a solicitor, could establish the relationship between the birth mother, the known donor and the child. This latter requirement would confirm that two of the parties to the home-insemination agreement were in fact the ultimate genetic progenitors of the child, as intended, thus ensuring protection of the child's right to knowledge of genetic identity through the registration of accurate details on the birth certificate (as regards the birth mother and intended co-parent) and in the National Donor-Conceived Person Register (as regards all three parties) that fully correspond with the home-insemination agreement that was pre-approved by the AHRRA.

Legislation could provide that every entry in the Register of Births of a child born via home insemination should be linked to the National Donor-Conceived Person Register. The Registrar could be required to furnish the AHRRA with written confirmation that, based on confirmed DNA evidence that was provided, a child was born as a result of a certain home-insemination agreement previously sanctioned by the authority and that their birth has been registered to reflect such agreement. On receipt of this written confirmation, the AHRRA could be required by statute to register information pertaining to all of the parties, including, at this stage, the child, in the National Donor-Conceived Person Register. The AHRRA could obtain this information from the copy of the home-insemination agreement retained by it at the time of the approval process and could verify it with the DNA evidence attached to the written confirmation of birth registration received from the Registrar's office. The child's details as registered on the birth certificate could be provided by the Registrar's office to enable them being recorded by the

AHRRA. Such important information could then be made available to the donor-conceived adult at 18, just as it is in the case of children conceived through DAHR that takes place in a clinical setting under the 2015 Act.[266]

XVII. Alternative Proposals for Regulating Non-Clinical DAHR

Bracken also proposes a mode of regulating non-clinical DAHR that attempts to balance the rights of all parties – the intended parents, known donor and the child. When registering the birth, Bracken proposes that the intended parents could provide the Registrar with a statutory declaration stating that they are the mother and intended parent of a child born via home-insemination; that they have recorded the identity and details of the known donor and transmitted these to the National Donor-Conceived Person Register; that the donor did not intend to be recognised as a parent of the child and that they have evidence to this effect.[267] Under Bracken's proposal, the Registrar would then be required to contact the known donor in writing requiring him to attend at the Registrar's office declaring that he is not a legal parent of the child within 28 days of written notice, and providing a statutory declaration to that effect. Once the registrar has both statutory declarations and is satisfied that the donor's details have been recorded on the National Donor-Conceived Person Register, they can register the mother and intended parent as the child's legal parents on the birth certificate.[268]

More recently, O'Mahony proposed a model of regulation whereby legislative provision could be made for the second parent of a child born through non-clinical DAHR to apply to the District Court at any time after the birth of the child for either parentage or guardianship.[269] He argues that the court should be empowered to grant parentage where information regarding the sperm donor has been provided to the National Donor-Conceived Person Register, subject to a best interests assessment by the court.[270] He believes that provision should be made in law allowing the parents to provide the requisite information on the gamete donor to the National Donor-Conceived Person Register.

All the abovementioned proposals reflect noble attempts to address the situation of same-sex couples who have recourse to home-insemination with sperm from a known donor, and they might provide the basis for a way forward given how they seek to balance the rights of all parties. However, there are a number

---

[266] However, the 2022 Bill proposes to amend the 2015 Act to reduce the age at which a child can access information to 16. See n 112.

[267] Bracken, n 253 above, 4, available at: https://lgbt.ie/wp-content/uploads/2018/10/LGBT-Pathways-to-Parenthood-Proposals-for-Reform.pdf.

[268] Ibid.

[269] C O' Mahony, n 94 above, 48.

[270] ibid.

of important points worth noting in relation to each proposal. They all rely on the National Donor-Conceived Person Register being operational, something that has only recently occurred, and they also all envisage some level of interaction between that Register and the Register of Births. In particular, Bracken's proposal places a significant onus on civil registrars and there might be some opposition to this from such registrars or, at the very least, further training required.[271] While my proposal envisages a more limited role for registrars, it would also require them to be trained regarding their role when presented with DNA evidence and a home-insemination agreement that has previously been approved by the AHRRA. Further, my proposal envisages a greater role for the AHRRA, and is very much dependent on input from that body, even though it has not yet been established by law, although the recent publication of the 2022 Bill has brought this significantly closer to fruition. Indeed, my proposal and Bracken's proposal might be objectionable because they do not involve a court in deciding parentage in cases of non-clinical DAHR, although my proposal envisages the legal division of the AHRRA meticulously carrying out this task at the pre-conception stage, and recent recommendations from the UK and New Zealand favour a rather streamlined administrative approach to acquiring legal parentage in AHR situations.[272] Although O'Mahony's proposal envisages the question of parentage being decided in the District Court, it does not state on what basis the second parent's application is to be grounded in order to enable the court to decide the issue of parentage, and while it requires the known donor to be put on notice of the application, it is somewhat confusing as it envisages non-clinical DAHR being easily incorporated within the 2015 Act, an Act which only applies to the separate context of physician-assisted DAHR.[273] In the absence of evidence such as written consents to parental status (or indeed donor status) that would be part of any DAHR procedure that takes place in a controlled clinical setting, or this author's proposed home-insemination agreement which provides robust pre-insemination safeguards for the parties, it is difficult to ascertain how a court is expected to adjudicate on a second parent's intention-based 'parent' status under O'Mahony's proposal, or verify that the evidence pertaining to the 'donor' that has been provided to the National Donor-Conceived Person Register actually pertains to a person genetically related to the child.

Bracken's proposal could similarly be frustrated – it requires intending parents to submit 'evidence' to the registrar that the known donor did not intend to be recognised as a legal parent.[274] However, one wonders what might constitute such

---

[271] Indeed, in 2018, one of the reasons given by the Department of Employment Affairs and Social Protection for the delay in the commencement of Part 9 of the CFRA 2015, which enables both same-sex parents of a donor-conceived child to be registered on the child's birth certificate, was that Civil Registration service staff in the HSE needed to be' fully trained and ready to implement the provisions of the legislation'. See N Baker,' Parental Rights for Gay Couples' *Irish Examiner*, 5th June 2018, 20.

[272] See New Zealand Law Commission (n 43) and Law Commission (n 66).

[273] C O' Mahony, n 94 above. 42 and 48.

[274] L Bracken, 'Pathways to Parenting' (2019) 4.

evidence, given that the Supreme Court has previously declared private agreements between parties that allocate parentage in cases of home-insemination as unenforceable? Indeed, private 'home insemination' agreements may vary considerably and some might not adequately ensure that the male progenitor is giving a fully informed consent to his 'donor' status, the waiver of his legal parental rights and the allocation of parentage to the intended parents at birth. Registrars would most likely resist any role in determining the validity of this type of evidence, and it is submitted that the State would not allocate them such a role as they are not in a position to make a welfare or best interests assessment. Further, under Bracken's proposal it is possible that the known donor might have had a change of heart and wish to identify as a parent of the child when contacted by the Registrar, and might simply refuse to complete a statutory declaration stating that he is not the father of the child, although the author does indeed envisage that recourse might be had to the courts to resolve such complicated situations.[275]

My proposal ensures that the child's legal parentage would be approved by the AHRRA prior to conception, and established at birth,[276] and that legislation would be enacted to ensure that a *state-approved* home-insemination agreement that complies with certain safeguards and establishes legal parentage could be accepted by the registrar (along with DNA evidence) when the intending parents are registering the birth. Thus, there would be evidence of the fully informed consent of all parties to their assigned legal status, and every home-insemination agreement received by the Registrar would be virtually identical and have prior state approval. Indeed, from the Registrar's perspective the process would be similar to accepting a court-approved declaration of parentage when registering or re-registering a child's birth. Under my proposal, the Registrar's role is clear, as limited as possible, akin to their role in other birth registration processes, and less likely to be disputed. The Registrar's role in linking in with the AHRRA is also clear, limited and not too dissimilar to what is envisaged of the interaction between these state bodies under the 2022 Bill as regards domestic surrogacy.[277] However, my proposal would only apply to *prospective* arrangements.

XVIII. Conclusion

The CFRA 2015 was an important milestone on the path to establishing parental rights for same-sex couples. However, the parents of children conceived via reciprocal IVF, non-clinical DAHR and international surrogacy were left behind by the Act and subsequent, relevant legislative initiatives.[278] The Health (Assisted Human

---

[275] ibid, 5.
[276] Although this may be subject to a cooling-off period for the known donor, as a genetic progenitor who may be viewed as akin to a traditional surrogate in that respect.
[277] See the Health (Assisted Human Reproduction) Bill 2022, s 66.
[278] See the Children and Family Relationships (Amendment) Act 2018, the General Scheme of the Assisted Human Reproduction Bill 2017 and the Health (Assisted Human Reproduction) Bill 2022.

Reproduction) Bill 2022 ignores these methods of family formation. Reciprocal IVF arrangements could explicitly be recognised by the state via legislation amending the 2015 Act, although recent developments indicate that, in practice, these arrangements are being recognised by the courts as falling within the ambit of the Act, based on legal advice from the Attorney General. The recognition of international commercial surrogacy agreements poses a more complex dilemma for policy-makers given the ethical concerns associated with these arrangements and the need for the state to be cognisant of international law obligations and international best practice when legislating in this area. Finding a means of regulating international commercial surrogacy in a manner that would alleviate the legal and ethical concerns associated with this practice while also respecting the right of the child to have its intended family structure recognised by Irish law is a difficult, unenviable task. However, the state's ongoing reluctance to tackle the myriad issues raised by international surrogacy via legislation is unacceptable from a child-centric perspective.

The Health (Assisted Human Reproduction) Bill 2022 seeks to establish a complex, hybrid legislative model for the regulation of domestic surrogacy arrangements that would involve both administrative *and* judicial processes, and unduly favour the position of the gestational surrogate over all of the other parties. This chapter has proposed an alternative, fully administrative means of regulating such arrangements, one that is influenced by proposals emanating from law reform bodies elsewhere, cognisant of developments in international law and best practice, and arguably more likely to encourage intended parents to avail of domestic over international surrogacy.

The Supreme Court's decision in *McD v L* clearly influenced the approach to regulating DAHR that was adopted in Parts 2 and 3 of CFRA 2015. However, this chapter has proposed that, akin to domestic surrogacy, regulating non-clinical DAHR could be achieved through a fully administrative process that would seek to protect the rights of all parties to the arrangement. The impending establishment of the AHRRA will be crucial to the type of regulatory model proposed in this chapter for non-clinical DAHR procedures and domestic surrogacy arrangements. The child's right to knowledge of genetic identity would also be vindicated by the measures proposed herein for regulating non-clinical DAHR and domestic surrogacy arrangements, because a streamlined, coherent interaction between the Register of Births, the AHRRA and both the National Donor-Conceived Person and National Surrogacy Registers is envisaged.

5

Same-Sex Relationships, Marriage and Parental Rights under the ECHR

I. Introduction

This chapter will explore the impact of Articles 8, 12 and 14 of the European Convention on Human Rights (ECHR) on same-sex families, but with a particular focus on Ireland. The ECHR is a product of the Council of Europe (CoE), which was founded in the aftermath of World War II in order to ensure respect for democracy, the rule of law and human rights, and which is comprised of 47 Contracting States. All 27 of the European Union's Member States are parties to the ECHR, as is Ireland's non-EU neighbouring jurisdiction, the UK. The ECHR was given some domestic effect in Ireland under the European Convention on Human Rights Act 2003 (the '2003 Act'). The chapter demonstrates that Article 8, which concerns, inter alia, a right to respect for private and family life, and Article 14, which provides that the rights under the ECHR shall be enjoyed free from discrimination, have helped to engender positive change at the national level for LGBT+ *individuals* because of the need for Contracting States to respect their private life; however, these provisions have thus far had a limited effect on same-sex *family life*, particularly in the context of parental rights. More recently, the European Court of Human Rights (ECtHR) has been instrumental in promoting the establishment of legal familial ties between intended parents and surrogate-born children as an aspect of the child's right to respect for private life under Article 8. Nonetheless, the chapter demonstrates that because the ECtHR accords Contracting States a wide margin of appreciation in this sensitive area, Ireland appears to be largely in compliance with its obligations under Article 8 of the ECHR when it comes to legally recognising a person's parental rights in relation to surrogate-born children.

The chapter also analyses the evolution of the right to marry and to found a family under Article 12 as it applies to LGBT+ persons. The chapter examines the Court's reasoning in *Goodwin v United Kingdom*, in which a trans person's right to marry a person of the opposite sex under Article 12 was established, and the Court's subsequent, unconvincing refusal to extend this reasoning in the same-sex marriage case of *Schalk and Kopf v Austria*. As there now exists an 'emerging consensus' on same-sex marriage in the Council of Europe, the chapter proffers an interpretation of Article 12 that could encompass same-sex marriage while respectfully consigning to the annals of history the historical argument that only favours the recognition of opposite-sex marriage under the ECHR.

II. The Margin of Appreciation

Once all domestic remedies have been exhausted an applicant can, because of the right of an individual to make an application, proceed with their case to the ECtHR in Strasbourg, where any alleged national violations of rights that are protected under the provisions of the ECHR will be adjudicated on. The ECtHR has repeatedly stressed that 'the Convention is a living instrument, to be interpreted in the light of present-day conditions',[1] but success by applicants before the Strasbourg Court has often been dependent on the 'margin of appreciation', a doctrine that signifies the area of discretion or 'elbow room' afforded to the Contracting States when alleged infringements of the ECHR are being assessed. Indeed, Brown has emphasised that 'although it is certainly true that the [ECtHR] takes a broader and less marriage-centred view of family life than the Irish Constitution, the margin of appreciation has the potential to mitigate against more radical judgments by the Strasbourg Court'.[2]

Essentially, where the law and practice differ widely amongst the Contracting States, a state that finds itself before the ECtHR for an alleged breach of the ECHR may be granted a rather broad margin of appreciation by the Court. This leeway is oft-considered appropriate by the Court, which has reiterated on many occasions that the national authorities are best placed to assess and respond to the needs of their societies.[3] Van Dijk and Van Hoof observe that there are no 'hard and fast rules governing the scope of the margin of appreciation',[4] yet the ECtHR has repeatedly made it clear in the case law that the Contracting States' margin will be broad where there is *no* European consensus, 'particularly where the case raises sensitive moral or ethical issues',[5] which can be the case where same-sex relationships, marriage and parental rights for LGBT+ couples are concerned. However, the converse is also true, and 'consensus has therefore been invoked to justify a dynamic interpretation of the Convention'.[6] This will be demonstrated later in this

---

[1] *EB v France* (2008) 47 EHRR 21; *Schalk and Kopf v Austria*, App No 30141/04 (ECtHR, 24 June 2010).

[2] E Brown, 'Committed Relationships and the Law: The Impact of the European Convention on Human Rights' in O Doyle and W Binchy (eds), *Committed Relationships and the Law* (Dublin, Four Courts Press 2007) 279.

[3] *Schalk and Kopf v Austria* (n 1) [62]. As Baroness Hale pointed out in *Re P*, the 'national authorities are better able than Strasbourg to assess what restrictions are necessary in the democratic societies they serve': see *Re P* [2008] UKHL 38 [118] (Baroness Hale).

[4] P Van Dijk and JGH Van Hoof, *Theory and Practice of the European Convention on Human Rights*, 3rd edn (Amsterdam, Kluwer, 1998) 87.

[5] *A, B and C v Ireland* App No 25579/05 (ECHR, 16 December 2010) [232]; *H v UK* App No 32185/20 (ECtHR, 31 May 2022) [51].

[6] ibid [234].

chapter when the Court's approach to a trans person's right to respect for private life under Article 8 and their right to marry under Article 12 in *Goodwin v United Kingdom* is analysed.[7] Further, the ECtHR has made it clear that 'the margin will tend to be narrower where the right at stake is crucial to the individual's effective enjoyment of intimate or key rights'[8] protected under the ECHR and its Protocols, where there is a difference in treatment based on sex or sexual orientation,[9] or 'where a particularly important facet of an individual's identity was at stake, such as when the legal parent-child relationship was concerned'.[10]

III. Article 8

Article 8(1) of the Convention provides that 'everyone has the right to respect for his private and family life, his home and his correspondence'.[11] The ECtHR has frequently pronounced that the notion of 'private life' under Article 8 is a broad concept which encompasses, inter alia, the right to establish and develop relationships with other human beings,[12] the right to 'personal development'[13] and 'gender identification, sexual orientation and sexual life'[14] which constitute 'a most intimate part of an individual's private life'.[15]

In considering 'family life' under Article 8 the ECtHR has held that this concept does not safeguard the mere desire to found a family; it presupposes the existence of a family. Draghici describes the ECtHR's approach to Article 8 as embracing an 'anti-formalistic and inclusive approach to the notion of "family"'.[16] Indeed, the Court has often confirmed that Article 8 'is not confined solely to families based on marriage and may encompass other *de facto* relationships'[17] and that 'the existence or non-existence of 'family life' is essentially a question of fact depending upon the real existence in practice of close personal ties'.[18] Consequently, Article 8 recognises a far more *diverse* range of families than the marital family recognised by

---

[7] *Goodwin v United Kingdom* (2002) 35 EHRR 18.

[8] *Connors v United Kingdom* App No 66746/01 (ECtHR, 27 May 2004) [82].

[9] *Karner v Austria* (2003) 38 EHRR 528 [49]; *X v Austria* (2013) 57 EHRR. 14 [99].

[10] Advisory Opinion concerning the Recognition in Domestic Law of a Legal Parent-Child Relationship between a Child born through a Gestational Surrogacy Arrangement Abroad and the Intended Mother, P-16-2018-001 (ECtHR, 10 April 2019) [44].

[11] Article 8(2) nonetheless permits the curtailment of this right by the State if this is 'in accordance with the law and is necessary in a democratic society in the interests of national security, public safety or the economic well-being of the country, for the prevention of disorder or crime, for the protection of health or morals, or for the protection of the rights and freedoms of others'.

[12] *Niemitz v Germany* App No 13710/88 (ECtHR, 16 December 1992) [29].

[13] *Bensaid v United Kingdom* (2001) 33 EHRR 205.

[14] *EB v France* (n 1) [43].

[15] *Smith and Grady v United Kingdom* (2000) 29 EHRR 493 [89].

[16] C Draghici, *The Legitimacy of Family Rights in Strasbourg Case Law – 'Living Instrument' or Extinguished Sovereignty?* (Oxford, Hart, 2017) 30.

[17] *X, Y and Z v United Kingdom* (1997) 24 EHRR 143 [36]; *Marckx v Belgium*, App no 6833/74 (ECtHR, 13 June 1979) [31].

[18] *K & T v Finland* App No 25702/94 (ECtHR, 12 July 2001) [150].

Article 41 of the Irish Constitution. The concept of 'family life' under Article 8 has been found to extend to, inter alia, cohabiting opposite-sex couples, an unmarried mother and her child, an unmarried father and his child, a cis-trans opposite-sex couple and their child, and a same-sex couple with children.

IV. Article 14

Article 14 of the Convention provides that

> the enjoyment of the rights and freedoms set forth in this Convention shall be secured without discrimination on any ground such as sex, race, colour, language, political or other opinion, national or social origin, association with a national minority, property, birth or other status.

Although sexual orientation discrimination was not explicitly referred to by the drafters, it falls within 'other status' and the ECtHR has declared that such discrimination is indeed 'covered by Article 14 of the Convention'.[19] This is because the list of grounds on which discrimination is not permitted, as set out in the provision is 'illustrative and not exhaustive, as is shown by the words "any ground *such as*"'.[20] As is apparent from the wording of Article 14, it is not free-standing; it can only be relied upon when another provision of the ECHR or one of the Convention's Protocols is engaged. As I shall demonstrate, Article 14 has assisted LGBT+ applicants challenging national laws that discriminate against them on the basis of their sexual orientation in aspects of their private or family life, as protected under Article 8. Nonetheless, the ECtHR has often reiterated that differential treatment under national law is only discriminatory for the purposes of Article 14 'if it has no objective and reasonable justification, which means that it does not pursue a 'legitimate aim' or if there is no 'reasonable proportionality between the means employed and the aim sought to be realised'.[21]

The Court has also stated that 'if the reasons advanced for such a difference in treatment were based *solely* on considerations regarding the applicant's sexual orientation this would amount to discrimination under the Convention.'[22] However, the margin of appreciation also plays a significant role in the ECtHR's Article 14 assessment such that differences in treatment under national laws that are based on sexual orientation have occasionally been upheld by the Court *when coupled with* a lack of European consensus.[23]

---

[19] *EB v France* (n 1) [50].

[20] *Fretté v France*, App No 36515/97 (ECtHR, 26 February 2002) [32]; emphasis added.

[21] *X v Austria* (n 9) [98].

[22] *EB v France* (n 1) [93]; emphasis added. In *Salgueiro da Silva Mouta v Portugal* App No 33290/96 (ECtHR, 21 December 1999) the Court found that the Contracting State's refusal to award the LGBT+ applicant custody of his biological child was based solely on his sexual orientation and this violated his right to respect for family life *with his child* under Article 8 on grounds prohibited by Art 14.

[23] *Fretté v France* (n 20).

V. Same-Sex Relationships and the ECtHR: Respect for Private and Family Life, but not yet Wedded Bliss

Despite its tendency to generally be progressive in its interpretation of rights under Article 8, the ECtHR only recognised childless same-sex unions as being embraced by the 'family life' aspect of this provision as recently as 2010. Further, 'family life' under Article 8 was only afforded to same-sex unions with children in 2012. To date, the ECtHR has not held that Article 12, or Article 8 when read in conjunction with Article 14, require a right to same-sex marriage to be recognised by the Contracting States. The journey from the recognition of consensual same-sex sexual activity under the respect for 'private life' limb of Article 8 to the recognition of same-sex relationships as 'family life' took a staggering 30 years and, in spite of the limited advances made since 2010, the court remains reluctant to vindicate the Article 8 rights of same-sex couples who are raising children.

VI. Consensual Same-Sex Sexual Activity and Relationships as Private Life under Article 8

In 1988 the ECtHR held in *Norris v Ireland* that the Irish legislation criminalising private consensual same-sex sexual activity between consenting male adults was in breach of the right to respect for one's private life under Article 8.[24] Indeed, legislation in Northern Ireland penalising such activity had already been deemed contrary to Article 8 in 1980 in *Dudgeon v United Kingdom*.[25] It is indubitable that the applicant's success in *Norris* was instrumental in paving the way for the legalisation of private same-sex sexual activity between consenting male adults in Ireland, and a range of subsequent legislative protections for LGBT+ persons. In 1993, five years after the *Norris* decision, the Criminal Law (Sexual Offences) Act came into force, abolishing the offences of buggery and gross indecency between males.[26] Legislative protections for LGBT+ persons were subsequently imposed in the fields of insurance,[27] employment[28] and goods and services.[29]

---

[24] *Norris v Ireland* (1988) 13 EHRR 186.

[25] *Dudgeon v United Kingdom* (1982) 4 EHRR 149.

[26] In 1993, the then Minister for Justice, Máire Geoghegan-Quinn, was instrumental in bringing about the decriminalisation of consensual same-sex sexual activity when, on 15 June 1993, she published the Criminal Law (Sexual Offences) Bill 1993, which was enacted and signed into law weeks later by President Mary Robinson as the Criminal Law (Sexual Offences) Act 1993.

[27] Health Insurance Act 1994.

[28] Employment Equality Act 1998.

[29] Equal Status Acts 2000–04. For a thorough analysis of the statutory protections afforded to LGBT+ individuals by the Oireachtas since decriminalisation see F Ryan 'Sexual Orientation Discrimination' in Cotter and Moffatt (eds), *Discrimination Law* (London, Cavendish 2005) ch 7.

In Strasbourg, an LGBT+ individual's right to respect for private life under the ECHR was further bolstered post-*Dudgeon* and *Norris* in two significant cases taken against the UK, when a different legal age of consent for opposite-sex and same-sex sexual activity under domestic law, and one's dismissal from employment on grounds of their sexual orientation, were respectively found to be in breach of Article 8.[30]

A. Pension Rights for a Surviving Same-Sex Partner and Article 8

The ECtHR might have come to protect same-sex intimacy between consenting adults, but the next logical step, the recognition of intimate, committed same-sex relationships as an aspect of 'family life' under Article 8, was not taken by the Court until *three decades* later. Even shortly after the turn of the millennium, in *Mata Estevez v Spain*,[31] the ECtHR held that the Spanish Government's refusal to grant the applicant a survivor's pension after his male partner's death was permissible, as this benefit was predominantly available to opposite-sex married couples. A non-marital opposite-sex partner was only eligible to claim this benefit following a partner's death if the parties were unable to marry because of the lack of Spanish divorce laws prior to 1981. The Court found that marriage constituted an essential precondition for eligibility for a survivor's pension and, even in the situation of the non-marital opposite-sex partner who was unable to marry, it was a notional condition for recognition of eligibility, which under Spanish law at the time it was not for same-sex couples. Although the applicant claimed that the Spanish authorities were acting in breach of his right to respect for 'family life', the ECtHR pronounced that because there was little agreement between the Contracting States on the issue of relationship recognition for same-sex couples, this was an area where they still enjoyed a wide margin of appreciation, and accordingly 'long-term homosexual relationships between two men do not fall within the scope of the right to respect for family life guaranteed by Article 8 of the Convention'.[32]

The Court further held that any discrimination between same-sex couples (and *most* cohabiting opposite-sex couples) and married couples was justified under Article 14 because the Spanish Government was pursuing a 'legitimate aim', ie protection of the family based on marriage bonds. Indeed, it is still acceptable under the ECHR for states to treat married and non-marital relationships differently in law.[33]

---

[30] See *Sutherland v UK* App No 25186/94 (ECmHR, 1 July 1997) and *Smith and Grady v UK* App No 33985/96 and 33986/96 (ECtHR, 27 September 1999). Further, in *Salgueiro da Silva Mouta v Portugal* App No 33290/96 (ECtHR, 21 December 1999) the Court recognised under Art 8 an LGBT+ father's right to respect for family life with his biological child from a previous opposite-sex relationship.

[31] *Mata Estevez v Spain* App No 56501/00 (ECtHR, 10 May 2001).

[32] ibid.

[33] *Gas and Dubois v France* App No 25951/07 (ECtHR, 15 March 2012).

As to whether the statutory restriction interfered with the applicant's right to respect for his private life, the ECtHR acknowledged that his emotional and sexual relationship with the deceased was protected under this tier of Article 8. Nonetheless the Court simply held that if there was any interference then this was justified by Article 8(2) of the ECHR, but the Court failed to identify which aspect of this provision the prima facie discriminatory treatment was saved by.[34]

B. Succession to a Tenancy for a Surviving Same-Sex Partner and Article 8

In *Karner v Austria*,[35] decided in 2003, the ECtHR stipulated that where domestic legislation allows a non-marital opposite-sex partner yet precludes a same-sex partner from succeeding to a tenancy, it will be in breach of the ECHR. This is because treating an unmarried same-sex partner differently to an unmarried opposite-sex partner would result in an interference with the former's right to respect for their home under Article 8 solely on the grounds of sexual orientation, contrary to Article 14. Since the Court decided the case under the respect for one's home limb of Article 8 it did not have to consider the application of the concepts of private life or family life contained therein. The Government had submitted that the discrimination was justified because the impugned statutory provision had an 'objective and reasonable justification', namely protection of the traditional family. The ECtHR cited its previous decision in *Mata Estevez* and accepted that 'protection of the family in the traditional sense is, in principle, a weighty and legitimate reason which might justify a difference in treatment'.[36] However, the Court went on to demonstrate a stringent approach to sexual orientation discrimination, one requiring a considerable nexus between the 'reasonable justification' and the means employed by the Contracting State to realise it, as

> the aim of protecting the family in the traditional sense is rather abstract and a broad variety of concrete measures may be used to implement it. In cases in which the margin of appreciation afforded to Member States is narrow, as is the position where there is a difference in treatment based on sex or sexual orientation, the principle of proportionality does not merely require that the measure chosen is in principle suited for realising the aim sought. It must also be shown that it was necessary in order to achieve that aim to exclude certain categories of people – in this instance persons living in a homosexual relationship – from the scope of application of section 14 of the Rent Act.[37]

The Court found that the Austrian Government had not proffered convincing and weighty reasons that justified excluding the surviving partner of a same-sex couple

---

[34] Article 8(2) permits the curtailment of rights protected by Art 8(1) on certain grounds. See n 11.
[35] *Karner v Austria* (n 9).
[36] ibid [40].
[37] ibid [41].

from the ambit of the impugned tenancy legislation, and consequently there had been a violation of Article 8 when taken in conjunction with Article 14.

C. Are *Mata Estevez* and *Karner* Compatible?

Bamforth has argued that in *Karner*, 'the Court's decision made it hard to see how the denial in *Estevez* that same-sex couples enjoyed family rights when it came to claiming social security entitlements could easily be distinguished.'[38] However, it is respectfully submitted that the two decisions are not in any way inconsistent. *Karner* was an easier case for the Court to decide because, unlike *Mata Estevez*, where the relief sought was arguably more controversial since the Court has often held that the Convention does not guarantee 'any right to a pension at all',[39] the right to respect for one's home is expressly protected under Article 8. This obviated the necessity to make pronouncements on the existence or non-existence of family life between same-sex partners. In any event, it is submitted that had the Court considered whether family life exists between same-sex partners in *Karner* it would have reached the same conclusion as in *Mata Estevez* because there had been very little movement in the *interim* towards providing for legislative recognition of same-sex relationships amongst the Contracting States.

Further, because the discrimination in *Karner* was between the surviving member of an opposite-sex couple (whether married or unmarried) who was entitled to succeed to a tenancy, and the survivor of a same-sex couple who was not so entitled, it was clearly based on sexual orientation alone. In *Mata Estevez*, subject to a minor exception, only the survivor of a married opposite-sex couple was entitled to claim a survivor's pension so unmarried couples, *whether of the same or the opposite sex*, were predominantly treated the same by the law. Hence the discrimination in that case was actually between married and unmarried couples, which is acceptable under the Convention.[40] Clayton and Tomlinson have observed that it is well-established in the ECtHR case law that 'the Convention confers preferential status to the traditional marriage' and consequently 'married couples are ... not treated as being in an analogous position with unmarried couples in relation to their right to found a family or where complaints of discrimination are made'.[41]

Arguably, *Karner* sees the ECtHR adopting a middle ground as regards same-sex relationships. It had recognised the sexual relationship between same-sex partners as an aspect of private life over 20 years earlier and it would come to recognise committed same-sex relationships as amounting to family life seven

---

[38] N Bamforth, 'Families but not (yet) Marriages? Same-Sex Partners and the Developing European Convention "Margin of Appreciation"' (2011) 23 *Child and Family Law Quarterly* 128.

[39] Indeed, this was recently reiterated by the Court in *Savickis v Latvia* App No 49270/11 (ECtHR, 9 June 2022).

[40] *Gas and Dubois v France* (n 32).

[41] R Clayton and H Tomlinson, *The Law of Human Rights: Volume 1*, 2 edn (Oxford, OUP, 2009) [13.71]. See also Bamforth, 'Families but not (yet) Marriages?' (2011).

years later.[42] In *Karner*, by requiring Contracting States to permit an LGBT+ individual to succeed to the tenancy of their deceased same-sex partner where this right is available to a non-marital opposite-sex partner, the Court was really obliging states to enact or amend existing legislation that would retrospectively recognise the familial ties between committed same-sex partners for the purpose of protecting an LGBT+ individual's express right to respect for their home under Article 8. Bamforth provides an apt summation of the case law prior to 2010 where Articles 8 and 14 were pleaded by an individual LGBT+ applicant, in that the ECtHR

> seems almost to be saying that lesbians and gay men may readily secure Convention protection when it comes to sexual activity or matters related to their private lives as individuals … but not when their deeper emotional and familial relationships are directly in issue.[43]

D. Article 8 and the Right to Respect for One's Home in England and Wales, and Ireland

The reactions to the *Karner* decision in England and Wales, and Ireland, are noteworthy. Although the *Karner* case was taken against Austria, in England and Wales, the judicial and legislative arms of Government responded swiftly. In *Ghaidan v Godin-Mendoza*[44] the House of Lords confirmed the Court of Appeal's earlier interpretation of tenancy legislation as embracing both an opposite-sex and a same-sex partner's right to succeed to a tenancy, despite the fact that the legislation only allowed a 'wife' or a 'husband' or a person living with the original tenant as such to succeed.[45] Their Lordships held that one could succeed to a tenancy if one was living with the original tenant *as if* they were his or her wife or husband, ie cohabiting in a committed relationship, irrespective of their sexual orientation. Their Lordships so acted in order to bring the statute in line with England and Wales' post-*Karner* obligations under the Convention. Lord Millett dissented, arguing that the terms 'husband' and 'wife' in the statute were gender-specific and that to succeed to the tenancy the LGBT+ appellant would have to demonstrate that he had been living with the tenant in a relationship as if he was the tenant's wife because a man cannot have a husband.[46] A more satisfactory solution to this dilemma came about in December 2005 when the Civil Partnership Act 2004 came into force. This is because Schedule 8 of this statute amended Schedule 1 of the Rent Act 1977 so that a same-sex cohabitant could succeed to their partner's tenancy if they were living together 'as if they were civil partners'. In any event, since the

---

[42] See *Dudgeon v United Kingdom* (n 24); *Schalk and Kopf v Austria* (n 1).
[43] Bamforth (n 38) 142.
[44] *Ghaidan v Godin-Mendoza* [2004] 2 AC 557.
[45] See also the discussion in F Ryan, 'Case Note: *Ghaidan v. Godin-Mendoza*' (2005) 27 *Journal of Social Welfare and Family Law* 355.
[46] [2004] 2 AC 557 [80] (Lord Millett).

introduction of marriage equality in England and Wales, a same-sex cohabitant can succeed to their partner's tenancy if they were living together 'as if they were a married couple', because Schedule 3 of the Marriage (Same-Sex Couples) Act 2013 provides that 'a reference to a married couple is to be read as including a reference to a married same sex couple' in existing legislation in England and Wales.[47]

However, in Ireland, the Residential Tenancies Act 2004 was enacted, and was in clear contravention of the state's obligations under Article 8 following the ECtHR's *Karner* decision. The gender-specific language contained in section 39 of the 2004 Act enabled only a person who was living with the tenant as 'husband and wife' in the dwelling for six months prior to their death to succeed to the tenancy. The state's obligation to respect one's 'home' under Article 8 was only brought in line with *Karner* in 2011 when the Civil Partnership and Certain Rights and Obligations of Cohabitants Act 2010 entered into force and amended the 2004 Act so that in addition to a spouse or an opposite-sex cohabitant, a civil partner or same-sex cohabitant could finally succeed to a tenancy.[48]

VII. Same-Sex Couples and Family Life under Article 8

In 2010 the ECtHR finally declared that same-sex couples enjoyed a right to respect for their 'family life' under Article 8 of the Convention. In *Schalk and Kopf v Austria*, the applicants, a cohabiting same-sex couple living in a stable de facto partnership, queried whether same-sex marriage could be embraced by Article 12 and, if not, whether a right to marry could instead be derived from Article 8 of the ECHR.[49] If this latter interpretation was possible, they claimed that their exclusion from the institution of marriage by Austrian domestic law amounted to sexual orientation discrimination contrary to Article 14. The ECtHR reiterated that same-sex relationships fell within the notion of 'private life' under Article 8 and, for the first time, the Court found that such unions could also constitute 'family life' under this provision. This was because, in the nine years since the decision in *Mata Estevez v Spain*,[50] a rapid evolution of social attitudes towards same-sex couples had occurred in many states, which had resulted in a large number granting legal recognition to such couples.[51] While 19 out of 47 Contracting

---

[47] See the Marriage (Same Sex Couples) Act 2013, Sch 4, Pt 1, para 1(1)(b).

[48] Civil Partnership and Certain Rights and Obligations of Cohabitants Act 2010, ss 40, 172 and 203. Today, given marriage equality, a same-sex spouse would simply fall within the definition of 'spouse' in the 2004 Act.

[49] *Schalk and Kopf v Austria* (n 10). The potential for the recognition of same-sex marriage under Art 12 of the ECHR will be examined later in this chapter.

[50] *Mata Estevez v Spain* (n 31).

[51] *Schalk and Kopf v Austria* (n 1) [93]. Indeed, in the later case of *Vallianatos v Greece* App Nos 29381/09 and 32684/09 (ECtHR, 7 November 2013) [73] the ECtHR recognised the right to respect for family life of stable same-sex couples who lived apart – the Court held that 'the fact of not cohabiting

States providing legal recognition for same-sex relationships was not even a bare majority to declare a 'consensus', the Court deemed this 'an *emerging* European consensus towards legal recognition of same-sex couples'.[52] In addition, the Court observed that certain provisions of EU law reflect a growing tendency to include same-sex couples in the notion of 'family'.[53] However, despite same-sex couples now enjoying 'family life', the possibility of recognising same-sex marriage under Article 8 was dismissed because the Court held that the ECHR 'is to be read as a whole and its Articles should therefore be construed in harmony with one another' and accordingly because

> Article 12 does not impose an obligation on Contracting States to grant same-sex couples access to marriage, Article 14 taken in conjunction with Article 8, a provision of more general purpose and scope, cannot be interpreted as imposing such an obligation either.[54]

This is consistent with the Court's earlier finding in *Parry v United Kingdom* that 'Article 12 is the *lex specialis* for the right to marry'[55] and, because a right to same-sex marriage could not even be derived from Article 8, Article 14 was not engaged.

At the time of their application, the applicants in *Schalk and Kopf* also claimed that by denying them the right to have their relationship formally recognised *other than through marriage*, the Austrian Government was discriminating against them on grounds of sexual orientation. However, since registered civil partnership laws had been enacted in Austria six months prior to the case being heard, the ECtHR held that it no longer had to examine whether the lack of any means of legal recognition for same-sex couples was in violation of Articles 8 and 14. Nonetheless, the Court was not swayed by the applicants' argument that if a state chooses to provide same-sex couples with an alternative means of relationship recognition, it is obliged to confer a status on them which – though carrying a different name – corresponds to the institution of marriage in every respect. The Court held that, when recognising same-sex relationships, 'States enjoy a certain margin of appreciation as regards the exact status conferred by alternative means of recognition'.[56] This indicated that Contracting States may not even need to introduce civil partnership, let alone marriage, to accord same-sex relationships respect for family life under Article 8. Indeed, it appeared possible that a statutory redress model for cohabiting couples akin to that which was about to be enacted in Ireland at the time might even have sufficed to respect the family life of same-sex couples.

However, the Court's position on the appropriate means of recognising same-sex relationships became clearer, albeit incrementally. In 2013, in *Vallianatos v Greece*, the ECtHR confirmed that where a state is introducing civil partnership

---

does not deprive the couples concerned of the stability which brings them within the scope of family life within the meaning of Article 8'.
[52] *Schalk and Kopf v Austria* (n 1) [105]; emphasis added.
[53] *Schalk and Kopf v Austria* (n 1).
[54] ibid [101].
[55] *Parry v United Kingdom* App No 42971/02 (ECtHR, 28 November 2006).
[56] *Schalk and Kopf v Austria* (n 1) [108].

for opposite-sex couples, it must make it available to same-sex couples also.[57] In this case, Greece had introduced civil partnership for opposite-sex couples and the Court held that this violated Articles 8 and 14. Thus, a state was only obliged to make civil partnership equally available to same-sex couples where it *chose* to provide a means of recognising formalised relationships outside marriage.

Nonetheless, by the time *Oliari v Italy* was decided in 2015, the Court observed 'the movement towards legal recognition of same-sex couples which had continued to develop rapidly in Europe since the Court's judgment in *Schalk and Kopf*, and it observed that 'twenty-four countries out of the forty-seven CoE Member States have already enacted legislation permitting same-sex couples to have their relationship recognised as a legal marriage or as a form of civil union or registered partnership.[58] Consequently, the Court finally confirmed that the lack of *any legal mechanism* for a same-sex couple to formalise their relationship in Italy was in breach of Article 8 of the Convention and,[59] quite significantly, it emphasised that

> in the absence of marriage, same-sex couples like the applicants have a particular interest in obtaining the option of entering into a form of civil union or registered partnership, since this would be *the most appropriate way* in which they could have their relationship legally recognised.[60]

In *Oliari*, the Court may have been willing to indicate that a form of civil partnership was the most appropriate way to formally recognise same-sex relationships outside of marriage because a thin majority of CoE states had either legislated for marriage or such a functional equivalent for recognising same-sex relationships.[61] Thus, one is inclined to agree with Scherpe that any legal framework introduced by a Council of Europe Contracting State aimed at recognising same-sex relationships 'will for the most part have to be a true and full functional equivalent of marriage' to comply with Article 8.[62]

VIII. The Evolution of the Right to Marry under Article 12

Article 12 of the Convention does not define marriage, but it nonetheless stipulates that 'men and women of marriageable age have the right to marry and to found a family, according to national laws governing the exercise of this right'.

---

[57] *Vallianatos and Others v Greece* App Nos: 29381/09 and 32684/09 (ECtHR, 7 November 2013).

[58] *Oliari and Others v Italy*, App Nos 18766/11 and 36030/11 (ECtHR, 21 July 2015) [55].

[59] *Oliari and Others v Italy*, App Nos 18766/11 and 36030/11 (ECtHR, 21 July 2015). The Court recently reiterated this finding in *Fedotova and Others v Russia*, App Nos 40792/10, 30538/14 and 43439/14 (ECtHR, 13 July 2021).

[60] ibid, [174]; emphasis added.

[61] ibid, [178].

[62] JM Scherpe, 'The Legal Recognition of Same-Sex Couples in Europe and the Role of the European Court of Human Rights' (2013) 10 *The Equal Rights Review* 83, 92.

In a series of cases between 1986 and 1998, the ECtHR refused to recognise the reassigned gender of trans persons as an aspect of their right to respect for private life under Article 8, and it also refused to recognise their right to marry a person of the opposite sex under Article 12. Thus, a male-to-female trans person could not marry a male under Article 12, or vice versa, because this was seen by the Court as a marriage between two persons of the same biological sex.[63] Further, the Court emphasised the link between marriage and procreation by stating that 'Article 12 is *mainly concerned* to protect marriage as the basis of the family'.[64] An appreciation of the reasoning in the ECtHR's case law concerning a trans person's right to marry is crucial to understanding the potential for recognising same-sex marriage under Article 12.

A. *Goodwin v United Kingdom*: A Progressive Article 12 for a New Millennium

In 2002 the Grand Chamber of the ECtHR handed down judgment in the landmark trans rights case of *Goodwin v United Kingdom*.[65] Christine Goodwin was a post-operative trans person seeking the vindication of her rights under Articles 8 and 12, and she was successful before the court. By 2002, 33 of the then 43 Council of Europe Contracting States legally recognised the reassigned gender of trans persons. In addition, gender reassignment was legally recognised in Singapore, Israel, South Africa, Canada, Australia, New Zealand and all but two of the 50 US States. The ECtHR noted that there was no common European approach as to how to address the repercussions of the legal recognition of gender reassignment, but that 'the lack of such a common approach among forty-three Contracting States with widely diverse legal systems and traditions is hardly surprising'[66] and hence in its judgment the Court proceeded to attach

> less importance to the lack of evidence of a common European approach to the resolution of the legal and practical problems posed than to the clear and uncontested evidence of a continuing international trend in favour not only of increased social acceptance of transsexuals but of legal recognition of the new sexual identity of post-operative transsexuals.[67]

---

[63] In *Rees v United Kingdom* (1986) 9 EHRR 56, the ECtHR held, at [49], that 'in the Court's opinion, the right to marry guaranteed by Article 12 refers to the traditional marriage between persons of opposite biological sex'. This was the second trans rights case to go before the ECtHR. *Van Oosterwijck v Belgium*, App No 7654/76 (ECtHR, 6 November 1980) was the first case taken to Strasbourg by a trans person, but the ECtHR refused to hear the merits of the case because the applicant had failed to exhaust all of the available *domestic* remedies in Belgium.

[64] ibid.

[65] *Goodwin v United Kingdom* (2002) 35 EHRR 18.

[66] ibid, [85].

[67] ibid. The terminology used by the Court in this passage reflects the understanding of gender identity at the time and the fact that it was not yet possible for a trans person to have their identity legally recognised anywhere in the world in the absence of medical/surgical interventions.

Additional evidence before the Court in *Goodwin* demonstrated that trans persons had been accorded the right to marry in their acquired gender in 54 per cent of the Contracting States as well as in the countries of Australia and New Zealand.[68] Thus, there was evidence of a thin European consensus on allowing a trans person to marry in their assigned gender, given that a majority of the Contracting States provided for this. In addition, there was slight evidence of an international tendency to move in this direction. Hence the Court acknowledged that

> fewer countries permit the marriage of transsexuals in their re-assigned gender than recognise the change of gender itself. The Court is not persuaded however that this supports an argument for leaving the matter entirely to the Contracting States as being within their margin of appreciation. This would be tantamount to finding that the range of options open to a Contracting State included an effective bar on any exercise of the right to marry. The margin of appreciation cannot extend so far.[69]

The Court was critical of the reasoning that had been employed in an earlier trans rights case, *Cossey v United Kingdom*, 12 years earlier:

> [I]t is artificial to assert that post-operative transsexuals have not been deprived of the right to marry as, according to law, they remain able to marry a person of their former opposite sex. The applicant in this case lives as a woman, is in a relationship with a man and would only wish to marry a man. She has no possibility of doing so. In the Court's view, she may therefore claim that the very essence of her right to marry has been infringed.[70]

Consequently, the ECtHR handed down a landmark judgment and decided that not only does a trans person's right to respect for private life under Article 8 require that their reassigned gender be recognised under the Contracting States' laws, but they should also be allowed to marry a person of the opposite sex by virtue of Article 12.[71] Thus, the Court expanded the definitional confines of the right to marry by holding that a trans woman could marry a man. Regarding the express reference in Article 12 to the right of men and women to marry, the Court was 'not persuaded that at the date of this case it can still be assumed that these terms must refer to a determination of gender by purely biological criteria'.[72]

---

[68] ibid, [57].

[69] ibid, [103].

[70] ibid, [101]. The terminology used by the Court in this passage reflects the understanding of gender identity at the time and the fact that it was not yet possible for a trans person to have their identity legally recognised anywhere in the world in the absence of medical/surgical interventions.

[71] Merely two days prior to the *Goodwin* decision being handed down, the High Court in Ireland concluded that a trans person had neither a right to have their reassigned gender recognised nor a right to marry a person of the opposite sex under the provisions of Irish Law: see *Foy v An t-Ard Chláraitheoir* [2002] IEHC 116. For a discussion of the *Goodwin* and *Foy* cases, see R O'Gorman, 'A Change will do you Good: The Evolving Position of Transsexuals under Irish and European Convention Law' (2004) 7 *Trinity College Law Review* 41. In 2007, the High Court in Ireland declared that, post-*Goodwin*, Irish law was incompatible with the provisions of the ECHR, and a Declaration of Incompatibility was issued under the European Convention on Human Rights Act 2003, s 5: see *Foy v An t-Ard Chláraitheoir* [2007] IEHC 470. The enactment of the Gender Recognition Act 2015 finally brought Irish law in line with the requirements of the ECHR.

[72] ibid [100].

B. Reactions to *Goodwin* in England and Wales, and Ireland

In the aftermath of the decision in *Goodwin*, same-sex couples seeking recognition of their foreign same-sex marriages under domestic law raised Article 12 before the superior courts in England and Wales, and Ireland, as being capable of requiring same-sex marriage. In 2006, Wilkinson and Kitzinger sought to have their Canadian same-sex marriage recognised under the law in England and Wales, while in Ireland that same year Zappone and Gilligan wished for theirs to be recognised under Irish law.[73] In these cases, the plaintiffs essentially claimed that the refusal of each respective Contracting State to recognise their Canadian same-sex marriage under domestic law contravened Article 12 of the ECHR, because technically the ECtHR in *Goodwin* had 'recognised that there is under the Convention an entitlement of two people who both by birth and biology are of the same sex to have the right to marry'.[74]

In *Wilkinson v Kitzinger*, the plaintiffs argued that the ECtHR's decision in *Goodwin* cut free the traditional approach to marriage which was 'rooted in biological determinism',[75] and this made it possible for an English court to interpret Article 12 as a 'living instrument' which recognised the right to marry of two persons of the same, as well as of the opposite, sex. However, this argument was refuted by Potter P, who felt that the ECtHR in *Goodwin* had in fact recognised 'the phenomenon of *re-assigned gender* whereby the applicant became eligible to marry, *as a woman*, a man of her choice'.[76] In the *Zappone* case Dunne J, in considering Article 12, relied heavily on the judgment in *Wilkinson v Kitzinger* because she felt that it 'set out clearly the position in relation to the right of marriage as identified by the European Court of Human Rights'[77] in *Goodwin*. Dunne J found Potter P's decision in respect of the Article 12 argument in that case to be 'compelling'[78] and she proceeded to endorse it without hesitation in the case before her. Thus the UK and Irish superior courts interpreted the ECtHR's approach to Article 12 in *Goodwin* as meaning that the parties must legally be recognised as male and female, respectively. Indeed, this interpretation of Article 12 was confirmed that same year because also in 2006, in *Parry v United Kingdom*, the ECtHR reiterated that Article 12 'enshrines the traditional concept of marriage as being between a man and a woman' and this is the case whether the parties' gender 'derives from attribution at birth or from a gender recognition procedure. Same-sex marriages are not permitted'.[79]

---

[73] See *Wilkinson v Kitzinger* [2007] 1 FLR 295 and *Zappone v Revenue Commissioners* [2008] 2 IR 417.
[74] *Zappone v Revenue Commissioners* (n 73) [249].
[75] *Wilkinson v Kitzinger* (n 73) [60].
[76] ibid [61].
[77] *Zappone v Revenue Commissioners* (n 73) [250].
[78] ibid.
[79] *Parry v United Kingdom* (n 55).

The Court continued by stating that

> while it is true that there are a number of Contracting States which have extended marriage to same-sex partners, this reflects their own vision of the role of marriage in their societies and does not, perhaps regrettably to many, flow from an interpretation of the fundamental right as laid down by the Contracting States in the Convention in 1950.[80]

Indeed, 'it is of course open to Member States to provide for rights more generous than those guaranteed by the Convention'[81] in their domestic laws. The Contracting States' ability to do so is recognised by Article 53 of the ECHR, which provides that 'nothing in this Convention shall be construed as limiting or derogating from any of the human rights and fundamental freedoms which may be ensured under the laws of any High Contracting Party'. While countries like Ireland and the UK have recently moved beyond Article 12 of the Convention by extending marriage to same-sex couples via their domestic laws, the following analysis of *Schalk and Kopf v Austria* illustrates that a right to same-sex marriage can now be derived from Article 12, but is not yet *required* by this provision. Contracting States with traditional views on marriage are not obliged to embrace same-sex marriage in order to comply with any obligation under Article 12 of the ECHR, though this may change in the future in light of evidence of an 'emerging' European consensus on the issue.

IX.   Same-Sex Marriage and Article 12 of the ECHR – *Schalk and Kopf v Austria*

As recently as 2010, the ECtHR gave its premier ruling on same-sex marriage and Article 12. In *Schalk and Kopf v Austria* the Court acknowledged that it had 'not yet had an opportunity to examine whether two persons who are of the same-sex can claim to have a right to marry'.[82] The applicants sought to test whether Austrian law's refusal to allow them to enter into a same-sex marriage violated Article 12 or as discussed, Article 8 taken in conjunction with Article 14. The applicants argued that the text of Article 12 did not necessarily have to be read in the sense that 'men' could only marry 'women' and vice versa. In response, the ECtHR observed that 'looked at in isolation, the wording of Article 12 might be interpreted so as not to exclude the marriage between two men or two women'.[83] Although the ECtHR recognised the literal potential of Article 12 to embrace same-sex marriage,

---

[80] ibid.

[81] *R (Ullah) v Special Adjudicator* [2004] UKHL 26 [20].

[82] *Schalk and Kopf v Austria* (n 1).

[83] *Schalk and Kopf v Austria* (n 1) [55]. Indeed, this point was acknowledged by Walsh and Ryan in 2006 when they observed that Art 12 'does not explicitly state that men and women may only marry *each other*': see J Walsh and F Ryan, *The Rights of de facto Couples* (Dublin, IHRC, 2006) 56.

it qualified this by stating that the drafters' references to 'men' and 'women' therein must be regarded as deliberate because

> all other substantive articles of the Convention grant rights and freedoms to "everyone" … moreover, regard must be had to the historical context in which the Convention was adopted. *In the 1950s marriage was clearly understood in the traditional sense of being a union between partners of different sex.*[84]

It is possible that in 1950 the drafters of the ECHR may have intended to restrict the rights to marry and to found a family to opposite-sex couples by expressly referring to 'men' and 'women' rather than 'everyone' in Article 12. Further credence is given to this argument when one considers the drafters' reference to the regulation of '*this right*' by the national authorities, as this envisages a connection between the rights to marry and to found a family such that the rights would be restricted to those adult relationships where procreation was possible *in principle*. Thus, it is arguable that the rights to marry and to found a family were intentionally linked, and gendered, in Article 12.

However, it is equally possible that the drafters may not have decided to deny same-sex couples access to marriage by stipulating all of the above, but rather the issue of same-sex marriage may not even have been within their contemplation because homosexuality, like gender identity, was likely viewed as an 'ethical problem, but certainly not a legal issue' in 1950.[85] This is also a possible explanation as to why sexual orientation discrimination was not expressly included in Article 14 of the ECHR.[86] Further, assisted procreation techniques like donor-assisted reproduction and gestational surrogacy, which same-sex couples now commonly have recourse to, were neither possible nor practised at the time, so by linking the rights to marry and to found a family, the drafters were likely reflecting in Article 12 their clear understanding of the only type of couple that could possibly 'found' a family in 1950, rather than engaging in any intentional exclusion. Indeed, Draghici has observed that 'the legal recognition of the family rights of same-sex couples and transsexuals did not constitute the object of negotiation in the fora adopting the major international human rights treaties'.[87]

A. The Court's Historical Argument in *Schalk and Kopf*: Lacking Credibility and Coherence

The Court's reliance on the clear, 'traditional' understanding of marriage in the 1950s to skirt the request to recognise same-sex marriage under Article 12 is somewhat disingenuous. In 1950, a 'traditional' marriage under Article 12 was

---

[84] ibid; emphasis added.
[85] *Cossey v United Kingdom*, (1990) 13 EHRR 622 [4.4.2] (Judge Martens, dissenting).
[86] Indeed, discrimination on grounds of gender identity is also not expressly included in Art 14.
[87] Draghici, *The Legitimacy of Family Rights in Strasbourg Case Law* (2017) 187.

hardly understood as being between a trans person and a person of the opposite sex. Indeed, even in 1986, almost 50 years later, the ECtHR in *Rees v United Kingdom* made it clear that 'the right to marry guaranteed by Article 12 refers to the traditional marriage between persons of opposite *biological* sex'.[88]

However, as discussed, the ECtHR in *Goodwin* recognised a trans person's right to marry by articulating an understanding of 'men' and 'women' under Article 12 that extended beyond biological sexual dimorphism, even though this was not the type of traditional, opposite-sex marriage that was understood by the drafters, or the societies of 1950s Europe. Therefore, the Court's subsequent retreat in *Schalk and Kopf* to a narrow historical argument in order to avoid a further, progressive interpretation of Article 12 that would extend the right to marry to same-sex couples is quite unconvincing.

Further, the Court in *Goodwin* had expressly *separated* the rights guaranteed by Article 12 by pronouncing that 'Article 12 grants the right to marry to men and women … furthermore, Article 12 grants the right to found a family'[89] while declaring that

> the second aspect is not however a condition of the first and the inability of any couple to conceive or parent a child cannot be regarded as *per se* removing their right to enjoy the first limb of this provision.[90]

This constituted a remarkable departure from earlier judgments concerning the right to marry because by separating it from the ability to found a family the ECtHR was undoubtedly rejecting the argument that the institution of marriage is primarily designed to facilitate the procreation of children and, by doing so, it abolished any necessity for the parties to a civil marriage to be of the opposite biological sex.[91] Wintemute believed that such language left 'the door open to acknowledge same-sex marriage at some point in the future',[92] and I was inclined to agree, arguing that the Court's reasoning was significant on more than one level.[93] First, the Court used broad, gender-neutral constructions by referring to 'any couple' and 'their right', rather than a man and a woman, and second, the Court's reasoning, while applicable to trans persons who cannot, without assistance, 'conceive' children with a person of the opposite sex, could equally apply to same-sex partners who also cannot procreate without assistance. Thus, if the reasoning in *Goodwin* is followed through to its logical conclusion, trans persons and LGBT+ persons should *all* enjoy a right to marry under Article 12. However, in *Schalk and Kopf* the ECtHR was quick to simply point out that this previous divesting of marriage from procreation and parenting in *Goodwin* did not

---

[88] *Rees v United Kingdom* (n 63) [49]; emphasis added.

[89] ibid [54].

[90] *Goodwin v United Kingdom* (n 65) [98].

[91] See further B Tobin, 'Same-Sex Couples and the Law: Recent Developments in the British Isles' (2009) 23 *International Journal of Law, Policy and the Family* 309, 314.

[92] R Wintemute, 'The Massachusetts Same-Sex Marriage Case: Could Decisions from Canada, Europe, and South Africa Help the SJC?' (2004) 38 *New England Law Review* 505, 510.

[93] Tobin, 'Same-Sex Couples and the Law' (2009) 316–17.

'allow any conclusion regarding the issue of same-sex marriage'.[94] Given that the Court in *Schalk and Kopf* had already held that same-sex marriage is possible on one literal interpretation of Article 12, it is unclear as to why it was adamant that its previous disjunctive reading of this provision supports a trans person's right to marry but not same-sex marriage, when such reasoning appears apt to engender both. Indeed, as Faffelberger and Huber have pointed out 'it is at least questionable whether [an opposite-sex, cis-trans marriage] can be called a more 'traditional' marriage than the one between two same-sex partners, as also in this relationship parenthood is biologically impossible'.[95]

B. Article 9 of the Charter of Fundamental Rights of the European Union

In *Schalk and Kopf*, the Court expanded upon its previous analysis in *Goodwin* of an analogous provision guaranteeing the right to marry and the right to found a family, Article 9 of the Charter of Fundamental Rights of the European Union. In *Goodwin* the Court had observed that Article 9 departs 'no doubt deliberately' from the wording of Article 12 of the ECHR in removing the reference to men and women.[96] It is also intriguing that the ECtHR's dynamic reinterpretation of Article 12 in *Goodwin* brought it more in line with Article 9, which states that 'the right to marry *and* the right to found a family shall be guaranteed in accordance with the national laws governing the exercise of *these* rights'.[97]

As I observe elsewhere, the rights to marry and to found a family are separate and distinct rights under Article 9, as under Article 12 post-*Goodwin*.[98] In *Schalk and Kopf* the Court brought Article 12 further in line with Article 9. The Court quoted from the commentary to Article 9, which acknowledges that although the provision poses no obstacle to the recognition of same-sex marriage 'there is however no explicit requirement that domestic laws should facilitate such marriages'. In light of this, the Court held that

> regard being had to Article 9 of the Charter, therefore, the Court would no longer consider that the right to marry enshrined in Article 12 must in all circumstances be

---

[94] *Schalk and Kopf v Austria* (n 1) [56].

[95] G Faffelberger and S Huber, 'Marriage between Homosexuals: Equal Treatment and Right to Marriage' (2008) 2 *Vienna Online Journal on International Constitutional Law* 61, 64. However, *since* the judgment in *Schalk and Kopf*, self-identification laws enabling trans persons to have their gender identity recognised through a legal self-identification procedure without the need for sterilisation procedures and hormonal treatment have been passed in a small number of Council of Europe Contracting States: Denmark (2014); Ireland (2015); Malta (2015); Norway (2016); Belgium (2017); Greece (2017); Portugal (2018); Luxembourg (2018); Iceland (2019); and Switzerland (2022). Consequently, procreation is now possible in *same-sex* cis-trans marriages and relationships in these Contracting States, but it was not when the *Goodwin* or *Schalk and Kopf* cases were decided.

[96] *Goodwin v United Kingdom* (n 65) [100].

[97] Charter of Fundamental Rights of the European Union, Art 9; emphasis added.

[98] Tobin (n 91) 316–17.

limited to marriage between two persons of the opposite sex. Consequently, it cannot be said that Article 12 is inapplicable to the applicants' complaint. However, as matters stand, the question whether or not to allow same-sex marriage is left to regulation by the national law of the Contracting State.[99]

Hence the Court reiterated that Article 12 is capable of recognising same-sex marriage, like the analogous Article 9 of the EU Charter but, because of the impact of the margin of appreciation doctrine, to which I shall now turn, the Court remained entirely deferential to the national authorities by providing that regulation of the matter is for now best dealt with by them as 'Article 12 of the Convention does not impose an obligation on [Contracting States] to grant a same-sex couple … access to marriage'.[100] Given that the Court's reasons for declining to vindicate a right to same-sex marriage under Article 12 in *Schalk and Kopf* arguably lack credibility and coherence, I would agree with Wintemute's observation that 'When, despite the weakness of the justifications for excluding same-sex couples from marriage, an international or highest national court finds no discrimination, it will often be clear that a lack of consensus has trumped principle'.[101]

C. The Margin of Appreciation and Same-Sex Marriage in *Schalk and Kopf v Austria*

In *Schalk and Kopf* the recognition of a right to same-sex marriage under Article 12 seems largely to have foundered because of judicial recourse to the 'margin of appreciation'. In *Cossey v United Kingdom*, one of the early cases on trans rights, Judge Martens described the margin of appreciation as representative of 'judicial self-restraint'[102] because the Court is conscious of its position as an international court when called on to develop the law in a sensitive area, and he pointed out that

> the Court, at least as far as family law and sexuality are concerned, moves extremely cautiously when confronted with an evolution that has reached completion in some Member States, is still in progress in others but has seemingly left yet others untouched.[103]

When *Schalk and Kopf* was being decided, merely six Contracting States provided for same-sex marriage, thirteen others provided for registered civil partnership while most jurisdictions offered no legal protection to same-sex couples. The Court

---

[99] *Schalk and Kopf v Austria* (n 1) [61].
[100] ibid [63].
[101] R Wintemute, 'Same-Sex Marriage in National and International Courts – "Apply Principle Now" or "Wait for Consensus?"' (2020) 1 *Public Law* 134, 143.
[102] *Cossey v United Kingdom* (n 85) [3.6.4] (Martens J, dissenting).
[103] ibid, [5.6.3].

observed that there was 'no European consensus regarding same-sex marriage'.[104] Indeed, as Bamforth has pointed out,

> *Schalk and Kopf* provides an almost textbook illustration of the extent to which the Court's interpretation of key rights of the European Convention on Human Rights can turn on its analysis of the 'margin of appreciation', something which often rests on its perception of whether there exists a consensus among signatory states concerning the legal treatment of the issue in question, especially when that issue is of a socially sensitive nature.[105]

However, it is important to note that 'consensus' is but one factor and may not always be decisive of the scope of the margin of appreciation. Another factor may help to either reinforce or counterbalance this factor. In *Schalk and Kopf*, once the lack of a European consensus had been established by the Court, this was buttressed by the fact that 'marriage has deep-rooted social and cultural connotations which may differ largely from one society to another'.[106] As Potter P observed in *Wilkinson v Kitzinger*,

> the European Court of Human Rights has consistently declared itself to be slow to trespass on areas of social, political and religious controversy where a wide variety of national and cultural traditions are in play and different political and legal choices have been made by the Members of the Council of Europe.[107]

This is true of the Court's approach to the margin of appreciation in *Schalk and Kopf*. Although the Court literally identified the potential for same-sex marriage under Article 12, it then retreated and found that there was no obligation on states to recognise such marriages given the lack of a European consensus on the issue, *and* the differing social and cultural perceptions of marriage in the 47 Contracting States. However, Draghici argues that within the 'horizontal, consent-based international society, the existence of widespread European consensus is a critical legitimising factor for progressive ECHR construction', and thus the Court's invocation in *Schalk and Kopf* of the judicial self-restraint mechanism that is the margin of appreciation doctrine is arguably defensible as it encourages continued compliance with the ECHR by the Contracting States.[108] Indeed, as Wintemute observes, the UK has already resisted a judgment made against it in *Hirst v United Kingdom* and he argues that this course of action has effectively amended Article 46(1) of the ECHR, which provides that governments undertake to abide by the final judgment of the Court, by adding the proviso 'unless they strongly disagree with it'.[109] Wintemute believes it is possible that 'other European countries will follow the UK's lead'.[110] Therefore, Lau is perhaps wise to urge caution because if

---

[104] *Schalk and Kopf v Austria* (n 1) [58].
[105] Bamforth (n 38) 141.
[106] *Schalk and Kopf v Austria* (n 1) [62].
[107] *Wilkinson v Kitzinger* (n 73) [44].
[108] Draghici (n 16) 238.
[109] R Wintemute, 'Same-Sex Marriage in National and International Courts' (2020) 154.
[110] ibid.

the ECtHR 'were to forego judicial restraint and demand immediate implementation of marriage equality, it would risk alienating Contracting States, undermining their overall cooperation with the Court'.[111]

However, irrespective of one's view on the margin of appreciation doctrine, by declining to recognise same-sex marriage under Article 12 in *Schalk and Kopf*, the Court not only permitted the very essence of the applicants' right to marry to remain infringed but conveyed to the 47 Contracting States that an effective bar on the right to marry of many LGBT+ persons is acceptable under the ECHR. Many LGBT+ persons, like the applicants, may be inherently incapable of marrying a person of the opposite sex, yet in Contracting States where they have no possibility of marrying a person of the same sex, whom they are capable of entering into an intimate, committed relationship with on a physical, emotional and psychological level, the message from Strasbourg is that it is not in breach of Article 12 to infringe the *very essence* of their right to marry.[112] Thus, in *Schalk and Kopf*, it is opined that the ECtHR 'by nevertheless exercising judicial self-restraint, sadly failed its vocation of being the last resort protector of oppressed individuals'.[113]

D. The Fallacy of *Schalk* and *Kopf v Austria*

In *Schalk and Kopf*, when deciding the issue of 'family life' under Article 8 of the ECHR, the Court recognised 'that same-sex couples are just as capable as different-sex couples of entering into stable committed relationships' and as a result they have a 'need for legal recognition and protection of their relationship'.[114] Thus, what the Court really recognised is that same-sex relationships can, in essence, be *marriage-like*. It is submitted that the Court's reasoning exposes its moral viewpoint on same-sex marriage. The Court's willingness in *Schalk and Kopf* to recognise 'family life' between same-sex couples under Article 8, but not '*marital* family life' under Article 12 could not be supported by relying on a 'consensus' across Europe in favour of the former, because at the time there was simply no consensus on *either*. Even combining the number of Contracting States (19 out of 47) that recognised 'family life' via registered partnership or same-sex marriage did not provide the Court with the thin consensus needed to legitimise recognising 'family life' for same-sex couples under Article 8, so the Court deemed this an 'emerging' consensus.

Thus, despite not really having a basis for recognising either, the Court was prepared to endorse same-sex couples as non-marital family units worthy of respect

---

[111] H Lau, 'Rewriting Schalk and Kopf: Shifting the Locus of Deference' in E Brems (ed), *Diversity and European Human Rights: Rewriting Judgments of the ECHR* (Cambridge, CUP, 2013) 243, 250.

[112] The very essence of the right is denied to all gay and lesbian persons (whether cisgender or trans) who would only wish to marry a person of the same sex, but the issue is not as pronounced for bisexual persons unless they wish to exercise their right to marry a person of the same sex.

[113] *Cossey v United Kingdom* (n 85) [3.6.4].

[114] *Schalk and Kopf v Austria* (n 1) [99].

for family life under Article 8, but not marital family units under Article 12, even though the stability and commitment which the Court itself deems them capable of are self-evident characteristics of *both* types of relationship. Essentially, same-sex couples in an analogous situation to opposite-sex couples are being treated differently on the basis of sexual orientation by the Court itself which, ironically, has repeatedly warned the Contracting States that 'differences based on sexual orientation require particularly serious reasons by way of justification'.[115] The Court's reliance on the 'consensus' approach to justify protection under Article 8 rather than Article 12 is unconvincing because by its own admission there was 'not yet a majority of States providing for legal recognition of same-sex couples'[116] and, another way of interpreting the 'emerging consensus' is that it was an emerging consensus in relation to recognising same-sex relationships as being *marriage-like* in substance, because the 19 Contracting States provided for marriage or its near-equivalent – civil partnership – for same-sex couples. Arguably, the Court could have found that since there was an 'emerging consensus' in relation to allowing same-sex couples to *formalise* their relationships through *marriage or marriage-like* institutions, then a same-sex couple should enjoy the right to marry under Article 12.

The Court was prepared to downplay a clear lack of consensus because it was morally comfortable with according same-sex unions recognition as 'family life' under the ECHR. However, when it came to marriage, it is arguable that it suited the Court to *embrace* a clear lack of consensus coupled with the subject matter of marriage and its 'deep-rooted social and cultural connotations' which differ from state to state to reinforce its own moral view that marriage remains an opposite-sex institution. Indeed, the Court's refusal to extend the reasoning in *Goodwin* is also indicative of a moral viewpoint on the definition of marriage, as is its willingness to allow a broad margin of appreciation and continue the discrimination against same-sex couples in the area of marriage regardless of the judicially recognised situational analogy with opposite-sex couples. Judge Martens' dissenting remarks, uttered two decades earlier in *Cossey v United Kingdom* when trans persons were being denied access to marriage in Strasbourg, seem equally apt to critique the Court's approach to the interpretation of Articles 8 and 12 in *Schalk and Kopf*:

> It is hardly compatible with the modern, open and pragmatic construction of the concept of 'family life' which has evolved in the Court's case-law ... to base the interpretation of Article 12 merely on the traditional view according to which marriage was the pivot of a closed system of family law. On the contrary, that evolution calls for a more functional approach to Article 12 as well, an approach which takes into consideration the *factual conditions* of modern life.[117]

---

[115] *Karner v Austria* (n 9) [37].
[116] *Schalk and Kopf v Austria* (n 1) [105].
[117] *Cossey v United Kingdom* (n 85) [4.4.3] (Martens J, dissenting).

E. Article 12 Post-*Schalk and Kopf*

The Court cannot make the gender-specific Article 12 of the ECHR the true doppelganger of Article 9 of the EU Charter of Fundamental Rights through simply de-gendering its language. However, once satisfied that a consensus exists, the Court could show respect for the historical context in which the ECHR was adopted *and* reach the logical outcome of the reasoning employed in *Goodwin* over two decades ago, while further aligning the spirit of Article 12 with that of Article 9 of the EU Charter. All of this could be achieved by the Court simply having recourse to international developments, which it is increasingly prone to do.[118]

Therefore, when a future same-sex marriage case presents itself, the Court could expand the scope of Article 12 of the ECHR by embracing the novel approach of the South African Constitutional Court when it reinterpreted Article 16 of the Universal Declaration on Human Rights of 1948 to encompass same-sex marriage in *Minister for Home Affairs v Fourie*.[119] Both of these provisions are virtually identical, most likely because, as the ECtHR itself acknowledged in *Johnston v Ireland*, 'the text of Article 12 was based on that of Article 16'.[120] Thus, perhaps the ECtHR could one day assert that the drafters' reference to 'men and women' in Article 12 was *descriptive* of an assumed reality in 1950 (ie marriage between persons of opposite biological sex) rather than *prescriptive* of a normative structure for all time, just as the South African Constitutional Court did in relation to Article 16 in *Fourie*.[121] Indeed, Sachs J stated in *Fourie* that 'as the conditions of humanity alter and as ideas of justice and equity evolve, so do concepts of rights take on new texture and meaning'.[122] This reasoning would respect the historical context while also allowing the Court to fully embrace the liberal, inclusive interpretation of Article 12 briefly touched upon in *Schalk and Kopf*. Bamforth points out that 'Article 12 tends to follow rather than to lead the way',[123] and this was certainly true given that the Court in *Goodwin* waited for a bare European consensus to recognise a trans person's right to marry. However, 17 of the 47 Contracting States now recognise same-sex marriage, so there exists an 'emerging consensus' of the type endorsed by the Court in *Schalk and Kopf* in relation to recognising 'family life' in Article 8.[124] Thus, if the ECtHR once again embraces an 'emerging consensus', marriage for same-sex couples might be *required* by Article 12 in the very near future.

---

[118] Advisory Opinion P-16-2018-001 (n 10); *Savickis v Latvia* App No 49270/11 (ECtHR, 9 June 2022).

[119] [2005] ZACC 19.

[120] *Johnston v Ireland* (1986) 9 EHRR 203 [52].

[121] *Minister of Home Affairs v Fourie and Another* (2006) 3 BCLR 355 (CC) [100]. Article 16(1) of the Universal Declaration on Human Rights provides that 'men and women of full age, without any limitation due to race, nationality or religion, have the right to marry and to found a family. They are entitled to equal rights as to marriage, during marriage and at its dissolution'.

[122] ibid, [102].

[123] Bamforth (n 38) 147.

[124] Switzerland became the most recent Contracting State to recognise same-sex marriage on 1 July 2022.

X. Second-Parent Adoption by a Same-Sex Partner and the ECHR

Having previously been called upon to find in violation of Articles 8 and 14 of the Convention national laws and practices that discriminated against LGBT+ *individuals* seeking to adopt a child, in *Gas and Dubois v France* and *X v Austria* the Court was tasked with considering whether national laws that restricted second-parent adoption to opposite-sex married couples, or to opposite-sex married and cohabiting couples, were in compliance with the provisions of the ECHR. In this section, I shall demonstrate that the Court has adopted an inconsistent and somewhat incoherent approach in cases where restrictive second-parent adoption laws were challenged by same-sex civil or cohabiting partners when compared to opposite-sex couples, and that the Court has sometimes failed to be cognisant of the best interests of the child in these cases.

A. *Gas and Dubois v France*

In *Gas and Dubois v France*,[125] the ECtHR had to consider the case of a civil partner who sought to establish parental rights by adopting a child being raised by her and her civil partner. The child was conceived by means of artificial insemination from an anonymous gamete donor and had been raised by the applicants, Gas and Dubois, since her birth in the year 2000. In 2006, Gas applied for a simple adoption order. In France, simple adoption enables a second legal parent-child relationship to be established in addition to the original parent-child relationship based on genetic ties. Essentially, this results in the sharing of parentage and parental responsibility between the child's genetic parent and their second parent, but, at the time, this could only occur if the parties were husband and wife. In the case of adoption by civil partners, whether of the same sex or opposite sex, and cohabiting opposite-sex or same-sex couples, a simple adoption by a second parent would not have resulted in the sharing but in the transfer of parentage and parental responsibility to that parent, thus extinguishing the original legal parent-child relationship between the genetic parent and the child.[126]

Therefore, the Nanterre tribunal de grande instance refused the order because in this instance the adoption would have legal implications which ran counter to the applicant's intentions and the child's best interests. This conclusion was later upheld by the Versailles Court of Appeal. Gas and Dubois argued before the ECtHR that the French authorities' refusal to grant a simple adoption order breached their right to respect for private and family life under Article 8 on the ground of sexual orientation contrary to Article 14.

---

[125] *Gas and Dubois v France* (n 33).
[126] See Art 365 of the French Civil Code.

B. Family Life between Same-Sex Couples and their Children

The Court had already held that 'family life' can exist between an unmarried couple of the opposite sex (by birth or gender recognition) raising the genetic child of one member of the union[127] and, in this case, the Court, following an examination of the applicants' situation, deemed Article 8 applicable because 'family life' was present between the same-sex civil partners and their child.[128] Given this, the outcome was disappointing. *Gas and Dubois* involved direct discrimination on grounds of marital status, yet the ECtHR found that the applicants were not discriminated against when compared to opposite-sex married couples. The Court held that the applicants' situation as regards second-parent adoption was not comparable to that of a married couple in view of the 'special status' of marriage and the (rather nebulous) concept of the 'social, personal and legal consequences' associated with that institution.[129] Further, the Court reiterated its earlier findings in *Schalk and Kopf* that the ECHR does not require the Contracting States to grant same-sex couples access to marriage and that they enjoy a certain margin of appreciation in determining the exact status conferred on such couples by any alternative means of legal recognition.[130] In other words, when enacting civil partnership laws France was in no way obliged to grant same-sex couples like the applicants all the rights usually linked to marriage, such as the right to apply for a simple adoption order and share parentage and parental rights in relation to each other's children.

The Court also found that there was no difference in treatment based on sexual orientation because an opposite-sex couple who had entered into a civil partnership was also prohibited from obtaining a simple adoption order. Although there was no direct discrimination on the basis of sexual orientation, indirectly there was because French law permitted an opposite-sex couple with a child in exactly the same situation to marry and circumvent the prohibition related to simple adoption, whereas a same-sex couple like Gas and Dubois could not avail of this option. Nonetheless, the ECtHR concluded that there had been no violation of Article 14 taken in conjunction with Article 8.

C. Marriage and Civil Partnership – Separate or Equal Institutions?

The Court's decision in *Gas and Dubois* would appear to be somewhat at odds with the earlier decision in *Burden v United Kingdom*, where the Grand Chamber qualitatively equated civil partnership in the UK with marriage.[131] In *Burden*, the

---

[127] *Emonet v Switzerland* (2009) 49 EHRR 11; *X, Y and Z v United Kingdom* (1997) 24 EHRR 143.
[128] *Gas and Dubois v France* (n 33) [37].
[129] ibid, [68].
[130] ibid, [66].
[131] *Burden v United Kingdom* (2008) 47 EHRR 51.

Grand Chamber held that the legal consequences of marriage and civil partnership 'set these types of relationship apart from other forms of cohabitation'[132] and reached the conclusion that 'there can be no analogy between married and *Civil Partnership Act* couples, on one hand, and heterosexual or homosexual couples who choose to live together but not to become husband and wife or civil partners, on the other hand'.[133] Scherpe observed that following *Burden*, 'in the eyes of the ECtHR opposite-sex marriage and same-sex civil partnership were to be considered *the same type of relationship*'.[134] However, it is debatable as to whether this was the Court's general intention because it seemed to be equating the specific marriage-like type of civil partnership that is available under the Civil Partnership Act 2004 in the UK with marriage, not the two institutions more generally. Indeed, following *Burden*, in *Manenc v France* the ECtHR had held that it was permissible for France to exclude a same-sex civil partner from obtaining a survivor's pension that was only available to married couples under French law.[135] *Gas and Dubois* makes it clear that, despite being formalised relationships, marriage and civil partnership are certainly not viewed as one and the same by the Court once children enter the equation because it refused to find that there was any discriminatory treatment between a married couple and same-sex civil partners in the context of second-parent adoption.

Historically, the reason behind the severance of the existing legal relationship between the adopted child and its genetic parent was to provide for certainty and avoid any conflict of interest that might arise for the adopted person as a result of their new legal status as a child of the adoptive parents. However, such reasoning is not valid in the case of second-parent adoption by a person who is married to or in a civil partnership with the child's parent, and with whom the child will usually have a long-standing, pre-existing familial relationship – hence why the child's relationship with its genetic parent is not extinguished where the adoptive parent is married to the child's parent. The Court's reluctance to equate marriage and civil partnership in situations where donor-conceived children are being raised in the latter union is dissatisfying from a child-centric perspective because, as O'Mahony observes,

> the strongest argument in favour of creating a positive obligation to recognise [family ties between a child and its second parent] is to look at the issue as one of children's rights rather than parents' rights – *ie*, that it is in the best interests of a child, whose relationship with a non-biological parent qualifies as family life within the meaning of Article 8, to have that family life legally recognised in domestic law.[136]

---

[132] ibid, [65].

[133] ibid; emphasis added.

[134] Scherpe, 'The Legal Recognition of Same-Sex Couples in Europe' (2013) 89.

[135] *Manenc v France* App No 66686/09 (ECtHR, 21 September 2010).

[136] C O'Mahony, 'Irreconcilable Differences? Article 8 ECHR and Irish Law on Non-Traditional Families' (2012) 26 *International Journal of Law, Policy and the Family* 31, 40.

The Court's ruling in *Gas and Dubois* failed to vindicate the best interests of the child at the centre of the case, who had been conceived via anonymous gamete donation and raised in a committed same-sex relationship since birth, and it is difficult to reconcile with the Court's earlier pronouncements in cases such as *Kroon v Netherlands* that

> where the existence of a family tie with a child has been established the State must act in a manner calculated to enable that tie to be developed and legal safeguards must be established that render possible as from the moment of birth or as soon as practicable thereafter the child's integration in his family.[137]

Indeed, in *Gas and Dubois*, Judge Villiger (dissenting) believed that parental responsibility was best shared in the interests of the child because all children, *regardless of the situation of their parents*, should receive the same treatment in law.[138] Thus, the Court should have adopted a child-centric approach, equated formalised same-sex relationships with marriage in cases involving second-parent adoption, and found France in violation of Articles 8 and 14.

D. A Comparison with *Emonet v Switzerland*

The decision in *Gas and Dubois v France* is difficult to reconcile with the Court's decision three years earlier in *Emonet v Switzerland*,[139] which demonstrates what could have happened if Gas had been granted a simple adoption order. Emonet had already adopted the disabled adult daughter of his long-term cohabiting opposite-sex partner when the parties learned that this had the effect of extinguishing the legal mother-child relationship and legally making the young woman Mr Emonet's daughter. Under Swiss law, the mother-child relationship would have survived the adoption process if Mr Emonet had been married to the child's mother. The mother and daughter objected to the termination of their legal relationship and requested that it be restored, but the Swiss authorities refused to do so. In Strasbourg, the applicants claimed that their right to respect for family life under Article 8 had been breached by the Swiss authorities and, in contrast to the *Gas and Dubois* case, here the Court found that there had been a violation of Article 8 of the ECHR.

In reaching this conclusion the Court had regard to the provisions of the Revised European Convention on the Adoption of Children, which had not even entered into force at the time.[140] Ironically, the Court ignored this Convention in

---

[137] *Kroon v. Netherlands* (1995) 19 EHRR 263 [32].
[138] *Gas and Dubois v France* (n 33) (Villiger J, dissenting).
[139] *Emonet v Switzerland* (2009) 49 EHRR 11.
[140] The Court has previously had recourse to other relevant Council of Europe Conventions in decisions pertaining to family life and Article 8. In *Johnston v Ireland* (1987) 9 EHRR 203 [74] the ECtHR had recourse to the Preamble to the European Convention on the Legal Status of Children born out of Wedlock in arriving at its conclusion that Ireland had breached the right to respect for family life of a

the later case of *Gas and Dubois*, even though it had entered into force six months previously.[141] Article 7(1) of the Convention provides that a child can be adopted by two persons of different sex who are married to each other or have entered into a registered partnership together, or a child can be adopted by one person. In addition, Article 7(2) of the Convention provides that:

> States are free to extend the scope of this Convention to same-sex couples who are married to each other or who have entered into a registered partnership together. They are also free to extend the scope of this Convention to different sex couples and same sex couples who are living together in a stable relationship.

Article 11(1) allows for the termination of the legal relationship between the adopted child and its genetic parents, but this is subject to Article 11(2), which states that '*the spouse or registered partner of the adopter* shall retain his or her rights and obligations in respect of the adopted child if the latter is his or her child, unless the law otherwise provides'.[142]

Following a consideration of Article 11(2), the Court made something of an overstatement by deeming the provision a sign of growing recognition in the Council of Europe's Member States for adoptions such as that at the centre of Emonet's case. Article 11(2) is not concerned with sanctioning the retention of the existing legal parent-child relationship in adoptions by *cohabitants* like Emonet; it is more limited, as it only sanctions such retention in formalised, registered relationships like marriage or civil partnership. Nonetheless, in that respect, Article 11(2) qualitatively equates marriage and civil partnership for adoption purposes, contrary to the Court's approach to the issue in *Gas and Dubois*. Ironically, when coupled with Article 7(2), Article 11(2) clearly sanctions the recognition in the Council of Europe's Member States of the type of adoption outcome sought in *Gas and Dubois* rather than that at issue in *Emonet*. However, in *Gas and Dubois*, rather than make an overstatement in relation to the significance of Articles 11(2) or 7(2) of the Convention, the Court failed to consider these provisions at all, even though in that case Dubois was the *civil partner* of the potential adopter, Gas, and the provisions were clearly of greater relevance.

Further, the Court in *Emonet v Switzerland* held that

> respect for the applicants' family life required that biological and social reality be taken into account to avoid the blind, mechanical operation of the provisions of the law to this very particular situation for which they were clearly not intended.[143]

In contrast, in *Gas and Dubois*, while the applicants were also entitled to respect for their family life, the Court did not accord weight to the 'biological *and* social

---

non-marital child by failing to provide a legal mechanism that would allow her to have her relationship with her natural father recognised under domestic law. However, this Convention had entered into force when the *Johnston* case was decided in 1986.

[141] The Revised European Convention on the Adoption of Children entered into force on 1 September 2011 and the *Gas and Dubois* case was decided six months later, in March 2012.

[142] Emphasis added.

[143] *Emonet v Switzerland* (n 139) [86].

reality' of the child's upbringing and ultimately find in their favour. Hence 'the blind, mechanical operation' of the law prevailed. In *Emonet*, the Court emphasised that 'it should be remembered that the aim of the Convention is to guarantee not rights that are theoretical or illusory but rights that are practical and effective'.[144] This aim of the ECHR was not realised by the Court's conclusion in *Gas and Dubois*, as the Court failed to vindicate a practical, effective right to respect for family life for the same-sex applicants or their child.

In *Emonet*, unlike *Gas and Dubois*, it was not argued that there was any discriminatory treatment between the cohabiting applicants and a married couple in the context of second parent adoption under Swiss law, so the ECtHR did not have to consider the application of Article 14 in conjunction with Article 8. Nonetheless, the Court proceeded to proffer an opinion as to whether any difference in treatment between married and unmarried adopters was justified at the national level in contemporary times, and it reached the conclusion that 'the Government's argument that the institution of marriage guaranteed the adopted person greater stability than adoption by an unmarried couple who lived together is not necessarily relevant nowadays'.[145] One wonders whether the Court would have made such a progressive statement if Emonet and his partner were of the same sex, or if it would instead have agreed with the Government's argument and conveniently stressed the difference between unmarried adopters and their married counterparts because of the somewhat abstract 'social, personal and legal consequences' associated with marriage, just as it later did in *Gas and Dubois*?

E. *X v Austria*

This case was somewhat similar to *Gas and Dubois* in that the applicant sought to adopt a child being raised by she and her same-sex partner.[146] However, in this case the couple were *cohabiting* and the child had not been born via assisted human reproduction but had a genetic father from his mother's previous relationship, with whom he maintained regular contact. The child had been raised by his mother and the applicant since the age of five. The child's father would not consent to the adoption by the applicant, so she and the child's mother asked the courts to override the need for his consent. Similar to the situation in *Gas and Dubois*, the Austrian authorities refused to allow second-parent adoption by the applicant, so she and her partner claimed before the Court that they were being discriminated against in the enjoyment of their family life as protected by Article 8, on the grounds of sexual orientation contrary to Article 14. Building on its earlier, progressive pronouncement in *Gas and Dubois*, in this case the Court held that the

---

[144] ibid, [77].
[145] ibid, [81].
[146] *X v Austria* (n 9).

relationship between the applicant, her long-term *cohabiting* same-sex partner and the child constituted 'family life' under Article 8.[147]

It was established by the Court in *Gas and Dubois* that where second-parent adoption is only available to married couples there will be no violation of Articles 8 and 14 because of the 'special status' of marriage. The Court merely reiterated this conclusion in the *X* case and once again eschewed its previous finding in *Emonet* that arguments favouring marriage over cohabitation in an adoption context were 'not necessarily relevant' nowadays. In this respect the decisions in both *Gas and Dubois* and *X v Austria* are rather noteworthy because, when presented with same-sex civil or cohabiting partners seeking to adopt children, marriage becomes 'special', something that it was not in *Emonet* when the Convention rights of unmarried opposite-sex adoptive parents were at issue.

However, the Court held that while the ECHR does not guarantee a right to adopt, 'a State which creates a right going beyond its obligations under Article 8 of the Convention may not apply that right in a manner which is discriminatory within the meaning of Article 14'.[148] Therefore, because Austrian Law permitted the possibility of second-parent adoption by an unmarried opposite-sex partner, the case could easily be distinguished from *Gas and Dubois*. Article 8 was engaged, as was Article 14 because it 'applies to those additional rights, falling within the general scope of any Convention article, for which the state has voluntarily decided to provide', such as adoption for unmarried couples.[149] The Court proceeded to engage in a rather robust scrutiny of the legitimacy and proportionality of the absolute prohibition on second parent adoption by same-sex couples in Austria.

F. The ECtHR's Robust Article 14 Analysis

The Court observed that there was a 'lack of evidence adduced by the Government in order to show that it would be detrimental to the child to be brought up by a same-sex couple or to have two mothers or two fathers for legal purposes'.[150] Second, the Court noted the incoherence of Austrian adoption law because adoption by single LGBT+ persons, even those in registered or cohabiting same-sex relationships, was possible, and 'the legislature therefore accepts that a child may grow up in a family based on a same-sex couple, thus accepting that this is not detrimental to the child'.[151] The Court also found force in the applicant's argument that the social reality in Austria was such that '*de facto* families based on a same-sex couple exist but are refused the possibility of obtaining legal recognition and protection'.[152] In this regard the Court made an observation that it neglected to

---

[147] ibid, [96].
[148] ibid, [135].
[149] *EB v France* (n 1) [48].
[150] *X v Austria* (n 9) [146].
[151] ibid, [144].
[152] ibid, [145].

make previously in *Gas and Dubois*, by acknowledging that second-parent adoption serves to promote the development of de facto family ties that have already been established, because

> in contrast to individual adoption or joint adoption, which are usually aimed at creating a relationship with the child previously unrelated to the adopter, second-parent adoption serves to confer rights *viv-à-vis* the child on the partner of one of the child's parents.

In light of all of this, the Court held that 'considerable doubt' was cast on 'the proportionality of the absolute prohibition on second-parent adoption by same-sex couples' in Austria.[153] Consequently, the Court concluded that there had been a violation of Articles 8 and 14 of the ECHR because the Austrian Government

> failed to adduce particularly weighty and convincing reasons to show that excluding second-parent adoption in a same-sex couple, *while allowing that possibility in an unmarried different-sex couple*, was necessary for the protection of the family in the traditional sense or for the protection of the interests of the child.[154]

The Court's reasoning in the *X* case goes some way towards explaining why it did not have recourse to the Revised European Convention on the Adoption of Children in *Gas and Dubois*. The Court observed that 'given the low number of ratifications so far, it may be open to doubt whether the Convention reflects common ground among European States at present'.[155] Currently, 10 of the Council of Europe's 47 Contracting States have ratified this instrument.[156] Indeed, it is arguable that the Court should not have had regard to this instrument at all in either the *Emonet* or *X* cases because it has not yet been ratified by the respondent Contracting State in either case, Switzerland or France. Regarding the ECtHR's reliance in its case law on a Treaty that has not been ratified by the Contracting State that is before the Court, Draghici points out that:

> Relying on a Treaty to which the respondent is not a party, which is inconsistent with the principle of consent governing international law obligations, may be overcome to the extent that the Treaty has received a *substantial* number of ratifications.[157]

However, that was not the case with the Revised European Convention on the Adoption of Children when either *Emonet* or *X* was decided by the Court, and nor is it the case today. Nonetheless, the Court in *X* found that Article 7(2) of the

---

[153] ibid, [144].

[154] ibid, [151]; emphasis added. However, on 1 August 2013 the Law amending the Civil Code and the Registered Partnership Act, BGBl. I Nr 179/2013 entered into force in Austria. By amending the respective provisions of the Civil Code and the Registered Partnership Act, second-parent adoption by same-sex cohabiting couples or those in registered partnerships is now possible without the termination of family relationships with the natural parent (see Section 197, paras 2, 3 and 4). The new provisions apply also retrospectively to those adoption contracts concluded before 1 August 2013. Same-sex marriage has been recognised in Austria since 2019, and thus a second parent adoption by a spouse in a same-sex marriage will now similarly not terminate the child's legal relationship with the genetic parent.

[155] ibid, [150].

[156] See www.coe.int/en/web/conventions/full-list?module=signatures-by-treaty&treatynum=202.

[157] Draghici (n 16); emphasis added.

Convention 'does not mean that States are free to treat heterosexual and same-sex couples who live in a stable relationship differently' when extending the right to apply for second-parent adoption to such couples,[158] and concluded that there had been a breach of Article 8 taken in conjunction with Article 14.

G. A More Child-Centric Approach?

Draghici observes that *X* was primarily concerned with the issue of discrimination between opposite-sex and same-sex cohabitants in the context of second-parent adoption, and 'consideration of the best interests of the child remains marginal' in the Court's decision.[159] Nonetheless, the Court's decision urged Austria to extend eligibility under its second-parent adoption laws so that the domestic courts would at least be in a position to consider whether it is in the best interests of the child to be adopted by the same-sex applicant with whom he was residing, and if his father's consent should be dispensed with. Thus, the court at least accepts that a child can possibly have two unmarried legal parents who are of the same sex.[160] The ECtHR was somewhat sensitive to the child's right to respect for 'family life' both with his same-sex parents *and* his genetic father, while remaining deferential to the national authorities in deciding these matters by emphasising that

> the Court deems it appropriate to stress the fact that the present case does not concern the question whether or not the applicants' adoption request *should* have been granted in the circumstances of the case. Consequently, it is not concerned with the role of the [child's] father or whether there were any reasons to override his refusal to consent. All these issues would be for the domestic courts to decide, were they in a position to examine the merits of the adoption request.[161]

Aside from this, the decision in *X* is not a significant step forward from that in *Gas and Dubois*, or in the Court's willingness to protect the ECHR rights of same-sex couples more generally. The decision merely continues the Court's approach in *Karner v Austria*, decided a decade previously, because again the Court only found a violation of Articles 8 and Article 14 due to the fact that a Contracting State had chosen to extend to unmarried persons of the opposite sex a right protected by Article 8, while withholding same from unmarried persons of the same sex.[162] Indeed, the Court was keen to taper its decision and emphasised

---

[158] ibid.

[159] Draghici (n 16) 222.

[160] I have argued that in *EB v France* (n 1) in 2008 the Court implicitly endorsed what were, at the time, un-'Convention'-al families consisting of two female same-sex parents and a child when it found that France's refusal to allow the individual LGBT+ applicant to adopt a child and raise it in the home she shared with her same-sex partner violated Arts 8 and 14, albeit that the applicant would be the child's sole *legal* parent: see B Tobin, '*EB v France*: Endorsing Un-'Convention'-al Families?' (2008) 11 *Irish Journal of Family Law* 78.

[161] *X v Austria* (n 9) [132].

[162] While the right to respect for one's home is *expressly* protected by Art 8, when a state chooses to provide for second-parent adoption this generally falls within the ambit of Art 8 and a state cannot

that it was not making any general pronouncements on same-sex couples' parental rights:

> [A]lthough the present case may be seen against the background of the wider debate on same-sex couples' parental rights, the Court is not called upon to rule on the issue of second-parent adoption by same-sex couples as such, let alone on the question of adoption by same-sex couples in general. What it has to decide is a narrowly defined issue of alleged discrimination between unmarried different-sex couples and same-sex couples in respect of second-parent adoption.[163]

When one compares the reticent approach to second-parent adoption in the *Gas and Dubois and X* cases with that in *Emonet* a few years previously, one is inclined to agree with Rainey, Wicks and Ovey's conclusion that 'there appears to remain some moral discomfort within the Court … in providing equal protection for family life irrespective of sexual orientation.'[164] Nonetheless, in *X* the Court closely scrutinised the justifications put forward by Austria for discriminating against different types of unmarried couples on the basis of sexual orientation. When considered in conjunction with the court's approach in *Karner* and *Vallianatos*, this strongly indicates that the Court believes that all family units outside of marriage should receive equal treatment under national laws, irrespective of the parties' sexual orientation, albeit only in circumstances where states *choose* to extend legal privileges beyond marriage. However, this is at least encouraging for future cases where a discriminatory approach is taken by a Contracting State when legislating to voluntarily extend parental and other rights that fall under Article 8 beyond the marital family unit.

XI. Surrogacy and the ECHR

A. International Surrogacy and Parentage Established Abroad

The ECtHR has identified that there is a lack of consensus across the Council of Europe's Contracting States as regards surrogacy arrangements, as

> according to a comparative law survey undertaken in 2019, surrogacy arrangements were permitted in nine of the forty-three Contracting States which responded to the survey, they appeared to be tolerated in a further ten and they were explicitly or implicitly prohibited in the remaining twenty-four Contracting States.[165]

---

unjustifiably discriminate in the application of the right under Art 14. This approach was continued later in 2013 in *Vallianatos*, where the Court found that Greek legislation extending civil partnerships to opposite-sex couples, but not same-sex couples, violated Arts 8 and 14.

[163] *X v Austria* (n 9) [134].

[164] B Rainey, E Wicks and C Ovey, *Jacobs, White and Ovey's The European Convention on Human Rights*, 6th edn (Oxford: OUP, 2014) 348.

[165] Advisory Opinion P-16-2018-001 (n 10).

Nonetheless, when compared to second-parent adoption by same-sex couples, the Court has taken a more child-centred approach when international surrogacy agreements are at issue. Accordingly, the Court has reduced the margin of appreciation available to the Contracting States in this controversial area by recognising that 'whenever the situation of a child is in issue, the best interests of that child are paramount'[166] and that respect for their private life under Article 8 requires that a surrogate-born child should be able to establish details of their identity as an individual human being.[167] The Court has held that this 'includes the legal parent-child relationship, since an essential aspect of the identity of individuals is at stake where the legal parent-child relationship is concerned'.[168]

While most of the Court's pronouncements in this area to date have involved opposite-sex intended parents who availed of such arrangements, the Court's reasoning appears equally applicable to same-sex intended parents. Essentially, where a legal parent-child relationship has been established between the intended parents and the child in the jurisdiction in which the surrogacy arrangement took place, Contracting States must provide a mechanism to recognise that relationship under domestic law in order to vindicate the child's right to respect for private life under Article 8.[169]

In *Mennesson v France*, the ECtHR found that, by failing to recognise the legal parent-child relationship that had been established abroad between twins born through international surrogacy and their genetic, intended father, France had violated the children's right to respect for their private life in Article 8.[170] In 2019, the Court went even further in its Advisory Opinion, issued in response to a request from France to clarify the implications of the *Mennesson* judgment regarding the legal status to be accorded to the intended mother.[171] The Court found that the children's right to respect for private life under Article 8 also 'requires that domestic law provide a possibility of recognition of a legal parent-child relationship with the intended mother'.[172] However, the Court has made it clear that Contracting States enjoy a wide margin of appreciation regarding the 'choice of means by which to permit recognition of the legal relationship between the child and the intended parents'.[173] In the Advisory Opinion and subsequent case law, the Court emphasised that adoption by the intended mother may be used to give effect to the child's right to respect for private life, provided that the adoption procedure 'enables a decision to be taken rapidly, so that the child is not kept for a lengthy period in a position of legal uncertainty as regards the relationship'.[174]

---

[166] ibid, [38].
[167] *H v United Kingdom*, App No 32185/20 (ECtHR, 31 May 2022) [45].
[168] ibid.
[169] Advisory Opinion P-16-2018-001 (n 10).
[170] *Mennesson v France*, App No 65192/11 (ECtHR, 26 September 2014) [100]–[101].
[171] Advisory Opinion P-16-2018-001 (n 10).
[172] ibid, [46].
[173] ibid, [51].
[174] ibid, [54].

In its Advisory Opinion, the ECtHR emphasised that it is in the child's best interests for the uncertainty surrounding the legal relationship with their intended mother to be 'as short-lived as possible', because 'unless and until that relationship is recognised in domestic law, the child is in a vulnerable position'.[175] Regarding the surrogate-born child's legal vulnerability, the Court held that, inter alia, 'there is a risk that such children will be denied the access to their intended mother's nationality which the legal parent-child relationship guarantees', and that 'their right to inherit under the intended mother's estate may be impaired'.[176] The Court also found that the surrogate-born child's 'continued relationship with [the intended mother] is placed at risk if the intended parents separate or the intended father dies'.[177] The Court's Advisory Opinion was concerned with an intended mother who was not the genetic mother of the surrogate-born twins, and thus the reasoning could equally apply to a non-genetic intended father in a same-sex relationship. Indeed, Bracken forcefully argues that 'the Advisory Opinion could be used to *demand* that a mechanism is made available to recognise the legal parental status of the second father'.[178]

B. Domestic Surrogacy and Birth Registration Requirements

However, a recent decision of the ECtHR confirms that, in domestic surrogacy cases, it is not a breach of the child's rights under Article 8 if domestic law requires the registration of the surrogate's husband on the child's birth certificate instead of the genetic, intended father, *provided* that the child has not been deprived of the possibility of establishing a legal relationship with their intended parents and details of their identity.

In *H v United Kingdom*, the applicant claimed that the registration of the surrogate's husband, rather than the genetic, intended father, as her 'father' on her birth certificate, as required by sections 35 and 38 of the Human Fertilisation and Embryology Act 2008 (HFEA), violated her right to respect for private life under Article 8.[179] The case involved a domestic surrogacy arrangement between a male same-sex couple and the surrogate and her husband. A donor egg was used in the arrangement. Relations between the parties broke down before the child's birth and, following the birth, the surrogate and her husband registered themselves as the child's parents on the birth certificate, as they were legally obligated to do. However, they later refused to consent to a Parental Order being made in favour of the child's same-sex intended parents, so the latter did not apply for one and, consequently, the surrogate and her husband remained as the child's legal parents.

---

[175] ibid, [49].
[176] ibid, [40].
[177] ibid.
[178] L Bracken, *Same-Sex Parenting and the Best Interests Principle* (Cambridge, CUP, 2019) 207.
[179] *H v United Kingdom* (n 167).

In assessing whether there had been a breach of the applicant's rights under Article 8 due to the requirements of sections 35 and 38 of the HFEA, the ECtHR acknowledged that the surrogate and her husband were recorded as the child's legal parents on the birth certificate. In the Court's view, the UK Parliament's choice to 'confer parenthood on the gestational mother and her husband' from the moment of birth in cases of assisted reproduction 'fell within the *wide margin of appreciation* enjoyed by the State when deciding such matters'.[180] However, the Court observed that the impugned law had not resulted in the child being 'wholly deprived of a legal relationship' with her intended parents, her genetic father and intended co-father, A and B, because once they brought proceedings in the domestic courts,

> they were not only granted parental responsibility together with [the surrogate and her husband], but a child arrangements order was also made, as a consequence of which the applicant lives with A and B; she has their names incorporated into her surname; and A and B have the legal right to make all 'parenting decisions'.[181]

The Court also concluded that the applicant 'has not been deprived of the possibility of establishing the details of her identity'. The Court felt that there was nothing preventing A and B, her intended parents with whom she resides, 'from telling her about the circumstances of her birth and her national and cultural heritage'.[182] The Court found that the applicant had not experienced any 'practical or material disadvantages' as a result of the impugned law.[183] Consequently, the Court declared the applicant's complaint inadmissible as being manifestly ill-founded pursuant to Article 35 of the ECHR.

XII. Implications of ECtHR Case Law for Ireland's Approach to Surrogacy

The ECtHR's case law on surrogacy is not entirely clear. While it appears from *Mennesson* and the Advisory Opinion that the possibility for both of the intended parents to establish *parentage* is required to satisfy the child's Article 8 rights, in *H v United Kingdom* the Court deemed those cases 'readily distinguishable' as they involved intended parents who had 'no legal relationship *whatsoever*' with the child, due to their absolute inability to establish *any* legal relationship with the child under French law.[184] In *H v United Kingdom*, the Court noted that although the intended parents had not acquired parentage, the child had not been 'wholly deprived of a legal relationship' with them, as they had been granted *parental*

---

[180] ibid, [54]; emphasis added.
[181] ibid, [47].
[182] ibid, [47].
[183] ibid.
[184] ibid, [46]; emphasis added.

responsibility (guardianship under Irish law). Further, the *H* case indicates that the concerns which the Court associated with the lack of a legal parent-child relationship between a child and its intended mother (and, possibly, a non-genetic intended father) in its Advisory Opinion, such as a lack of inheritance rights and access to that parent's nationality, will not result in any violation of the child's right to respect for private life unless it can be established that the child has suffered '*practical or material disadvantages*'.[185] In *H*, the Court agreed with the UK domestic courts and noted that the child had not suffered any such disadvantage as there was no evidence of any harm to her from not acquiring her intended father's nationality, and any impact on her inheritance rights was 'speculative' and 'in any event capable of being overcome by way of testamentary provision'.[186]

Essentially, one cannot be certain that the ECtHR's case law on surrogacy *requires* Ireland to greatly disturb the current status quo for legally recognising the familial ties between intended parents and their surrogate-born children in order to be ECHR-compliant. In Ireland, a genetic intended father can be recognised as a parent and guardian and, in light of the above, recognising the *guardianship* rights of an intended mother or non-genetic intended father, as Irish law does, might be within a state's margin of appreciation. Guardianship enables such an intended parent to care for a child until they reach adulthood, ensuring that the child is not 'wholly deprived' of a legal relationship with this intended parent, a minimum requirement under the ECHR. Holding the status of legal guardian obviates many of the practical difficulties commonly associated with a lack of parentage and, if the intended parents split up or the genetic intended father dies, the intended mother or non-genetic intended co-father can apply to the Irish courts seeking custody and access.[187] Indeed, in *H*, although the Court acknowledges that it was not called on to consider the Convention-compatibility of the mechanism for establishing familial ties between the child and its intended parents in the UK, the Court nonetheless indicates that parental responsibility (guardianship) is envisaged within the *type* of possibility for 'the legal recognition of the intended parents' required by Article 8:

> [I]t has not been necessary for the Court to consider whether there existed in the United Kingdom a possibility for the legal recognition of the intended parents (*for example, through an application for parental responsibility, a child arrangements order or a parental order*), as this was not the subject of the applicant's complaint.[188]

---

[185] ibid; emphasis added.

[186] ibid. Indeed, in another recent case involving a same-sex couple seeking Polish nationality for their surrogate-born child whose parentage had been established in the US, the ECtHR declared the application inadmissible because there was no evidence any *hardship* had been suffered as a result of the decision by the Polish authorities to refuse their request: see *SH v Poland*, App Nos 56846/15 and 56849/15 (ECtHR, 16 November 2021).

[187] See the Guardianship of Infants Act 1964, ss 11B and 11E, as inserted the Children and Family Relationships Act 2015, ss 55 and 58.

[188] *H v United Kingdom* (n 167) [58].

However, despite this statement by the Court, guardianship as the sole means of recognising the legal relationship between *both* intended parents and the child would be unlikely to comply with Article 8 because the child would have no legal parent under domestic law, even where one of the parties is their genetic father. This does not appear to be the intention of the Court because earlier in the judgment in *H*, the Court extended the reasoning employed in its decisions on international surrogacy to the context of domestic surrogacy, and required Contracting States to provide a possibility for the genetic father to establish *parentage* in respect of the surrogate-born child, as

> according to the Court's case-law, which principally concerns surrogacy arrangements abroad, where a child is born through a surrogacy arrangement and the intended father is also the biological father, Article 8 of the Convention only requires that domestic law provide a possibility of recognition of the legal relationship between him and the child.

The Court held that there was 'no reason to adopt a different approach in cases where a child was born to a surrogate in the respondent state'.[189] While this paragraph is unclear as to what is required of a Contracting State as again it only refers to recognising 'the legal relationship' between the genetic father and the child, subsequently in the same paragraph the Court stated that it is for each Contracting State to decide what 'formal means of recognition of *parentage* may satisfy Article 8 of the Convention'.[190] Thus, despite distinguishing *Mennesson* and the Advisory Opinion in the *H* case and arguably casting some doubt on the applicability of these significant decisions beyond France, the Court clarified that the requirement under Article 8 for a genetic intended father to have a possibility of establishing *parentage* in relation to the child applies to domestic and international surrogacy arrangements and extends across the 47 Contracting States.

However, *H* and other recent case law strongly implies that the ECtHR will closely and holistically scrutinise surrogacy-related complaints on a case-by-case, jurisdiction-by-jurisdiction basis, and that 'depending on the law of the Contracting State concerned, non-recognition of the legal parent-child relationship may entail certain practical and material disadvantages'. Where, as in Ireland, there is the possibility of guardianship for an intended mother or non-genetic intended father, it may be difficult to prove any practical or material disadvantages through non-recognition of the legal parent-child relationship. The ECtHR may very well be satisfied that by providing guardianship rights for such an intended parent, Irish law does not violate the child's right to respect for private life. When one considers that the Court in *H* distinguished the Advisory Opinion and appeared to endorse guardianship (parental responsibility) as a means of establishing 'the legal recognition of the intended parents' and that Article 5 of Protocol 16 of the ECHR stipulates that the Court's Advisory Opinions are *non-binding* in any event, then arguably this conclusion is not without merit.

---

[189] ibid. Thus, this aspect of the *Mennesson* decision is certainly not confined to France.
[190] ibid; emphasis added.

Nonetheless, while providing guardianship for intended mothers and non-genetic intended fathers of surrogate-born children might *generally* be acceptable to the ECtHR for a Contracting State to comply with Article 8, Ireland's provisions enabling persons who are not the legal parents of a child to apply for guardianship would most likely be non-compliant. In Ireland, intended mothers and non-genetic intended fathers who wish to apply to the Court to be appointed a guardian can only do so a minimum of two years after the child's birth.[191] This indicates that guardianship as currently provided for under Irish law is far from an appropriate mechanism to '*promptly and effectively*'[192] vindicate the surrogate-born child's right to respect for private life, and an expeditious legal mechanism for establishing familial ties between parent and child is certainly preferred, and likely required, by the ECtHR.

A. The Court's Imprecise Use of Language: Legal Parent–Child Relationship or an Alternative Form of Recognition?

While there is arguably some doubt *post-H* as to what exactly might be required of a Contracting State when it comes to vindicating the surrogate-born child's right to respect for private life vis-à-vis its intended mother or non-genetic intended father under Article 8, much of the confusion is generated by the Court's imprecise use of language in surrogacy case law. The Court shifts between referring to 'legal recognition of intended parents' to the 'legal parent-child relationship' to 'legal recognition to the family ties between the intended parents and a child', and it often does so within the same case, and on multiple occasions. In future decisions the Court needs to be mindful of its chosen terminology, because legally recognising a parent's relationship or 'family ties' with a child is not necessarily the same as legally recognising that person's *parentage*. The former can be satisfied through mechanisms such as guardianship, custody and access. Nonetheless, it seems incongruous that France would be required to go from an absolute prohibition on surrogacy to full legal recognition of *parentage* for *both* intended parents as a result of *Mennesson* and the Advisory Opinion, whereas Ireland's halfway-house approach of guardianship for an intended mother or non-genetic intended father under existing law might, but for the dubious temporal requirement, be largely Convention-compliant. Despite the apparent 'reining in' to some extent of *Mennesson* and the Advisory Opinion in *H*, perhaps the better interpretation is that because *guardianship* does not bestow *parentage* on an intended mother or intended co-father, it does not establish the 'legal parent-child relationship' envisaged in the ECtHR's case law.[193] Indeed, in the Advisory Opinion and subsequent

---

[191] See the Guardianship of Infants Act 1964, s 6C, as inserted by the Children and Family Relationships Act 2015 s 49.

[192] Advisory Opinion P-16-2018-001 (n 10) [55].

[193] Advisory Opinion P-16-2018-001 (n 10) [40].

case law, the ECtHR often refers to adoption as a viable means of establishing this type of relationship between the parties, which indicates that it is the establishment of *parentage* that is required by the Court in order to fully vindicate the child's Article 8 rights.[194] If this is the correct interpretation, then again, by providing for second-parent adoption, Ireland is *largely* compliant with its ECHR obligations.

Although an intended mother or non-genetic intended father of a surrogate-born child can apply to adopt the child as a spouse, civil partner or cohabitant of the child's parent, and thus establish the 'legal parent-child relationship' envisaged by the ECtHR, this mechanism is also subject to a two-year statutory waiting period.[195] While the Court's decision in *C and E v France* indicates that adoption can be a suitable mechanism for establishing the legal parent-child relationship between an intended parent and the child, it also noted that in France, the average waiting time for a decision was only 4.1 months in the case of full adoption and 4.7 months in the case of second-parent adoption. However, the significant waiting period before an intended parent can even *apply* for a second-parent adoption under Irish law could mean that it might be unlikely to be regarded by the ECtHR as an expeditious adoption mechanism that can vindicate the surrogate-born child's right to respect for private life under Article 8.[196] In international surrogacy situations, given the absence of a specific legal mechanism like a parental order that would establish a parent-child relationship between a child and an intended mother or non-genetic intended father, Irish policy-makers should at least consider reducing the waiting period before such intended parents can apply for guardianship or, more appropriately, second-parent adoption in order to more effectively vindicate the child's right to respect for private life under Article 8.[197] However, merely because a revised second-parent adoption procedure in Ireland might satisfy the requirements of Article 8 does not mean that this route should necessarily be taken to decide parentage in surrogacy situations. As discussed in the previous chapter, conceptually, adoption is not an appropriate mechanism to decide parentage in surrogacy situations and, in practice, having separate procedures for the genetic father (declaration of parentage, guardianship) and intended mother or non-genetic intended co-father (second-parent adoption) is far less streamlined than having either an administrative pre-conception State approval or judicial post-birth parental order model.

---

[194] *C and E v France*, App Nos 1462/18 and 17348/18 (ECtHR, 19 November 2019); *D v France* App No 11288/18 (ECtHR, 16 July 2020).

[195] See the Adoption Act 2010, s 23(2)(a), as inserted by the Adoption (Amendment) Act 2017, s 12, the Adoption Act 2010, s 33(a), as inserted by the Adoption (Amendment) Act 2017, s 16. In the absence of specific legislation governing the adoption of children born by surrogacy and DAHR, applications for the adoption of such children are treated on a case-by-case basis by the Adoption Authority.

[196] See *C and E v France* (n 194).

[197] I made this suggestion when giving oral evidence to the Joint Oireachtas Committee on International Surrogacy: see Joint Committee on International Surrogacy debate (26 May 2022), available at www.oireachtas.ie/en/debates/debate/joint_committee_on_international_surrogacy/2022-05-26/2.

B. Is Ireland's Proposed Post-Birth Parental Order Model ECHR-Compliant?

In *H v United Kingdom*, the Court's decision as regards the requirements of UK domestic law in the context of surrogacy and birth registration makes it clear that the virtually identical proposal in the Health (Assisted Human Reproduction) Bill 2022 for the surrogate to be the legal parent at birth is within a state's margin of appreciation and is compliant with the ECHR. The Court refused to find that the intended parents 'must immediately and automatically be recognised as such in law' in order to comply with the ECHR,[198] and it accorded Contracting States a *wide* margin of appreciation as regards the establishment of legal parentage. Therefore, current Irish law, whereby a genetic intended father can seek a Declaration of Parentage and Guardianship from the courts and an intended mother or non-genetic intended father can apply for second-parent adoption, or equally, the post-birth Parental Order model for such persons to establish parentage in domestic surrogacy cases, as proposed by the Health (Assisted Human Reproduction) Bill 2022, *both* appear to be ECHR-compliant (apart from the temporal requirement associated with second-parent adoption).

C. Limitations of the Decision in *H v United Kingdom*

Unfortunately, the Court in *H* was not presented with an opportunity to examine the *adequacy* of the legal mechanism available in the UK for establishing the legal parent-child relationship in domestic surrogacy arrangements, noting 'the limited manner in which the applicant has framed her Convention complaint'.[199] She had not sought to argue, before the domestic courts or the ECtHR, that section 54 of the HFEA, which is the 'existing mechanism for obtaining legal recognition of an intended parent through the making of a parental order'[200] by a domestic court in the UK, was incompatible with her rights under Article 8. The applicant's complaint was limited to challenging the birth registration requirements under the HFEA as they applied to surrogacy arrangements:

> [I]t has consistently and clearly been stated on behalf of the applicant that the complaint in the present case is solely concerned with the fact that, pursuant to sections 35 and 38 of the HFEA, [the surrogate's husband], rather than A, was recorded as her father on her birth certificate. Both before the domestic courts and before this Court it has further been asserted that the complaint does not seek to raise the Article 8 compatibility of section 54 of the HFEA.[201]

---

[198] ibid, [56].
[199] ibid, [48].
[200] *H v United Kingdom* (n 167) [57].
[201] ibid, [44].

The compatibility of section 54 with Article 8 was most likely not challenged in the domestic proceedings or in proceedings before the ECtHR because the intended parents had not tested the provision by seeking a parental order in the domestic courts. Although a DNA test had confirmed that A was indeed the applicant's genetic father, his and his partner's reluctance to apply for a parental order in the absence of consent from the surrogate and her husband is completely understandable in light of the recent decision in *Re AB (Surrogacy: Consent)*.[202] This confirms that the court has no ability under section 54 to dispense with the requirement for consent from the surrogate (and her husband, where applicable) except in the limited circumstances where the parties cannot be found or are incapable of giving agreement.[203] However, as the applicant had not challenged section 54 in the domestic courts and therefore exhausted all available domestic remedies, the outcome of her case would most likely have been the same had she challenged it in Strasbourg. The ECtHR would most likely have declared a complaint in relation to section 54 as inadmissible under Article 35 of the ECHR.

Although *H v United Kingdom* did not present the Court with the ample opportunity to do so, it is nonetheless disappointing that the ECtHR has not yet been called on to consider the compatibility of section 54 of the HFEA with the surrogate-born child's right to respect for their private life under Article 8 of the ECHR. As Ireland is proposing to introduce an identical provision as part of its domestic surrogacy laws, one can only hope that the ECtHR will have the opportunity to do so in the not-too-distant future. By enabling a surrogate to arbitrarily withhold consent to the making of a parental order, section 54 and equivalent provisions can fail to constitute an effective mechanism for an established parent-child relationship to be recognised in law, and this can indubitably result in an interference with the child's right to respect for private life under Article 8. The facts of *H v United Kingdom* demonstrate that the strength of the surrogate's position (and also that of her husband) under section 54 of the HFEA is what deterred the same-sex intended parents from applying for a parental order, and this denied the applicant the possibility of formally establishing the legal parent-child relationship with their genetic, intended father via a parental order in circumstances 'where the biological reality of that relationship had been established and the child and parent concerned demanded full recognition thereof'.[204] The applicant was also denied the possibility of establishing the legal parent-child relationship with her non-genetic intended father. Consequently, section 54 and equivalent provisions elsewhere are ripe for assessment by the ECtHR as regards their compliance with the ECHR.

---

[202] *Re AB (Surrogacy: Consent)* (2016) EWHC 2643 (Fam).
[203] ibid, [11] (Theis J).
[204] *H v United Kingdom* (n 167) [45].

XIII. Conclusion

To date, the ECtHR has been of little benefit in advancing the position of same-sex *families* across the Council of Europe's Contracting States. As regards same-sex couples, the Court's approach to family life and marriage under the ECHR could even be described as frustrating. Despite (arguably) hurriedly recognising 'family life' between childless same-sex partners over a decade ago, even in the absence of a legitimate consensus, the Court only encouraged the Contracting States to *respect* such family life by providing for civil partnership under their domestic laws once it was satisfied that a thin consensus on allowing same-sex couples to formalise their relationships had been established. The Court has similarly proven reluctant to involve itself in the vindication of parental rights for same-sex couples with children, only finding a violation of Articles 8 and 14 where Contracting States have voluntarily extended parental rights beyond marital families and discriminated between unmarried opposite-sex and same-sex couples when doing so. Margaria observes that:

> Despite the expansion of the scope of 'family life' to incorporate homosexual relationships, the case law that follows does not generally advance the position of homosexual (aspiring) parents – as well as of the children potentially involved – to any considerable extent. Marriage continues to be an insurmountable obstacle to fighting discrimination on grounds of sexual orientation.[205]

However, despite this reticence, the general thrust of the Court's case law since *Karner* makes it clear that once a Contracting State extends legal rights and privileges beyond marriage, then in the absence of all but the most compelling reasons, all non-marital families must receive equal treatment in law irrespective of the sexual orientation of the parties. Although very few of the decided cases thus far have concerned same-sex families, the Court's approach to protecting the rights of surrogate-born children in relation to their intended parents has been more child-centric, but uncertainty arguably remains regarding the *extent* of the Contracting States' duty towards recognising the familial ties between an intended mother or non-genetic intended father. Indeed, the Court grants the Contracting States such a wide margin of appreciation in the area of assisted human reproduction that it appears the existing and proposed mechanisms for acquiring parentage and/or guardianship in relation to surrogate-born children in Ireland are predominantly Convention-compliant.

In 2002, Article 12 was dynamically interpreted by the ECtHR such that the right to marry contained therein was no longer preoccupied with the parties' biological sexual dimorphism or their capacity to procreate. Despite this, the ECtHR very unconvincingly refused to extend this reasoning in 2010 and, consequently,

---

[205] A Margaria, *The Construction of Fatherhood – The Jurisprudence of the European Court of Human Rights* (Cambridge, CUP, 2019) 135.

Article 12 does not yet *require* Contracting States to introduce same-sex marriage. However, in relation to same-sex marriage, there now exists the type of 'emerging consensus' across the Contracting States akin to that which led to the Court recognising 'family life' between same-sex couples in 2010. This might suffice for the Court to require same-sex marriage under Article 12 if a case should come before it in the not-too-distant-future. However, given that the Court repeatedly acknowledges the 'special status' of marriage, it might await a thin majority consensus on the issue, just as it did regarding a trans person's right to marry.

6

Concluding Remarks

This book has highlighted that, although controversial, achieving marriage equality through modes of participatory democracy can have a phenomenal impact on same-sex couples where, *as in Ireland*, it results in a citizen-approved constitutionalisation of fundamental rights that legally insulates same-sex couples' right to marry from any future anti-LGBT+ administration, absent another constitutional referendum.

Nonetheless, the book has also demonstrated that, with calls for a referendum to extend the constitutional definition of the 'Family' *beyond marriage*, it is now timely to reconsider the value of civil unions for those same-sex (and opposite-sex) couples who seek an alternative means of formalising their relationships. Evidence indicates that it may be somewhat lamentable that conformity with the Constitution post-marriage equality meant that same-sex civil partnership was denied the opportunity to truly 'emerge' as a viable alternative to marriage, or be extended to opposite-sex couples.

Although marriage equality was achieved in Ireland in 2015, and represents the apex of legal relationship recognition for same-sex adults, it is clear that, irrespective of a couple's marital status, same-sex families with children are still very much an 'emerging' family form in law. Irish law does not adequately vindicate the familial ties between same-sex couples and their children born via donor-assisted human reproduction and surrogacy, and such couples represent the majority of same-sex parents.[1] Therefore, a significant proportion of same-sex families are without the optimal level of legal recognition.

Further, the European Court of Human Rights has adopted a reticent approach in case law concerning same-sex families with children. This indicates that the Court regards such same-sex families as constituting an 'emerging' family form across the Council of Europe, and might explain why it is unwilling to lead the way unless a Contracting State forces its hand. Nonetheless, the Court's child-centric approach to the position of surrogate-born children under the ECHR encourages

---

[1] A recent collaborative survey carried out between Dr Lydia Bracken of the University of Limerick and LGBT Ireland found that the most common pathways to parenting for same-sex couples were surrogacy and donor assisted reproduction, with 80% of survey respondents having availed of one or the other (67% DAHR; 13% surrogacy): see L Bracken, 'LGBTI+ Parent Families in Ireland: Legal Recognition of Parent-Child Relationships' (University of Limerick, 2021).

the Contracting States to take measures to vindicate the rights of such children vis-à-vis their intended parents, irrespective of the latter's sexual orientation.

Finally, one hopes that the detailed, pragmatic, balanced, child-centric recommendations for law reform proposed herein will at least lead to further debate on, and consideration of, the legal position of same-sex families with surrogate-born or donor-conceived children by policy-makers, academics, activists, NGOs, and all of the other relevant stakeholders in Ireland, and maybe even beyond.

BIBLIOGRAPHY

Adanan, A, 'Succession Law and Cohabitation after 10 Years of the Civil Partnership and Certain Rights and Obligations of Cohabitants Act 2010' (2020) 25 *Conveyancing and Property Law Journal* 70.

Alghrani, A, and Griffiths, D, 'The Regulation of Surrogacy in the United Kingdom: The Case for Reform' (2017) 29 *Child and Family Law Quarterly* 165.

All-Party Oireachtas Committee on the Constitution, 'Tenth Progress Report: The Family' (Stationery Office, 2006).

All-Party Parliamentary Group on Surrogacy, 'Report on Understandings of the Law and Practice of Surrogacy' (APPG, 2021).

Allan, S, 'The Review of the Western Australian Human Reproductive Technology Act 1991 and the Surrogacy Act 2008 (Report: Part 2)' (Government of Western Australia – Department of Health, 2019).

Andersson, G et al, 'The Demographics of Same-Sex Marriages in Norway and Sweden' (2006) 43 *Demography* 79.

Araujo, RJ, 'Same-Sex Marriage – From Privacy to Equality: The Failure of the "Equality" Justifications for Same-Sex Marriage' in S Fitzgibbon, LD Wardle and AS Loveless (eds), *The Jurisprudence of Marriage and Other Intimate Relationships* (Buffalo, WS Hein & Co, 2010).

Bailey, L, 'No-Fault Divorce – Beyond Good and Evil' (1972–1973) 4 *Colonial Law Review* 10.

Bala, N, 'Controversy over Couples in Canada: The Evolution of Marriage and Other Adult Interdependent Relationships' (2003) 29 *Queen's Law Journal* 41.

Bamforth, N, 'Families but not (yet) Marriages? Same-Sex Partners and the Developing European Convention "Margin of Appreciation"' (2011) 23 *Child and Family Law Quarterly* 128.

Beilfuss, CG, 'Southern Jurisdictions: Consolidation in the West, Progress in the East' in TJ Biblarz and J Stacey, 'How does the Gender of Parents Matter?' (2010) 72 *Journal of Marriage and Family* 3.

Boele-Welki, K and Fuchs, M (eds), *Same-Sex Relationships and Beyond: Gender Matters in the EU*, 3rd edn (Cambridge, Intersentia, 2017).

Bracken, L, 'Pathways to Parenting: Proposals for Reform' (LGBT Ireland, 2019).

—— *Same-Sex Parenting and the Best Interests Principle* (Cambridge, CUP, 2019).

—— 'LGBTI+ Parent Families in Ireland: Legal Recognition of Parent-Child Relationships' (University of Limerick, 2021).

Brazier, M, Campbell, A and Golombok, S, 'Surrogacy: Review for Health Ministers of current Arrangements for Payments and Regulation – Report of the Review Team' (HMSO, 1998).

Brown, A, and Wade, K, 'The Incoherent Role of the Child's Identity in the Construction and Allocation of Legal Parenthood' (2022) 42 *Legal Studies* 1.

Brown, E, 'Committed Relationships and the Law: The Impact of the European Convention on Human Rights' in O Doyle and W Binchy (eds), *Committed Relationships and the Law* (Dublin, Four Courts Press, 2007).

Byrne, R and Binchy, W, 'Family Law' in R Byrne and W Binchy (eds), *Annual Review of Irish Law 2010* (Dublin, Thomson Round Hall, 2011).

Carolan, E, 'Committed Non-Marital Couples and the Irish Constitution' in O Doyle and W Binchy (eds), *Committed Relationships and the Law* (Dublin, Four Courts Press, 2007).

Chan, W, 'Cohabitation, Civil Partnership, Marriage and the Equal Sharing Principle' (2013) 33 *Legal Studies* 46.

Citizen's Assembly, 'Report of the Citizen's Assembly on Gender Equality' (Citizen's Assembly, 2021).

Clayton, R and Tomlinson, H, *The Law of Human Rights: Volume 1*, 2nd edn (Oxford, OUP, 2009).

Commission on Assisted Human Reproduction, 'Report of the Commission on Assisted Human Reproduction' (Department of Health, 2005).

Constitution Review Group, 'Report of the Constitution Review Group' (Stationery Office, 1996).

Convention on the Constitution, 'Third Report of the Convention on the Constitution: Amending the Constitution to Provide for Same-Sex Marriage' (Convention on the Constitution, 2013).

—— 'Second Report of the Convention on the Constitution' (Convention on the Constitution, May 2013).

Cowden, M, '"No Harm, No Foul": A Child's Right to Know their Genetic Parents' (2012) 26 *International Journal of Law, Policy and the Family* 102.

Cox, N, 'A Question of Definition: Same-Sex Marriage and the Law' in O Doyle and W Binchy (eds), *Committed Relationships and the Law* (Dublin, Four Courts Press, 2007).

Crawshaw, M, Blyth, E. and van den Akker, O, 'The Changing Profile of Surrogacy in the UK – Implications for National and International Policy and Practice' (2012) 34 *Journal of Social Welfare and Family Law* 267.

Cretney, S, 'Comment: Sex is Important' (2004) 34 *Family Law* 777.

Crompton, L, 'Civil Partnership Bill 2004: The Illusion of Equality' (2004) 34 *Family Law* 888.

Dane, S, Short, L and Healy, G, 'Swimming with Sharks: The negative social and psychological impacts of Ireland's marriage equality referendum 'NO' campaign' Survey Report (University of Queensland, 7 October 2016).

Department for Culture, Media and Sport, 'Civil Partnership Review (England and Wales): Report on Conclusions' (DCMS, 2014).

Douglas, G, 'Case Report: *Re AB (Surrogacy: Consent)* [2016] EWHC 2643 Fam' (2017) *Family Law* 57.

—— 'The Intention to be a Parent and the Making of Mothers' (1994) 57 *Modern Law Review* 636.

Doyle, O, *Constitutional Equality Law* (Dublin, Thomson Round Hall, 2004).

—— 'Moral Argument and the Recognition of Same-Sex Partnerships' in O Doyle and W Binchy (eds), *Committed Relationships and the Law* (Dublin, Four Courts Press 2007).

—— *Constitutional Law: Text, Cases and Materials* (Dublin, Clarus Press, 2008).

—— 'Sisterly Love: The Importance of Explicitly Assumed Commitment in the Legal Recognition of Personal Relationships' in S Fitzgibbon, LD Wardle and AS Loveless (eds), *The Jurisprudence of Marriage and Other Intimate Relationships* (New York, WS Hein & Co 2010).

—— 'Minority Rights and Democratic Consensus: The Irish Same-Sex Marriage Referendum' (2020) 15 *National Taiwan University Law Review* 21.

Draghici, C, *The Legitimacy of Family Rights in Strasbourg Case Law – 'Living Instrument' or Extinguished Sovereignty?* (Oxford, Hart, 2017).

Dunne, P, 'Civil Partnership in an Ireland of Equal Marriage Rights' (2015) 53 *Irish Jurist* 77.

Eskridge Jr, WN, 'Equality Practice: Liberal Reflections on the Jurisprudence of Civil Unions' (2001) 64 *Albany Law Review* 853.

Faffelberger, G and Huber, S, 'Marriage between Homosexuals: Equal Treatment and Right to Marriage' (2008) 2 *Vienna Online Journal on International Constitutional Law* 61.

Fenton-Glynn, C, 'The Regulation and Recognition of Surrogacy under English Law: An Overview of the Case Law (2015) 27 *Child and Family Law Quarterly* 83.

—— 'International Surrogacy Arrangements: A Survey' (Cambridge Family Law, 2022).

Fenwick, H and Hayward, A, 'From Same-Sex Marriage to Equal Civil Partnerships: On a Path towards 'Perfecting' Equality?' (2018) 30 *Child and Family Law Quarterly* 97.

Finance and Public Administration References Committee, Parliament of Australia, 'Arrangements for the Postal Survey' (Commonwealth of Australia, 2018).

Foley, B, *Deference and the Presumption of Constitutionality* (Dublin, Institute of Public Administration, 2008).

Glennon, L, 'Fitzpatrick v Sterling Housing Association Ltd – An Endorsement of the Functional Family?' (2000) 14 *International Journal of Law, Policy and the Family* 226.

Golombok, S, *Modern Families* (Cambridge, CUP, 2015).

Graycar, R and Millbank, J, 'From Functional Family to Spinster Sisters: Australia's Distinctive Path to Relationship Recognition' (2007) 24 *Journal of Law and Policy* 121.

Green Party, 'Valuing Families: A Policy on Marriage and Partnership Rights' (Green Party, 2006).

Halpin, B and O' Donoghue, C, 'Cohabitation in Ireland: Evidence from Survey Data' Working Paper 2004-01 (University of Limerick, 2004).

Harding, M, '"Best Interests" as a Limited Constitutional Imperative' in *International Survey of Family Law 2019* (Cambridge, Intersentia, 2019).

Hayward, A, 'The Future of Civil Partnership in England and Wales' in JM Scherpe and A Hayward (eds) *The Future of Registered Partnerships* (Cambridge, Intersentia, 2017).

——— 'The Steinfeld Effect: Equal Civil Partnerships and the Construction of the Cohabitant' (2019) *Child and Family Law Quarterly* 283.

——— 'Relationships with Status: Civil Partnership in an Era of Same-Sex Marriage' in F Hamilton and G Noto La Diega (eds) *Same-Sex Relationships, Law and Social Change* (London, Routledge, 2020).

Healy, G, Sheehan, B and Whelan, N, *Ireland Says Yes: The Inside Story of how the Vote for Marriage Equality was Won* (Dublin, Merrion Press, 2015).

Hogan, G, 'The Supreme Court and the Equality Clause' (1999) 4 *Bar Review* 116.

Hogan G. and Whyte, G, *JM Kelly – The Irish Constitution*, 4th edn (Dublin, Butterworths, 2003).

Horsey, K. 'Challenging Presumptions: Legal Parenthood and Surrogacy Arrangements' (2010) 22 *Child and Family Law Quarterly* 449.

Hörster, HE, 'Does Portugal Need to Legislate on de facto Unions?' (1999) 13 *International Journal of Law, Policy and the Family* 274.

IHREC, 'Submission on the General Scheme of the Family Court Bill 2020' (IHREC, 2021).

Imrie, S and Golombok, S, 'Impact of New Family Forms on Parenting and Child Development' (2020) 2 *Annual Review of Developmental Psychology* 295.

Jackson, E, 'Assisted Conception and Surrogacy in the United Kingdom' in J Eekelaar and R George (eds), *Routledge Handbook of Family Law and Policy* (London, Routledge, 2014).

Jadva, V, 'Surrogacy: Issues, Concerns and Complexities' in S Golombok et al (eds), *Regulating Reproductive Donation* (Cambridge, CUP, 2016) 126.

Johnson, G, 'Civil Union, A Reappraisal' (2005) 30 *Vermont Law Review* 891.

Joint Committee on International Surrogacy, 'Final Report of the Joint Committee on International Surrogacy' (Dublin, Joint Committee on International Surrogacy, 2022).

Joint Committee on Justice, Defence and Equality, 'Report on hearings in relation to the Scheme of the Children and Family Relationships Bill' (Dublin, Joint Committee on Justice, Defence and Equality, 2014).

Kavanagh, A, 'Strasbourg, the House of Lords or elected Politicians: Who decides about rights after *Re P?*' (2009) 72 *Modern Law Review* 828.

Keane, R, (2008) 'The Constitution and the Family: The Case for a New Approach' in O Doyle and E Carolan (eds), *The Irish Constitution: Governance and Values* (Dublin, Thomson Round Hall, 2008).

Kiernan, K, 'The Rise of Cohabitation and Childbearing Outside Marriage in Western Europe' (2001) 15 *International Journal of Law, Policy and the Family* 1.

Kilkelly, U, 'Complicated Childhood: the Rights of Children in Committed Relationships' in O Doyle and W Binchy (eds), *Committed Relationships and the Law* (Dublin, Four Courts Press 2007).

Kralijić, S, 'Same-Sex Partnerships in Eastern Europe: Marriage, Registration or no Regulation' in K Boele-Welki and M Fuchs (eds), *Same-Sex Relationships and Beyond: Gender Matters in the EU*, 3rd edn (Cambridge, Intersentia, 2017).

Lau, CQ, 'The Stability of Same-Sex Cohabitation, Different-Sex Cohabitation, and Marriage' (2012) 74 *Journal of Marriage and Family* 973.

Lau, H, 'Rewriting Schalk and Kopf: Shifting the Locus of Deference' in E Brems (ed), *Diversity and European Human Rights: Rewriting Judgments of the ECHR* (Cambridge, CUP, 2013).

Law Commission, 'Cohabitation: The Financial Consequences of Relationship Breakdown' Law Com No 307 (2007).

——— ' The Review of the Western Australian Human Reproductive A New Law' Law Com No 244 (HMSO, 2019).

Law Reform Commission, 'Report on the Rights and Duties of Cohabitants' LRC 82-2006 (2006).

—— 'Fifth Programme of Law Reform' LRC 120-2019 (2019).

Leonard-Kane, M, 'Lesbian Co-Parenting and Assisted Reproduction: In an Age of Increasing Alternative Family Forms, Can Ireland Continue to Ignore the Need for Legislative Boundaries to be Placed on "Fertile" Ground?' (2010) 13 *Trinity College Law Review* 5.

Lewis, J, 'Debates and Issues Regarding Marriage and Cohabitation in the British and American Literature' (2001) 15 *International Journal of Law, Policy and the Family* 159.

Margaria, A, *The Construction of Fatherhood – The Jurisprudence of the European Court of Human Rights* (Cambridge, CUP, 2019).

Marsh, M, Suiter, J, and Reidy, T, 'Report on Reasons Behind Voter Behaviour in the Oireachtas Inquiry Referendum 2011' (Red C, 2012).

McCarthy, F, 'Cohabitation: Lessons from North of the Border?' (2011) 23 *Child and Family Law Quarterly* 277.

McCormick, C, and Stewart, T, 'The Legalisation of Same-Sex Marriage in Northern Ireland' (2020) 71 *Northern Ireland Legal Quarterly* 557.

Mee, J, 'Cohabitation, Civil Partnership and the Constitution' in O Doyle and W Binchy (eds), *Committed Relationships and the Law* (Dublin, Four Courts Press, 2007).

—— 'A Critique of the Cohabitation Provisions of the Civil Partnership Bill 2009' (2009) 12 *Irish Journal of Family Law* 83.

—— 'Cohabitation Law Reform in Ireland' (2011) 23 *Child and Family Law Quarterly* 323.

Miles, J, Wasoff, F and Mordaunt, E, 'Cohabitation: Lessons from Research North of the Border?' (2011) 23 *Child and Family Law Quarterly* 302.

Millbank, J, 'The Role of "Functional Family" in Same-Sex Family Recognition Trends' (2008) 20 *Child and Family Law Quarterly* 155.

Mulligan, A, 'From *Murray v Ireland* to *Roche v Roche*: Re-Evaluating the Constitutional Right to Procreate in the Context of Assisted Reproduction' (2012) 35 *Dublin University Law Journal* 261.

Nestor, J, *An Introduction to Irish Family Law,* 1st edn (Dublin, Gill and Macmillan, 2000).

New Zealand Law Commission, 'New Issues in Legal Parenthood' NZLC R88 (2005).

—— 'Review of Surrogacy' Issues Paper, NZLC IP47 (2021).

—— 'Review of Surrogacy' Report, NZLC R146 (2022).

Norrie, K 'Registered Partnerships in Scotland' in JM Scherpe and A Hayward (eds) *The Future of Registered Partnerships* (Cambridge, Intersentia, 2017).

O'Cinnéide, C, 'Equivalence in Promoting Equality: The Implications of the Multi-Party Agreement for the Further Development of Equality Measures for Northern Ireland and Ireland' (Equality Authority and Equality Commission for Northern Ireland, 2005).

O'Gorman, R, 'A Change will do you Good: The Evolving Position of Transsexuals under Irish and European Convention Law' (2004) 7 *Trinity College Law Review* 41.

O'Mahony, C, 'Societal Change and Constitutional Interpretation' (2010) 1 *Irish Journal of Legal Studies* 71.

—— 'Irreconcilable Differences? Article 8 ECHR and Irish Law on Non-Traditional Families' (2012) 26 *International Journal of Law, Policy and the Family* 31.

—— 'Principled Expediency: How the Irish Courts can Compromise on Same-Sex Marriage' (2012) *Dublin University Law Journal* 198.

—— 'A Review of Children's Rights and Best Interests in the Context of Donor-Assisted Human Reproduction and Surrogacy in Irish Law' (Department, of Children, Equality, Disability, Integration and Youth, 2021).

Parkinson, P, and Aroney, N, 'The Territory of Marriage: Constitutional Law, Marriage Law and Family Policy in the ACT Same-Sex Marriage Case' (2014) 28 *Australian Journal of Family Law* 160.

Pennings, G, 'Evaluating the Welfare of the Child in Same-Sex Families' (2011) 26 *Human Reproduction* 1609.

Perrin, E and Siegel, B et al, 'Promoting the Well-being of Children whose Parents are Gay or Lesbian' (2013) 131 *Paediatrics* 1374.

Probert, R, '*Hyde v Hyde*: Defining or Defending Marriage?' (2007) 19 *Child and Family Law Quarterly* 322.

Rainey, B, Wicks, E and Ovey, C, *Jacobs, White and Ovey's The European Convention on Human Rights,* 6th edn (Oxford, OUP, 2014).

Rokas, K, 'Greece' in K Trimmings and P Beaumont (eds) *International Surrogacy Arrangements: Legal Regulation at the International Level* (London, Bloomsbury, 2013).

Rosenfeld, M, 'Couple Longevity in the Era of Same-Sex Marriage in the United States' (2014) 76 *Journal of Marriage and Family* 905

Ryan, F, '"When Divorce is Away, Nullity's at Play": A New Ground for Annulment, its Dubious Past and its Uncertain Future' (1998) 1 *Trinity College Law Review* 15.

—— 'Sexuality, Ideology and the Legal Construction of Family: Fitzpatrick v. Sterling Housing Association' (2000) 3 *Irish Journal of Family Law* 2.

—— 'Case Note: *Ghaidan v. Godin-Mendoza*' (2005) 27 (3–4) *Journal of Social Welfare and Family Law* 355.

—— 'From Stonewall(s) to Picket Fences: The Mainstreaming of Same-Sex Couples in Contemporary Legal Discourses' in O Doyle and W Binchy (ed.), *Committed Relationships and the Law* (Dublin, Four Courts Press, 2007).

—— '21st Century Families, 19th Century Values: Modern Family Law in the Shadow of the Constitution' in Doyle, O. and Carolan, E. (eds), *The Irish Constitution: Governance and Values* (Dublin, Thomson Round Hall, 2008).

—— 'The General Scheme of the Civil Partnership 2008: Brave New Dawn or Missed Opportunity?' (2008) 11 *Irish Journal of Family Law* 51.

—— *Annotated Legislation: Civil Partnership and Certain Rights and Obligations of Cohabitants Act 2010* (Dublin, Thomson Round Hall, 2011).

—— 'The Rise and Fall of Civil Partnership' (2016) 19 *Irish Journal of Family Law* 50.

—— 'Repackaged Goods? - Interrogating the Heteronormative Underpinnings of Marriage' in F Hamilton and G Nota La Diega (eds) *Same-Sex Relationships, Law and Social Change* (London, Routledge, 2020).

Sáez, M. 'Same-Sex Marriage, Same-Sex Cohabitation and Same-Sex Families Around the World: Why "Same" is so Different' (2011) 19 *American University Journal of Gender Social Policy and Law* 7.

Scheib, JE, Riordan M and Rubiri, S, 'Choosing Identity - Release Sperm Donors: The Parents' Perspective 13–18 Years Later' (2003) 18 *Human Reproduction* 1115.

Scherpe, JM, 'The Legal Recognition of Same-Sex Couples in Europe and the Role of the European Court of Human Rights' (2013) 10 *The Equal Rights Review* 83.

Scherpe, JM and Fenton-Glynn, C, 'Surrogacy in a Globalised World: Comparative Analysis and Thoughts on Regulation' in JM Scherpe, C Fenton-Glynn and T Kaan (eds) *Eastern and Western Perspectives on Surrogacy* (Cambridge, Intersentia, 2019).

Schrama, WM, 'The Dutch Approach to Informal Lifestyles: Family Function over Family Form?' (2008) 22 *International Journal of Law, Policy and the Family* 311.

Schuz, R, 'Surrogacy in Israel' in JM Scherpe, C Fenton-Glynn and T Kaan (eds), *Eastern and Western Perspectives on Surrogacy* (Cambridge, Intersentia, 2019).

Scottish Law Commission, 'Aspects of Family Law - Discussion Paper on Cohabitation' Scottish Law Com No 170 (2020).

Shannon, G, *Child Law*, 2nd edn (Dublin, Thomson Round Hall, 2010).

Shannon, G, *Children and Family Relationships Law in Ireland: Practice and Procedure* (Dublin, Clarus Press, 2016).

Short, E et al, 'Lesbian, Gay, Bisexual and Transgender (LGBT) Parented Families: A Literature Review prepared for The Australian Psychological Society' (Melbourne, The Australian Psychological Society 2007).

Slabbert, M. and Roodt, C, 'South Africa' in K Trimmings and P Beaumont (eds), *International Surrogacy Arrangements: Legal Regulation at the International Level* (London, Bloomsbury, 2013).

Sloan, B, 'Registered Partnerships in Northern Ireland' in J Scherpe and A Hayward (eds), *The Future of Registered Partnerships* (Cambridge, Intersentia, 2017).

Sloth Nielsen, J, 'South Africa' in JM Scherpe, C Fenton-Glynn and T Kaan (eds), *Eastern and Western Perspectives on Surrogacy* (Cambridge, Intersentia, 2019).

Sperti, A, *Constitutional Courts, Gay Rights and Sexual Orientation Equality* (Oxford, Hart, 2017).

Stephenson, S, 'The Constitutional Referendum in Comparative Perspective: Same-Sex Marriage in Ireland and Australia', International Journal of Constitutional Law Blog (4 June 2015), available at www.iconnectblog.com/2015/06/the-constitutional-referendum-in-comparative-perspective-same-sex-marriage-in-ireland-and-australia.

Stith, R, 'On the Legal Validation of Sexual Relationships' in S Fitzgibbon, LD Wardle and AS Loveless (eds), *The Jurisprudence of Marriage and Other Intimate Relationships* (Buffalo, WS Hein & Co, 2010).

Surrogacy UK, 'Surrogacy in the UK: Myth Busting and Reform – Report of the Surrogacy UK Working Group on Surrogacy Law Reform' (Surrogacy UK, 2015).

Sutherland, EE, 'From "Bidie-In" to "Cohabitant" in Scotland: The Perils of Legislative Compromise' (2013) 27 *International Journal of Law, Policy and the Family* 143.

Tobin, B, 'EB v France: Endorsing Un-"Convention"-al Families?' (2008) 11 *Irish Journal of Family Law* 78.

—— 'Relationship Recognition for Same-Sex Couples in Ireland: The Proposed Models Critiqued' (2008) 11 *Irish Journal of Family Law* 10.

—— 'Same-Sex Couples and the Law: Recent Developments in the British Isles' (2009) 23 *International Journal of Law, Policy and the Family* 309.

—— 'The Revised General Scheme of the Children and Family Relationships Bill 2014: Cognisant of the Donor-conceived Child's Constitutional Rights?' (2014) 52 *Irish Jurist* 153.

—— 'A Critique of Re AB (Surrogacy: Consent): Can Ireland learn from the UK Experience?' (2017) 20 *Irish Journal of Family Law* 3.

—— 'Forging a Surrogacy Framework for Ireland: The Constitutionality of the Post-birth Parental Order and Pre-birth Judicial Approval Models of Regulation' (2017) 29 *Child and Family Law Quarterly* 133.

—— 'Regulating Non-Clinical Donor Assisted Human Reproduction in Ireland' (2018) 60 *Irish Jurist* 179.

—— 'An Appraisal of Ireland's Current Legislative Proposals for Regulating Domestic Surrogacy Arrangements' (2019) 41 *Journal of Social Welfare and Family Law* 205.

—— 'Assisted Reproductive Techniques and Irish Law: No Child left Behind?' (2020) 64 *Irish Jurist* 138.

Tobin, J and McNair, R, 'Public International Law and the Regulation of Private Spaces: Does the Convention on the Rights of the Child Impose an Obligation on States to Allow Gay and Lesbian Couples to Adopt?' (2009) 23 *International Journal of Law, Policy and the Family* 110.

UNHRC, 'Report of the Special Rapporteur on the Sale and Sexual Exploitation of Children' (UNHRC, 2018)

Van Dijk, P and Van Hoof, JGH, *Theory and Practice of the European Convention on Human Rights*, 3rd edn (Amsterdam, Kluwer, 1998).

Verrelli, S et al, 'Minority Stress, Social Support, and the Mental Health of Lesbian, Gay and Bisexual Australians during the Australian Marriage Law Postal Survey' (2019) 54 *Australian Psychologist* 336.

Wade, K, 'The Regulation of Surrogacy: A Children's Rights Perspective' (2017) 29 *Child and Family Law Quarterly* 113.

Walker, AJ and McGraw, LA, 'Who is Responsible for Responsible Fathering?' (2000) 62 *Journal of Marriage and Family* 563.

Wallbank, J and Dietz, C, 'Lesbian Mothers, Fathers and Other Animals: Is the Political Personal in Multiple Parent Families?' (2013) 25 *Child and Family Law Quarterly* 451.

Walsh, DJ, *Irish Public Opinion on Assisted Human Reproduction Services: Contemporary Assessments from a National Sample* (Dublin, RCSI, 2013).

Walsh, J and Ryan, F, *The Rights of de facto Couples* (Dublin, IHRC, 2006).

Wardle, LD, 'The Potential Impact of Homosexual Parenting on Children' (1997) *University of Illinois Law Review* 833.

—— 'Form and Substance in Committed Relationships in American Law' in O Doyle and W Binchy (eds), *Committed Relationships and the Law* (Dublin, Four Courts Press, 2007).

—— 'The Attack on Marriage as the Union of a Man and a Woman' (2007) 83 *North Dakota Law Review* 1365.

—— 'Gender Neutrality and the Jurisprudence of Marriage' in S Fitzgibbon, LD Wardle and AS Loveless (eds), *The Jurisprudence of Marriage and Other Intimate Relationships* (Buffalo, WS Hein & Co 2010).

—— 'The Boundaries of Belonging: Allegiance, Purpose and the Definition of Marriage' (2011) 25 *Brigham Young University Journal of Public Law* 287.

Wintemute, R, 'The Massachusetts Same-Sex Marriage Case: Could Decisions from Canada, Europe, and South Africa Help the SJC?' (2004) 38 *New England Law Review* 505.

—— 'Marriage or "Civil Partnership2 for Same-Sex Couples: Will Ireland Lead or Follow the United Kingdom?' in O Doyle and W Binchy (eds), *Committed Relationships and the Law* (Dublin, Four Courts Press, 2007).

—— 'Same-Sex Marriage in National and International Courts – "Apply Principle Now" or "Wait for Consensus?"' (2020) 1 *Public Law* 134.

Witzleb, N, 'Marriage as the "Last Frontier"? Same-Sex Relationship Recognition in Australia' (2011) 25 *International Journal of Law, Policy and the Family* 135.

Wojcik, ME, 'Wedding Bells Heard Around the World: Years from Now, Will we Wonder why we Worried about Same-Sex Marriage?' (2003–2004) 24 *Northern Illinois University Law Review* 589.

Working Group on Domestic Partnership, 'Options Paper' (Stationery Office, 2006).

Zervogianni, E, 'Greece' in JM Scherpe, C Fenton-Glynn and T Kaan (eds), *Eastern and Western Perspectives on Surrogacy* (Cambridge, Intersentia, 2019).

—— 'Lessons Drawn from the Regulation of Surrogacy in Greece, Cyprus and Portugal, or a Plea for the Regulation of Commercial Gestational Surrogacy' (2019) 33 *International Journal of Law, Policy and the Family* 160.

INDEX

Milton Keynes UK
Ingram Content Group UK Ltd.
UKHW021936101124
450918UK00004B/57